# VISION, RACE, AND MODERNITY

## A VISUAL ECONOMY OF THE ANDEAN IMAGE WORLD

*Deborah Poole*

PRINCETON UNIVERSITY PRESS
PRINCETON, NEW JERSEY

Copyright © 1997 by Princeton University Press
Published by Princeton University Press, 41 William Street,
Princeton, New Jersey 08540
In the United Kingdom: Princeton University Press,
Chichester, West Sussex
All Rights Reserved

*Library of Congress Cataloging-in-Publication Data*
Poole, Deborah, 1952–
Vision, race, and modernity : a visual economy of the Andean
image world / Deborah Poole.
p.   cm. — (Princeton studies in culture/power/history)
Includes bibliographical references (p.    ) and index.
ISBN 0-691-00646-6 (CL : acid-free paper). —
ISBN 0-691-00645-8 (PB : acid-free paper)
1. Visual anthropology—Andes Region.    2. Photography in ethnology—
Andes Region—History.    3. Indians of South America—Andes Region—
Pictorial works—History.    4. Race—Pictorial works—History.
I. Title.    II. Series.
GN347.P66    1997
305.8′0098′0222—dc21        96-45561

This book has been composed in Berkeley Book Modified

Princeton University Press books are printed
on acid-free paper and meet the guidelines for
permanence and durability of the Committee on
Production Guidelines for Book Longevity
of the Council on Library Resources

Printed in the United States of America
by Princeton Academic Press

2   4   6   8   10   9   7   5   3   1

2   4   6   8   10   9   7   5   3   1
(Pbk.)

# VISION, RACE, AND MODERNITY

EDITORS

Sherry B. Ortner, Nicholas B. Dirks, Geoff Eley

A LIST OF TITLES

IN THIS SERIES APPEARS

AT THE BACK OF

THE BOOK

PRINCETON STUDIES IN
CULTURE / POWER / HISTORY

For Chacho

# Contents

# Illustrations

# _Acknowledgments_

SINCE the day in 1985 when I first wrote down some unformed ideas about photography, representation, race, and the Andes, this book and I have traveled a long way. Many people have accompanied me on this journey into the Andean image world. Some graciously coached me in their different spheres of knowledge. Others lent support and friendship as I ventured deeper and deeper into what often felt like an endless sea of images and words.

Fran Antmann was my partner in the early stages of the research. We wrote our first research proposals on Andean photography as collaborative efforts; we shared the J. Paul Getty Postdoctoral Fellowship that launched my work on the Andean image world; we traveled together to the archives in London, Paris, Lima, and Cusco; and we jointly conceived and set up a permanent archive to house the plates and images we discovered in Cusco. Although our individual projects later took different forms, I am forever indebted to Fran for sharing with me her passion for photography, her knowledge of photographic history, and her skills as a photographer and researcher. Fran printed many of the photographs reproduced in chapters 7 and 8. Other friends who provided ideas and comments on my early forays into representational theory and colonial imagery include Ric Burns, Edward Said, Leyli Shayegan, Anne McClintock, Bruce Mannheim, Ruth Behar, Nancy Micklewright, Joanne Rappaport, Tom Zuidema, and Gary Urton.

The archive that Fran and I helped to form in Cusco now exists as the Fototeca Andina (Andean Photography Archive) at the Centro de Estudios Regionales Andinos "Bartolomé de Las Casas." Our work there would not have been possible without the encouragement and support of Adelma Benavente, Guido Delran, Ivan Hinojosa, and Henrique Urbano. Others who assisted in Cusco include Patricia Marín and the photographers Washington González, Cesar Meza, Eulogio Nishiyama, Horacio Ochoa, David Salas, and Gregorio Licuona. In Lima I benefited from the friendship and ideas of Nelson Manrique, Gustavo Buntinx, Marisol de la Cadena, and the late Alberto Flores-Galindo.

Of those who supported our work in Peru, I owe special debts to Luis Figueroa Yabar and Adelma Benavente. Luis and his mother, Ubaldina Yabar de Figueroa, shared with us the wonderful archive of photographic plates taken by his father, Juan Manuel Figueroa Aznar. Luis has graciously granted permission for me to publish his father's photographs in this book. Adelma Benavente guided me through Cusco society and helped in many of the interviews with Cusqueño photographers and collectors. She continues to be the best single source on Peruvian photographic history.

I am also grateful to those institutions that generously provided access to their photographic collections and archives. These include the Museo Histórico Regional in Cusco and the Archivo Courret and Biblioteca Nacional in Lima; the Bibliothèque Nationale de France, the Musée de l'Homme, the Société de Géographie, and Gérard Lévy in Paris; the Prints and Photography Division of the U.S. Library of Congress in Washington, D.C.; the George Eastman House in Rochester, New York; and the Royal Geographic Society in London.

During the final stages of writing, I benefited from the critical commentaries and hard work of colleagues and students at the New School for Social Research. Talal Asad, Steve Caton, Partha Chatterjee, Kate Crehan, David Gordon, Rayna Rapp, and Bill Roseberry provided insight, encouragement, and friendship. Research assistants who worked with me on different phases of the book include Joel Baumann, Juan Echeverri, Nina Hien, Erin Koch, Carmen Martínez, and Casey Walsh. Delphine Selles helped with some difficult French translations. Xavier Andrade, Tom Cummins, Johannes Fabian, Florencia Mallon, Ben Orlove, Gerardo Rénique, and Gary Urton provided insightful readings of the finished work. Michael Muse and Nina Hien helped to prepare the manuscript for publication. At Princeton University Press, I thank Mary Murrell, for her encouragement and support, and Elizabeth Gretz, for her superb editing.

Chapter Seven was originally published in a slightly different form in *Representations*, no. 38 (1992). Some of the material in Chapter Four was published in *Dialectical Anthropology* 12 (1988).

My research in Peruvian and European archives was funded by postdoctoral fellowships from the J. Paul Getty Foundation and the University of Michigan Society of Fellows. The Faculty Research Fund and the Provost's Office of the New School for Social Research provided monies to offset the cost of developing and printing the photographs for the book.

A final word of thanks goes to Gerardo Rénique, who saw this project through its many different phases, encouraged its completion, and tolerated its excesses.

VISION, RACE, AND MODERNITY

## CHAPTER ONE

# Introduction

ANTHROPOLOGISTS, as everyone knows, are people who "go to the field." Frequently pictured, or at least imagined, wearing the pith helmets and khaki clothing of someone's colonial past, anthropologists are charged with the task of recording native customs, deciphering savage tongues, and defending beleaguered traditions. Following the prescription of the founding father of ethnographic fieldwork, Bronislaw Malinowski, they are supposed to immerse themselves in the culture of the other and emerge decorously shaken but professionally unscathed to report their findings to scientific societies, professional associations, and crowded lecture halls.

The actual experience of fieldwork is, of course, quite different. As every fieldworker knows, the reality is far from romantic. The natives are sometimes far from friendly. The states in which natives live are far from welcoming. Even the reasons we do fieldwork itself are increasingly under siege. Finally, and often most perplexing of all, the natives tend to ask more and harder questions of the anthropologist than the other way around. Indeed, for me, the hardest questions about fieldwork have always come from the natives—in my case, Quechua-speaking peasants living in southern highland Peru. "Why are you here?" they would frequently ask. "And what are you doing?" "Are you looking for gold?" "What are you writing down now?" "Why didn't you write down what I just said?" Sometimes they asked if I was crazy. Why else, they reasoned, would anyone want to come there of her own free will (unless she were looking for gold).

The peasants with whom I lived in southern highland Peru were probably right to be perplexed about the mysterious nature of my mission (which was to study their fiestas, fairs, history, and culture). They did not take long, however, to find some more practical niche for me to fill: I became the resident community photographer. Indeed, some months I spent more time taking, developing, and distributing snapshots than anything else. At first I volunteered both my services and the photographs. Soon, however, as my dwindling grant monies flowed into the multinational coffers of Kodak and the somewhat more rustic cash registers of Cusco's photographic studios, I found that I needed rules. If a family wanted more than four poses, I made them pay for the extra pictures. If they wanted multiple copies, enlargements, or identity-card portraits, the same rule applied. I marveled at the rapidity with which they learned to exploit their local representative of what Walter Benjamin has dubbed the "age of mechanical reproduction."

I also marveled at the poses they chose. They were, of course, familiar with photographic portraiture. Calendars with photographs of everything from nude gringas to plumed Incas graced the walls of their houses. Newspapers, books, and magazines were treasured objects brought from Cusco or Lima. Some people had studio portraits of relatives or ancestors wrapped carefully in old scraps of textiles or tucked away in the niches of their homes' adobe walls. Despite the diversity of the photographs they had seen, the poses they chose for their own portraits were remarkably uniform. They stood stiffly, with their arms down at the side, facing the camera, with serious faces. Photographs with smiles were usually rejected, as were the unposed, or what we would call "natural," photographs I took on my own. My subjects were also committed to being photographed in their best clothes. I did a good deal of my interviews and other fieldwork while hanging around houses waiting for them to wash and braid their hair, scrub the baby, and even trim the horse's mane in preparation for the family portrait. I began to develop a theory about their understanding of what portraits were and their attachment to particular poses. According to my field notes, it had something to do with the history of photography (about which I knew virtually nothing at the time) and the types of poses required for the very old cameras still used in Cusco's public plazas and commercial studios.

As my curiosity about peasants and photographs grew, I began to experiment. I took books of photographs to the field to show people. I wanted to see how they judged the pictures. What would they say? I think I expected them to be either indifferent or disapproving. But their comments proved to be much more astute. One day while looking through Sebastiao Salgado's *Other Americas*, for example, my friend Olga surprised me.[1] I had chosen Salgado's work to discuss with her, in part, because I found it to be a book with no easy answers. The photographs were lush, lavish, textured, undeniably beautiful. As prints, they were technically perfect. They appealed to everything I knew, consciously or unconsciously, about what a beautiful photograph was supposed to be. Yet as an anthropologist, I also found them alienating. They showed unhappy or destitute-looking people doing what appeared to be weird things. Where, I asked (somewhat self-righteously) were the people plowing fields, working in factories, or organizing strikes who also make up the "other Americas"?

Olga, however, found my concerns uninteresting. She liked the book a lot. Here were photographs that looked nothing like her own stiff-bodied portraits. Moreover, they were in black and white, a format that my "clients" systematically rejected. Nonetheless, this was her favorite among the several different books we had looked at. "Why?" I asked. "Because," she said, "poverty is beautiful." She proceeded to dissect several photographs for me. She liked how Salgado's prints emphasized the texture of the peasants' ratty clothes. She liked the fact that he showed an old peasant couple from the back, because this drew attention to the raggedness of their clothes (as well as, I thought, their anonymity). She even liked Salgado's picture of cracked peasant feet—the one image on which my own negative opinion would not budge.

To this day, I'm not sure whether Olga convinced me with her praise for *Other Americas*. What she and her neighbors did do, however, was pique my curiosity about the ways in which visual images and visual technologies move across the boundaries that we often imagine as separating different cultures and classes. Clearly the peasants I photographed had their own ideas about photographs. These ideas shared much with my own. Yet they also differed in important ways. Olga's comments about poverty and beauty—and my reaction to them—suggested to me the importance of reexamining my own assumptions about how political ideologies intersect with visual images. Similarly, our shared appreciation of the photographs' formal qualities suggested something about the complex ways in which a European visual aesthetic had established its claims on our otherwise quite different ideas of the beautiful and the mundane.

Although Olga and the other people with whom I lived, talked, and worked in the Cusco provinces of Paruro and Chumbivilcas during the early 1980s will appear nowhere in the pages that follow, this book is, in many ways, indebted to them. Their understanding of the power—and magic—of photography helped me frame my own interests in the history of visual technologies in non-European settings. Their attitudes toward the photographic image made me think about the political problem of representation in a slightly more critical way. Finally, my own experience as community *retratista* (portraitist) was constantly in my mind as I stared at thousands of mute images of Andean peasants held in the photographic archives of New York, Washington, Rochester, London, Paris, Lima, and Cusco. How would I decipher the intentions of the photographers who took these, sometimes anonymous, images? How could I even begin to imagine what the subjects of these nineteenth- and early twentieth-century photographs were thinking? How would I talk about and theorize the different visual styles I began to detect in European and Peruvian photographs? Where else beyond the archive should I look for insights into the cultural and racial discourses that animated these silent images? What role did these photographs in fact play in shaping the identities and imaginations of the people who posed for them? What message about my own, late twentieth-century ideas of photography and the self were they sending back to me from their unique viewpoint on the Andean past? (Figure 1.1).

———

This book is an attempt to answer some of these questions. It is, in one sense, a contribution to a history of image-making in the Andes. In another, much broader sense, it uses visual images as a means to rethink the representational

Figure 1.1. Girl with
mirror (c. 1925)

politics, cultural dichotomies, and discursive boundaries at work in the encounter between Europeans and the postcolonial Andean world. In describing
this encounter, I am particularly concerned with investigating the role played
by visual images in the circulation of fantasies, ideas, and sentiments between
Europe and the Andes. One goal of the book is to ask what role visual discourses and visual images played in the intellectual formations and aesthetic
projects that took shape in and around the Andean countries in the nineteenth
and early twentieth centuries. A second goal is to examine the role of visual
images in the structuring and reproduction of the scientific projects, cultural
sentiments, and aesthetic dispositions that characterize modernity in general,
and modern racial discourse in particular. The visual materials analyzed here
include images from eighteenth-century novels and operas, engravings from
nineteenth-century scientific expeditions, *cartes de visite*, anthropometric photography, *costumbrista* painting, Peruvian *indigenista* art, and Cusqueño studio
photography from the 1910s and 1920s.

As this list of image forms and genres makes clear, my purpose is neither to write a history of visual representation in the Andes nor to compile a comprehensive inventory of the motifs, styles, technologies, and individuals implicated in constructing "an image of the Andes." The diversity, even unorthodoxy, of the images and image-objects that have circulated around and through the Andes dictates against any such singular histories. It calls instead for a consideration of the astounding number and variety of images and image-objects through which that place called "the Andes" has been both imagined and desired, marginalized and forgotten by people on both sides of the Atlantic.

The term "image world" captures the complexity and multiplicity of this realm of images that we might imagine circulating among Europe, North America, and Andean South America. With this term, I hope to stress the simultaneously material and social nature of both vision and representation. Seeing and representing are "material," insofar as they constitute means of intervening in the world. We do not simply "see" what is there before us. Rather, the specific ways in which we see (and represent) the world determine how we act upon that world and, in so doing, create what that world is. It is here, as well, that the social nature of vision comes into play, since both the seemingly individual act of seeing and the more obviously social act of representing occur in historically specific networks of social relations. The art historian Griselda Pollock has argued, "the efficacy of representation relies on a ceaseless exchange with other representations."[2] It is a combination of these relationships of referral and exchange among images themselves, and the social and discursive relations connecting image-makers and consumers, that I think of as forming an "image world."

The metaphor of an image world through which representations flow from place to place, person to person, culture to culture, and class to class also helps us to think more critically about the politics of representation. As I shall argue, the diversity of images and image-objects found in the Andean image world speaks against any simple relationship among representational technologies, surveillance, and power. Neither the peasants whose portraits I took, nor the many Peruvians with whom I later spoke while researching this book, nor the images I found in archives and books conformed to any simple political or class agendas. Nor were they immune to the seductions of ideology. Rather, like most of us, they seemed to occupy some more troublesome niche at the interstices of different ideological, political, and cultural positions. To understand the role of images in the construction of cultural and political hegemonies, it is necessary to abandon that theoretical discourse which sees "the gaze"—and hence the act of seeing—as a singular or one-sided instrument of domination and control. Instead, to explore the political uses of images—their relationship to power—I analyze the intricate and sometimes contradictory layering of relationships, attitudes, sentiments, and ambitions through which European and Andean peoples have invested images with meaning and value.

One way of thinking about the relationships and sentiments that give images their meaning is as a "visual culture." Indeed, this might seem the obvious route for an anthropologist engaged in visual analysis. The term "culture," however, brings with it a good deal of baggage.[3] In both popular and anthropological usage, it carries a sense of the shared meanings and symbolic codes that can create communities of people. Although I would not want to dispense completely with the term visual culture, I have found the concept of a "visual economy" more useful for thinking about visual images as part of a comprehensive organization of people, ideas, and objects. In a general sense, the word "economy" suggests that the field of vision is organized in some systematic way. It also clearly suggests that this organization has as much to do with social relationships, inequality, and power as with shared meanings and community. In the more specific sense of a political economy, it also suggests that this organization bears some—not necessarily direct—relationship to the political and class structure of society as well as to the production and exchange of the material goods or commodities that form the life blood of modernity. Finally, the concept of visual economy allows us to think more clearly about the global—or at last trans-Atlantic—channels through which images (and discourses about images) have flowed between Europe and the Andes. It is relatively easy to imagine the people of Paris and Peru, for example, participating in the same "economy." To imagine or speak of them as part of a shared "culture" is considerably more difficult. I use the word "economy" to frame my discussion of the Andean image world with the intention of capturing this sense of how visual images move across national and cultural boundaries.

The visual economy on which this book focuses was patterned around the production, circulation, consumption, and possession of images of the Andes and Andean peoples in the period running from roughly the mid-eighteenth to the early twentieth century. I have defined the chronological boundaries of this economy, on the one extreme, by the occurrence of certain shifts (about which I will have more to say in a moment) in the status of both vision and the observer in European epistemologies. On the other extreme, I have closed my inquiry in the decades preceding the advent of mass media and what Guy Debord has called the "society of the spectacle." The changes wrought in our understanding of images and visual experience by television and cinema have been dramatic. This book considers the visual economy that anticipated these changes in visual technology, public culture, and the forms of state power they presumed.[4]

In analyzing this economy, my goal is twofold: On the one hand, I want to understand the specificity of the types of images through which Europe, and France in particular, imagined the Andes, and the role that Andean people played in the creation of those images.[5] On the other hand, I am interested in understanding how the Andean image world participated in the formation of a modern visual economy. Two features in particular distinguished this visual economy from its Enlightenment and Renaissance predecessors. First, in the modern visual economy the domain of vision is organized around the continual production and circulation of interchangeable or serialized image objects and visual experiences. Second, the place of the human subject—or observer—is rearticulated to accommodate this highly mobile or fluid field of vision. These new concepts of observation, vision, and the visual image emerged toward the beginning of the nineteenth century at a time when Europe's capitalist economy and political system were undergoing dramatic change.

The complexity of the discursive and social fields within which this comprehensive reorganization of both vision and knowledge occurred poses a challenge to its description and theorization. This book frames the history of modern visuality through a discussion of specific sets of images and the individuals and societies that produced them. In this way, vision becomes a problem of social actors and societies, rather than of the abstract discourses, regimes of knowledge, sign systems, and ideologies that cloud much of the theoretical literature on the subject. Discursive regimes have a constitutive, even material presence in history. To understand how they shape our actions, beliefs, and dreams, however, we must look at the ways in which discourses intersect with specific economic and political formations. This is particularly true in the non-European world, where western European philosophical and scientific notions of representation, vision, and truth were molded to fit the particular political and cultural agendas of both the agents of imperial rule and the natives who resisted (and accommodated) their rule.

## PRINCIPLES OF VISUAL ECONOMY

Like other economies, a visual economy involves at least three levels of organization. First, there must be an organization of production encompassing both the individuals and the technologies that produce images. Regarding the production of images, I focus here on the individuals and, to a lesser extent, the institutions who made, circulated, and publicized images of the Andean world. In this respect, the book might well be approached as a historical ethnography of the intellectuals whose words and pictures shaped modern imaginings of the Andes.

Like other ethnographers, I have been selective in choosing the individuals whose work will represent the Andean image world.[6] In making these selections, I have been guided not by the idea of discovering a typical or representative set of either images or image-makers but, rather, by an understanding that each individual and image constitutes a particular instance within the remarkably broad range of representational practices and discourses that have gone into the construction of the Andean image world. The men and women whom we will meet range from famous personalities such as Voltaire, Humboldt, and Buffon to unfamiliar or even—some might argue—insignificant figures such as the anthropologist Arthur Chervin, the artist Juan Manuel Figueroa, and the studio photographers Filiberto and Crisanto Cabrera. Though weighed differently in history books, both groups had roles to play in shaping the visual discourses and economies that surfaced in the course of the Andean-European encounter. Although Humboldt's lush engravings were certainly seen by more people, Figueroa's private photographs or the Cabreras' studio portraits speak with equal—and perhaps greater—eloquence about the role the visual economy has played in the more intimate arena of feeling, desire, and emotion.

A second level of economic organization involves the circulation of goods or, in this case, images and image-objects. Here the technological aspect of production plays a determining role. During the nineteenth and twentieth centuries, two technologies have been of particular importance in producing an archive of images of the Andean world. Up through the early nineteenth century, Andean peoples and places were seen almost exclusively in engravings. Then, from roughly the mid-nineteenth century on, photography and lithography intervened as the preferred technologies for reproducing images of the Andes and its peoples.[7] The immediate effect of this technological innovation was a spectacular expansion of both the quantity and the accessibility of Andean images. Lithographs had circulated among the relatively limited number of people who could afford to purchase engravings and books. Photographs, however, were mass-produced in carte de visite, postcards, and after the perfection of halftone processing in the early 1880s, in popular magazines and newspapers.

This question of circulation overlaps with the third and final level on which an economy of vision must be assessed: the cultural and discursive systems through which graphic images are appraised, interpreted, and assigned historical, scientific, and aesthetic worth. Here it becomes important to ask not what specific images *mean* but, rather, how images accrue value. In the dominant European value system, for example, graphic images are evaluated in terms of their relationship to the reality they re-present. According to this realist discourse, the goal of all visual representation is to narrow the gap between the image and its referent. The image's value or utility is seen to reside in its ability to represent or reproduce an image of an original (or reality). Within the terms of the dominant realist discourse, this representational function of the image might therefore be thought of as its "use value."[8]

When thought of as part of a general economy of vision, however, an image must also be considered in terms of its exchange value. Here the object status of the graphic images produced through different technologies assumes an immediate importance. Photography and photoengraving, for example, in addition to producing more "realistic" images are also technologies for the mechanical and mass production of specific sorts of image-objects. These objects are characterized in the first place by their relative affordability, portability, and size. The peasants I photographed, for example, could own photographic portraits in a way they were not likely to have owned paintings. More important, they could secret their photographs away in niches or display them, as they wished. They could also reproduce them, make them larger or smaller, and give them away. Regardless of the technical quality or pictorial content, possession of photographs conferred a special status on their owners. When we consider such social uses of photographic objects or commodities, it becomes clear that the value of images is not limited to the worth they accrue as representations seen (or consumed) by individual viewers. Instead, images also accrue value through the social processes of accumulation, possession, circulation, and exchange.[9]

On some level, the exchange value of any particular image or image-object is, of course, intimately related to its representational content. We need only think of the very different valuations placed on family portraits and postcards. Both are based on photographic technologies; both circulate in society; yet both acquire different social and aesthetic values by virtue of the fact that one contains the likeness of people we know, while the other contains pictures of people or places we know only as images.

But there is also a heuristic argument to be made for considering the two forms of value separately, because each has something rather different to say about the social nature of images. One way to appreciate how this works is to ask what happens to our own understanding of images when we privilege one or the other of these forms of value in our analyses of images. Thus if we look at a postcard in terms of its representational content, its political and social importance would appear to be related to what it does or does not tell us about the particular place it shows—for example, La Paz. If we think about the postcard's exchange value, we think instead of the ways in which this picture of La Paz circulates in relationship to millions of other postcards of "other places," and the ways in which the fact of its circulation connects the viewer, however tenuously, both to the material, geographic fact of La Paz and to this other world of postcard images with which it will be archived and compared.

A similar separation of emphasis marks the literature on colonial representation.[10] These works tend to describe specific sets of images taken in the colonial or non-European world in terms of their representational function or use value. The next step is often to denounce the extent to which (and, less often, the ways in which) this content "mis-represents" the reality it claims to portray. It is through this process of misrepresentation that the image is then said to construct an "image" of the colonial world, for the European observer. This type of analysis suffers from two major problems. First, if we focus only on representation and its discontents, it remains virtually impossible to distinguish how (or if) the visual politics of colonialism differ from its textual politics. Second, a focus on content avoids the larger problem of how to judge the complex and sometimes conflicting interpretations brought to most images by different viewers.

With this problem in mind, more recent efforts to analyze the place of visual imagery in colonialism have moved away from the study of "representations" to focus instead on what I have glossed as the image's exchange value. Work has concentrated in particular on the analysis of two types of images: postcards and racial or ethnographic survey photography.[11] Most of this work shares a Foucauldian (or more generally poststructuralist) concern with unmasking the political functions of the colonial archive as a technology for regulating or normalizing colonial identities, or for compiling the statistical bases of imperial knowledge.[12] If we shift our attention from the image to the archive, it becomes possible to ask a very different set of questions about the ways in which vision and power intersect in the colonial world.

In exploring the Andean image world, I have tried to give equal weight to the representational content (or use value) of specific images and groups of images *and* to the forms of ownership, exchange, accumulation, and collection that characterize particular image forms as material objects. Because their graphic surfaces were read as representations of some (real or imagined) material referent in the Andean world, the images we will encounter contributed individually and collectively to create a shared discourse of what "the Andes" were. In other words, they conformed in some sense to a dominant European visual culture in which images were read as "representations" of a reality out there, beyond the image. They also conformed, not surprisingly, to contemporary understandings of racial difference and cultural evolution as well as to the civilizing missions and manifest destinies of European and North American imperialism. In pointing toward this complicity between imperial discourse and the representational function of images, my reading of the Andean visual archive shares a common interest with other recent works on the representation of native or working-class subjects from the non-European world. In emphasizing the collective and circulatory nature of the Andean image world, I also share a general poststructuralist concern with understanding the statistical and archival technologies that underwrite modern imperial power.

Where my analysis of the Andean image world departs from other studies of colonial representation is in its attempt to locate images within a more general economy of vision and then to relate this economy to the historically shifting discourse of race. More concretely, I suggest three arguments about visual modernity and race. First, by approaching images as material objects with sensuous characteristics of their own, I suggest specific ways in which the material and commodity character of such modern image forms as photographs shaped popular understandings of "race" as a material, biological fact.

Second, in addition to considering what we might think of as the "ideological" role of images, I also look at the particular ways in which fantasy and desire enter into the production and consumption of visual images. I gloss this dimension under the somewhat less concrete but, I will argue, no less "economic" term of pleasure. Finally, I consider non-European (in this case, Andean) images as more than passive "reflections" of discourses constituted in Europe. Instead I ask what role colonial images played in the formation and consolidation of the visual and racial discourses that formed the heart of European modernity.[13]

## VISION AND RACE

The particular forms of exchange value associated with mass-produced images took shape toward the middle of the nineteenth century. At this time, the fetish quality of reproducible images such as photographs and lithographs began to accrue value independently of the referential content or use value assigned to them as representations of particular persons, places, or objects (Figure 1.2). Most critics have pointed toward photography as the generative technology behind this rearticulation of the relation between image and representation. Of particular importance have been Walter Benjamin's essays on the revolution wrought by photography and cinema in the social field of art. Because photography was able to reproduce images mechanically and serially, Benjamin argues, it dismantled the aura (or "value") attached to the work of art as a singular representation. In its place there emerged what he sees as a (potentially) more democratic form of visual economy in which reproductions of works of art circulate freely in society, and in which "representations" refer to other images as often as to a singular referential reality.[14]

My initial research for this book was inspired, in part, by a similar interest in examining how photographic technology had altered the concepts of vision and visuality animating the Andean image world. As I began to engage the discursive histories and visual practices through which eighteenth- and early nineteenth-century Europeans had imagined the Andes, however, I perceived a shift in the organization of visual experience that anticipated the introduction of photography. As Jonathan Crary has pointed out in his study of visual modernity, the crucial rupture in European understandings of visual subjectivity and the observer took place in the first decades of the nineteenth century—just prior to Daguerre's 1839 invention of the photographic process and well before the introduction of positive-image photographic printing techniques. The defining characteristics of this epistemic break in the field of vision were the consolidation of particular forms of subjective vision and "a proliferation of circulating signs and objects whose effects coincide with their visuality."[15]

Figure 1.2. Peruvian soldier and wife (c. 1880)

Crary locates the origins of visual modernity in the European philosophical discourses and techniques associated with observation and the constitution of the observing subject. My task, however, has been to trace the origins of visual modernity and what Crary has called its "relentless abstraction of the visual" in the rather differently configured visual field of Andean imagery. Here, in the explosive terrain of (post)colonial relations, the notions of accumulation, serialization, and interchangeability that lay at the heart of both visual modernity and the capitalist economy were played out most dramatically in the domain of racial theory and the related physiognomic discourse of "types." The relevance of race for a study of visual culture is obvious. By phrasing identity in the rigorous methods and languages of the biological science of the time, nineteenth-century racial theory translated the politics of colonial subjugation into the visual—and aesthetic—calculus of embodied "natural" differences. In saying this, however, I do not want to imply that race operates only or even primarily through visual technologies and discourses. Nor do I want to say that either vision explains race, or race, vision. Rather, by looking at the historical intersections between visual and racial discourses, this book approaches vision and race as autonomous but related features of a broad epistemic field in which knowledge was organized around principles of typification, comparability, and equivalency.

Part of the scientific and voyeuristic fascination of the engravings and, especially, the photographs of non-European peoples and places that circulated in nineteenth-century Europe had to do with the ways in which their material nature as image objects lent support to an emerging idea of race as a material, historical, and biological fact. Racial theory built its classifications by comparing individuals with other individuals and then classifying them accordingly. Within each category or "race," individuals were considered equivalent to others as representatives of their kind. Across racial categories, individuals were compared for the purpose of assigning both identity and relative social worth. I suggest that the visual archive of colonial—or non-European—images participated in specific ways in the consolidation, dissemination, and popularization of this logic of comparability and equivalency. The writings of Peter Camper, Johannes Friederich Blumenbach, and Paul Broca, to name just a few of Europe's founding racial theorists, were read by a rather limited number of people. Photographs, however, circulated widely. In doing so, they not only reflected racial discourse, but also participated in the formation of the racial culture of European modernity. In his studies of modern disciplinary practices and regimes of governance, Michel Foucault has proposed that we look to the mundane practices of inscription, registration, and inspection for the origins of the modern clinical gaze. This book follows Foucault's genealogical method in looking to the archival and representational machineries of colonial image production and circulation for the origins of modern racial thought.

Foucault's work also provides guidance for thinking about the chronology of modern racial thought. In his later works, Foucault was concerned to outline the process through which a modern discourse of sexual or biological self-consciousness, surveillance, and discipline emerged together with the normalizing state in late eighteenth- and early nineteenth-century Europe. He suggests that this discourse and its attendant disciplinary technologies were instrumental in the formation of a specific kind of modern power called "biopower." For Foucault, biopower was distinctive in that, "for the first time in history," it "brought life and its mechanisms into the realm of explicit calculations and made knowledge-power an agent of transformation of human life." Biology, demography, medicine, and moral statistics took shape as the premier sciences of the nineteenth century. These scientific discourses, Foucault argues, constituted the political technologies that shaped those new forms of normalizing power concerned with "distributing the living in the domain of value and utility."[16]

This epochal shift in forms of power and knowledge was also marked by a shift in European discourses of identity from what Foucault characterizes as an "aristocratic" concern with blood and lineage to a modern "bourgeois" concern with progeny, reproduction, and population. Key to this shift was the modern biological concept of "race." What Foucault fails to point out, however, is that this new discourse on race—and the forms of "biopower" it enabled—did not take place within the bounds of Europe alone. Rather, as Ann Stoler has argued, modern racial and evolutionary thought must be studied in relation to the expanding colonial empires that Foucault effectively elides from his history of European sexuality and governmentality. As a tool of imperial expansion, "race" provided the scientific language through which "natives" could be described, classified, and subjugated as morally inferior (or childish) human types. As a disciplinary technology, the very concept of race provided a model (or stimulus) for the perfection of those disciplinary discourses of the bourgeois self that Foucault glosses as "sexuality."[17]

This book makes two specific interventions into the discussion that Stoler's book has helped to open on Foucault, race, and colonialism. The first concerns chronology; the second, the place of visual discourses and technologies in the constitution of modern racial thought. In the *History of Sexuality*, Foucault claims that the bourgeois disciplinary gaze was not involved with the surveillance of "others" until the late nineteenth century.[18] In his later lectures on race and the normalizing state, however, he begins to map a more complex scenario for the emergence of modern racial discourse. Although he does not give an exact "origin" for racial discourse, he points toward the new technologies of regularization and enumeration that emerged in the mid- to late eighteenth century.[19] Stoler has argued that Foucault's Eurocentric chronology must be rethought in light of the colonial histories, cultures, and administrative regimes where "race" was perfected as a normalizing technology. In this book I look at the historical problem of race and colonialism from a somewhat different angle. Specifically, I examine race as a visual technology founded on the same principles of equivalency and comparison that underwrote the statistical technologies, moral discourses, and regulatory power of the normalizing state.

Race is a slippery and often empty category: it occupies different strategic positions and carries substantively different meanings in different historical moments, scientific disciplines, national traditions, and intellectual contexts. It is both visual and nonvisual, scientific and "popular," fixed and ever-changing. To say this, however, is not to suggest that race does not exist either discursively or materially, in the sense that discursive concepts exert a material presence on society and history. Rather it is to suggest that we can perhaps come to understand race better by thinking about it as part of broader discursive economies or, in Foucault's language, epistemes. I focus on one such discursive economy: the visual economy of modernity. In thinking about how race figures in this visual economy, I am concerned with understanding, on the one hand, how European perceptual regimes have changed over time and in relation to an increasing interest in non-European peoples, and, on the other hand, how visual images have shaped European perceptions of race as a biological and material fact.

## THE PROBLEM OF PLEASURE

In our rush to uncover the complicitous ties among art, representation, and power (or, perhaps more appropriately in this case, race and representation) we frequently forget that images are also about the pleasures of looking. Visual images fascinate us. They compel us to look at them, especially when the material they show us is unfamiliar or strange. This is particularly true of photography and photographic-based images, such as photogravures, which exert a cultural claim to represent "reality." Indeed, photographs exert a peculiarly powerful hold on our imaginations. Michael Taussig has argued that the spell photography weaves around us is multiplied in images of people from the colonial or non-European world who appear both like and not like us. It is to this "intercultural optical space of magical power," Taussig says, that we should look when trying to understand our irresistible—and, Taussig argues, ultimately human—desire to gaze upon the other (Figure 1.3).[20]

The attraction we feel toward visual images may very well be universal—part of the mimetic faculty that Taussig describes so well. The particular ways in which we experience the pleasures of the visual, however, are both culturally and historically specific. Here I am concerned with the type of visual experience that emerged together with a particular European project of modernity in the late eighteenth and early nineteenth centuries. Recent studies have stressed two aspects of modern European visual culture. Critics of Enlightenment rationalism have pointed toward the relationship among Cartesian rationalism, graphic theories of perspective, and the practices and discourses of domination and surveillance that inform European philosophical and cultural understandings of alterity and "otherness."[21] It is this aspect of modern visual culture that we emphasize when analyzing images as either instruments or reflections of the ideological and discursive projects of colonialism, imperialism, and capitalism.

Other critics, however, have argued that alternative forms of visuality coexist with or punctuate the historically dominant regimes of rationalism and perspectivalism. Of particular importance is the argument of Roland Barthes

Figure 1.3. Bolivian woman (c. 1930)

that visual images operate according to an uncoded, or open, semiotic.[22] This argument suggests that—Cartesian perspectivalism notwithstanding—the value of a photograph or other visual image is not necessarily tied to its ability to represent a particular material referent. Once unleashed in society, an image can acquire myriad interpretations or meanings according to the different codes and referents brought to it by its diverse viewers. While available ideologies of gender and race effectively limit the range of interpretations applied to a photographic portrait, that photograph's "meaning" cannot be controlled in the sense that its image (signifier) remains tied to any one code or referent (signified). Barthes's provocative theory of the visual sign has important implications for an ideological analysis of images. Thus, for example, although a photograph of a bedraggled Indian woman or an empty Andean landscape can be interpreted as reflections of the racialism of colonial rule or the expansionist impulse of capitalism, neither photograph can be tied to a single ideological agenda.

If we combine Barthes's observations on the visual sign with other critical perspectives on the role of both sensuous imagination and fantasy in the shaping of European historical and visual imagination, it becomes possible to speculate about the existence of subaltern regimes in which vision is not necessarily tied to the repressive or disciplinary mechanisms of what Martin Jay has termed "Cartesian perspectivalism."[23] Jay has presented one of the most persuasive arguments for the existence of multiple "scopic regimes" in European modernity. He identifies two scopic regimes other than the dominant perspectival mode. In the first, vision is fragmented and focused on the material or empirical. As such, the hierarchical and spatial concerns of perspective are supposedly subverted, if not undone. Jay then identifies the second alternative regime with the irregular forms and tactile aesthetic of the baroque, in which "the body returns to dethrone the disinterested gaze of the disincarnated Cartesian spectator."[24]

To what extent do such alternative or subaltern regimes of vision function to oppose (or even undermine) the dominant visual regime? For Barthes himself, the fluid or open nature of the semiotic code allows images—in particular photographic images—to operate as spaces of fantasy and desire.[25] For Walter Benjamin, the non-narrative quality of visual images operates in a similar fashion to open up critical spaces from which dominant historical narratives can be questioned.[26] Some feminist critics have presented similar arguments for the fragmentary and inherently oppositional nature of feminine (or feminist) modes of seeing.[27] Finally, anthropologists and historians of art have argued for the need to consider the cultural bases of different perceptual and visual regimes.[28]

Pleasure is another concept that is crucial for understanding the unevenness of "dominant" visual regimes. Visual images give us pleasure. This is as true for the anthropologist as for the peasants she photographs. Pleasure, however, works in complex ways. By providing a nexus for the mimetic play of sympathy and imitation, images stimulate a potentially anarchic domain of fantasy and imagination. The pleasure that images give us, however, is itself molded by aesthetic ideologies whose histories are anything but innocent. Literature, art, and music have all served as vehicles for expressing and strengthening attachments to nation, race, and empire. Indeed, as Edward Said has eloquently argued, it is through the "pleasures of empire" that the imperial enterprise becomes most clearly engrained in the individual imagination and subjectivity.[29] In my exploration of the Andean image world, I have tried to keep constantly in mind the complexities and unpredictabilities of this domain of pleasure. As any analyst of colonial imagery can attest, it is almost too easy to consign all images to the task of reproducing (or perhaps even producing) imperial, racial, and sexual ideologies. The more challenging task is to think about the ways in which aesthetics and the "open code" of visual images occasionally disrupt the powerful hold that imperial discourse has over our imaginations.

Speculations regarding the role of pleasure and the existence of "alternative" or "subaltern" regimes of vision raise crucial questions about how agency and location enter into our analyses of images and visuality. Who sees the images? How do such factors as age, gender, race, class, and culture affect different reactions to images? If we are to argue for the oppositional nature of alternative visual regimes, then how does this "oppositionality" map onto different groups in space and time? And to return to my original questions about the value systems that make up the modern visual economy, who "attaches" value to an image or image-object? Is the "value" constructed by the discursive system itself (as, for example, occurs with money or gold in the capitalist economy) or is the "value" of an image-object more like fashion in varying with the specific historical and social location of its viewer?

One of the most important contributions that anthropology can make to a critical theory of visuality and the image is to stress the diversity of visual subjectivities at work in any given "image world." Those analyses that assume some version of Jay's Cartesian perspectivalism as the only visual regime in modernity assume a unitary visual subject. Seen from this perspective, the images that nineteenth- and early twentieth-century travelers brought back from the Andes assume the disciplinary function of normalizing or limiting the range of meanings it was possible to ascribe to the Andes and its peoples. This was, for example, one of the primary functions of the racial photographs and cartes de visite that were collected (and viewed) by upper- or middle-class Europeans. Indeed, I emphasize this "repressive" function in my analysis of the cartes de visite in Chapter Five. Nevertheless, it needs to be recognized that, for other non-European viewers or for the indigenous subjects of the photographs themselves, the images might very well have taken on different meanings.[30]

## VISION IN THE ANDEAN POSTCOLONIAL

Visual images, writes Griselda Pollock, fall "at the point . . . where the will to know and the resultant relations of power are furrowed by the more unpredictable . . . plays of fascination, curiosity, dread, desire and horror."[31] Part of the argument of this book is that this counterpoint between sensuous imagination and imperious knowledge acquired particular characteristics in the image world that was woven around the Andean-European encounter (Figure 1.4). This was so for two reasons. The first involves the ways in which images themselves were interpreted and valued in the type of visual economy that was generated from Europe from the late eighteenth to early twentieth

Figure 1.4. Priests on Inca's throne, Saqsawaman, Cusco (1920s)

century. The second involves the political and historical relationships linking the Andean republics of Ecuador, Peru, and Bolivia with the northern European and North American countries that dominated cultural production concerning Latin America.

This period might best be defined as the Andean postcolonial. Historically, it begins with the late eighteenth-century indigenous revolts and early nineteenth- century movements for national independence. It closes with the emergence of modern states in the early decades of the twentieth century.[32] The period coincides with the epochal or formative moments of European modernity. This moment was launched by the Enlightenment, modern nationalist discourse, and the new form of state power Foucault has called "biopower." The currents determining what "modernity" would be, however, did not flow only in one direction. Rather, the sentiments, practices, and discourses known as European modernity were themselves shaped in important ways by the constant flow of ideas, images, and people between Europe and the non-European—in this case, Andean—world. Just as the centers and peripheries of the global capitalist economy that underwrote modernity were linked by a constant flow of goods, capital, and people, the divergent interpretations (or cultures) of modernity that emerged in different parts of the world were connected and dependent phenomena. Circulation or exchange, not dependence, formed the dominant mode of their interconnection.

Chronologically, this book stands apart from other work on the Andes, in which issues of representation and cultural encounter have tended to be discussed almost exclusively in reference to the initial centuries of Spanish colonial rule.[33] Within that literature, the roots of everything from Andean indigenous culture to political violence and modern racism are routinely traced to the ethnic and cultural dichotomies generated by the Spanish colonial experience. My intention is to contribute a more critically informed, historical understanding of how modern visual and aesthetic discourses have shaped both European and Andean imaginings of the "Andean world."

Of the many different concepts, philosophies, and discourses that went into the making of the modern Andean image world, it is the notion of race that stands out for both its persistence and its universality. All Europeans or North Americans who traveled to South America did so with an understanding that some—not always well defined—"racial" divide separated their cultures, histories, religions, and bodies from the Andean peoples they would meet. Within the Andean republics themselves, notions of difference based on physical appearance, culture, and skin color have played a dominant role in the structuring of social identities and political-economic policies since at least the time of the conquest. During the colonial period, the principal divide was that separating "Indians" from Spaniards and the American-born *criollos* (creoles), who identified culturally and ethnically with the Europeans. Most anthropologists and historians have pointed to this colonial divide as the source of contemporary racial and ethnic relations.[34] In this scheme, "race" is understood to be, on the one hand, an empirical reality based in the historical fact that the Andean world was once (and for some analysts, is still) made up of two separate genetic and cultural groups and, on the other, an ongoing cultural tradition in which people's understanding of everything from national history to their own subjectivity is grounded in a "colonial" discourse of inequality.

In examining the history of race as a visual discourse, this book proposes a different genealogy of race in the Andean world. Rather than asking why racial divisions persist in the modern world—an impossible question to answer if we focus only on the origins of racial ideology—this book instead asks how the particular visual qualities that modern racial discourse has assigned to "race" have come to seem so natural. Other histories of race begin with the assumption that modern racial thought (or racism) emerged when Europeans began to give increasingly precise definitions or boundaries to observed differences in human populations.[35] In these works, modern racial science with its many false and gross generalizations is seen to have been motivated by a general impulse toward greater realism.

In opposition to this realist narrative, I ask how it was that "race" came to be seen at all. This question could be asked of virtually any part of the world where the colonizing mission of the European nations was sanctified by formal political and economic controls. What is particularly interesting about the Andean—or, on a broader scale, the Latin American—context, however, is that unlike Africa, where racial stereotypes and images were well inscribed in the European artistic and visual consciousness, the Americas confronted northern European travelers and scientists with relatively uncharted terrain.[36] Such early eighteenth-century theorists as Blumenbach, Georges Cuvier, and Johann Gottfried von Herder, for example, refused to form opinions on the "racial" classification of the Americas, claiming that too little was then known about the native Americans' physiognomies, biology and culture.[37] The opening of Spain's former South American colonies in the 1820s and 1830s to northern European scientists and travelers thus coincided with two crucial moments in the foundation of European modernity: the revolution in visual and observational technologies that accompanied what Foucault, Crary, and others have identifed as the emergence of the "modern observer," and the appearance of a new discourse of embodied racial difference grounded in the sciences of biology and comparative anatomy.

The following chapters trace the emergence of a racial language tailored to the specific political, geographic, and cultural realities of the Andes. Chapter Two considers the general absence of a visual language for describing South American bodies in eighteenth-century France. Here I am particularly interested in asking why women's bodies so often seem to provide the first sites from which "difference"—and somewhat later "race"—were theorized as visual problems in late eighteenth- and early nineteenth-century representations of Peruvians. Chapter Three examines the emergence of the substantively different physiognomic or typological mode of description that characterized early nineteenth-century approaches to the study of South America. It looks in some detail at the work of three Europeans who were influential in shaping a certain image of the Andes for future generations of European and Latin American intellectuals: the Comte du Buffon, Alexander von Humboldt, and Alcides d'Orbigny.

Chapter Four returns to the question of gender, to consider the images of Peruvian women produced by two early nineteenth-century European artists: Léonce Angrand and Johann Moritz Rugendas. In the early decades of Latin American independence, women provided, I suggest, a vehicle through which European artists and travelers began to map out the distinctive "racial types" that would shape all future European imaginings of the Andean republics, their economies and peoples. Chapter Five then examines how these racial types played in the distinct technological field of the *carte de visite*, or "calling card," photographs that dominated European photographic collections in the second half of the nineteenth century. In discussing the Andean carte de visite, I look at photography and race as related visual technologies in which the sensuous pleasures of collecting and the statistical language of equivalency converged.

The remaining chapters discuss how the visual politics of race were reworked by Peruvian intellectuals and photographers of the late nineteenth and early twentieth centuries. Here I am interested in examining the racial and national projects developed by South American intellectuals as forms of contestation that were nonetheless intimately connected to—and even dependent on—the European visual economy. In Chapter Six, I discuss the aesthetic workings of race and gender in Peruvian national discourse through an analysis of the work of a prominent Lima intellectual, Manuel Atanasio Fuentes. Chapter Seven examines the photographs and indigenista philosophy of Juan Manuel Figueroa. Like other highland artists of his time, this Cusco-based artist used photography as a means to invent new racial and cultural identities, yet rejected the dominant European concept of photography as a realist or documentary technology. Finally, in Chapter Eight I close with some reflections on the role of photography—and photographic portraiture in particular—in the consolidation of modern racial discourse.

## CHAPTER TWO

# The Inca Operatic

[The Incas] lack only our vices to be equal in every
respect to the Europeans.
(*Voltaire, 1736*)

IN 1745 Charles Marie de la Condamine of the French Royal Academy of Sciences published an account of the voyage he had recently completed from Ecuador to Guyana.[1] He divided his *Relation abrégée*, or "Short Account," of the journey into two parts.[2] In the first 216 pages he described the flora, fauna, geology, and settlements he had observed while in South America. This part of the book also mentioned the various Indian "nations" that the French academician had encountered along the shores of the Amazon and its tributaries. In the second part of the *Relation*, La Condamine reproduces a forty-five-page letter to "Madame * * *," in which he describes the murder of a French surgeon named Seniergues and his own failed attempts to obtain justice from Peru's colonial courts. In the 1745 edition, the letter, which is not mentioned on the book's title page, forms an integral part of the *Relation*. The title page of the second edition published in 1778, however, promotes the letter as an extra feature, entitled "An Account of the Popular Uprising in Cuenca, Peru."[3] The second edition also includes a previously unpublished letter written by Monsieur Godin des Odonais, a mathematician who accompanied La Condamine to South America. In the letter, Godin describes the perils encountered by his wife as she traveled from Cuenca to Manaus in search of her husband.

The 1745 edition also includes a foldout map of the Amazon and its tributaries. The 1778 edition includes, in addition to the map which serves as a frontispiece, another foldout plate facing the opening page of the book's preface. This plate shows a disorderly scene involving armed men, huddled priests, and many spectators seated in a grandstand surrounding a central plaza or square (Figure 2.1). Two numbered keys appear in the lower corners of the engraving. The one on the left identifies several of the men by name; the one on the right provides names for the churches and mountains that serve to locate the scene in the Andean portion of La Condamine's voyage. As visual devices, however, these two lists do more than name. Together they refer the plate to two curiously similar—and for the book's contemporary readers, equally familiar—iconographic conventions. The first convention was the

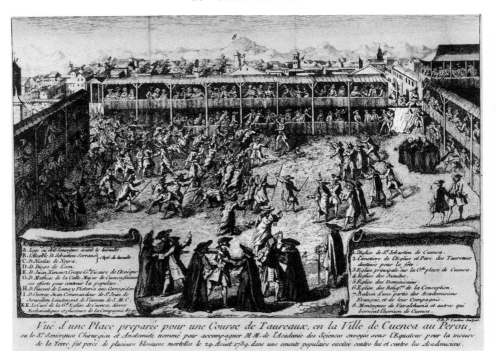

Figure 2.1. Incident at Cuenca (1778)

numbered keys that geologists and geographers had recently begun to append to their maps.[4] The second was the religious paintings through which European artists had, for centuries, narrated histories of martrydom and sainthood. The caption just below the boxes suggests that both labeling conventions may be appropriate to interpreting the engraving. It reads:

> View of the Plaza prepared for the Bullfight, in the City of Cuenca in Peru, where Sieur Seniergues, Surgeon and Anatomist appointed to accompany the Monsieurs of the Academy of Sciences sent to the Equator to measure the Earth, was pierced with several mortal wounds on August 29, 1739, in a popular riot incited against him and the Academicians.

On first inspection, La Condamine's engraving appears to be a rather unremarkable example of the type of sensationalism we have by now come to expect in European representations of the non-European world. As we learn in the letter that describes the event, Seniergues was killed as the result of a personal dispute involving a woman who had once been engaged to the son of Cuenca's mayor.[5] The engraving, however, entices the reader—who has presumably not yet read the letter to Madame * * *—with an unexplained picture of Spanish colonial subjects murdering a respected French surgeon. European scientists appear to be the unlucky victims of a barbarous horde; a bloody bullfight in Peru is contrasted with the secular mission of the French scientists; and Spain's American subjects are presented as inherently ungovernable. Especially for readers of the 1778 edition—in which the title page advertises that the book will deliver details of a "popular uprising"—the engraving may also have resonated with the North Americans' revolt against British rule just two years before and the expected implications of that revolution for France's political future.

On a first look, then, La Condamine's plate appears to conform quite easily to that general process of apprehension and preconception through which Europeans have seemingly always viewed non-European and colonial worlds. Yet what, exactly, do we mean when we talk about such a process—or project—of appropriation and representation? Does it mean that Europeans have always suffered from either a cultural predisposition or political will to "mis-represent" and belittle "the other"? Is it enough to say that a European image such as La Condamine's plate portrays non-Europeans as "barbarians"? Is it sufficient to explain representations in terms of their ideological utility for colonialism, capitalism, or, in the case of La Condamine's plate, French interest in Spain's restless American colonies? Is the cultural logic (and intentionality) that animates the production and consumption of visual representations such as this homologous with that of exploitation? Or do we need to think about a different way to theorize the relationship between visual images and worldly power?

One way to answer these questions is to consider how this plate differs from our own critically informed, twentieth-century expectations regarding European representations of non-Europeans. Here two observations immediately come to mind. The first is that the "others" portrayed in this particular plate do not actually look much different from their European victims. Their dress is essentially identical, and there is no particular emphasis on their physical appearance. Indeed part of the importance of the "key" is that it allows the viewer to discern which actors are European and which American. The second observation has to do with the historical fact that La Condamine's engraving pictured an area of the world that had previously occupied a marginal place in the social, political, and visual imagination of the book's predominantly French readers. What did it mean for French readers of the *Relation* to look at this plate? Did it matter for them that Seniergues was killed in the Andes as opposed to, for example, Africa or Mexico? When commissioning the image for his only pictorial plate, why did La Condamine privilege this tragic event rather than either his own scientific activities or some other more exotic "savages"?[6]

In this chapter I explore some of the issues that need to be considered if we are to answer such questions about visual images in general and La Condamine's eighteenth-century Andean image in particular. I consider how particular debates regarding the nation, the body, and sensory perception channeled the natural curiosity about "the other" that eighteenth-century Europeans shared with many other cultures around the world and across time. I also examine the types of expectations and desires that eighteenth-century French intellectuals projected on a particular part of the "non-European" world: the Andes or "Pérou." I suggest that an identifiable constellation of ideas, attitudes, impressions, and knowledge about the Andes and Peru took shape in France during precisely those years between La Condamine's initial journey (1735) and the second edition of his *Relation* (1778). In this period, some of France's leading intellectuals turned their attention, briefly, to the Andes and the Incas. The result was a small group of plays, operas, and novels in which Inca subjects engaged various Enlightenment debates about tolerance, governance, and the sensuous subject. These works were products of both a specific interest in the tragedy of the Inca conquest and a time when "difference" bore a conceptual relationship to the body different from the one it has acquired in our own biologically informed world view. Toward the end of this period, two events—Latin American independence and the emergence of the modern sciences of biology and comparative anatomy—transformed the ways in which Europeans would perceive and represent the Incas and other non-European peoples. Here, therefore, I situate eighteenth-century French representations of Peru, the Incas, and their "Virgins of the Sun" in the context of contemporary debates about perception, tolerance and the sensuous body. In Chapter Three, I turn to those theories of nature and vision that prefigured a modern visual discourse of (racial and national) type.

## THE SENTIENT CITIZEN

Our story begins in 1735 not, as one might imagine, with the Andes themselves, but with a bitter, nationalist-tinged dispute between followers of the British scientist Isaac Newton and the French *savant* Jean Dominique Cassini. Whereas Cassini had predicted that the earth was elongated, Newton's theory of gravity suggested that the earth was instead flattened at the poles. Intent on settling this thorny question once and for all, France's Royal Academy of Sciences voted to mount an expedition charged with measuring the length of the equatorial meridian. As the academicians scanned their maps for the perfect site, their eyes came to rest, eventually, on Spanish South America. There, near Quito, was a site that offered several advantages: it had been settled by Europeans for nearly two hundred years; it had an alpine, as opposed to tropical, climate; and, it was argued, the thin air of its mountainous terrain would facilitate the astronomical measurements through which the Newton-Cassini dispute was finally to be settled. Permission was obtained from the Spanish Crown, and on May 16, 1735, the expedition, headed by Charles Marie de La Condamine, set sail from La Rochelle. Accompanying La Condamine were the mathematicians Louis Godin des Odonais and Pierre Bouguer and the naturalist Joseph de Jussieu, whose collections would later enrich Paris's famous Jardin du Roi (see Chapter Three). To ensure that the French scientists did not collect other kinds of "data," Jorge Juan and Antonio de Ulloa went along as representatives of the Spanish Crown.[7]

The expedition's troubles began almost immediately upon its arrival in the New World. Hazardous travel conditions and obstinate bureaucrats colluded to slow the group's progress. After almost twelve months of slogging through jungles and mangrove swamps, the academicians finally arrived in Quito only to discover that they had run out of money. To cash their bills of exchange, La Condamine then had to undertake an additional five-month journey to the viceregal capital of Lima. Finally, on Easter Day, 1738, three years after their departure from France, the expedition members reached the slopes of the volcano Cotopaxi. They set up their instruments, went to sleep, and awoke— as so many other travelers would in centuries to come—to find that their Indian guides, cooks, and bearers had quietly disappeared. As they struggled to find new helpers, news arrived from Paris that another expedition, mounted shortly after La Condamine's departure, had already returned with measurements confirming Newton's theory. No longer was there any urgency to measure the meridian, and the once-celebrated mission found itself abandoned and forgotten in the equatorial Andes. Upon his return to Paris some ten years later, La Condamine himself was forced to confess that "the question of the earth's shape was finished."[8] With the *Relation abrégée*, he hoped to resurrect his scientific standing with an account of the voyage of exploration that now stood as his expedition's most important accomplishment.[9]

The *Relation*, however, did more than simply bolster its author's standing in the French Royal Academy. From its conception in 1735, the "Mission Condamine" had been front-page news for the expanding literate public of France. This was in part because, as a mission of unprecedented scientific importance, the expedition rallied the proto-nationalist sentiments of a relatively new and educated bourgeois readership.[10] As La Condamine himself notes in the preface to the first edition,

> No one is unaware that ten years ago, several Astronomers from the Academy were sent by order of the King to the Equator and the Polar Circle, to measure the terrestrial meridians, while other academicians undertook the same operations in France. . . .
>
> Under another reign, all those voyages with the equipment and the number of observers they required, could only have been the fruit of a long peace. Under that of Louis XV, they were conceived and successfully carried out during the course

of two bloody wars; while the King's armies rushed [*voloient*] from one end to the other of Europe to aid his Allies, his Mathematicians spread over the surface of the Earth [and] worked under the Torrid and Glacial Zones for the progress of the Sciences and the mutual benefit of Nations.[11]

La Condamine uses similar language when he explains his decision to publish his account of Seniergues's murder as an obligation "to defend the honor and the interests of my Sovereign, the Nation, and the Academy."[12]

The appeals of both La Condamine's Mission and his subsequent publications were thus addressed to a certain understanding of national interest and identity. To state this, however, is not to assert that the mission's significance was in any way limited to the ideological terrain of nationalism. Indeed, La Condamine's mission anticipated by some decades the emergence of the modern discourse—and sentiment—of nationalism, which took shape in the aftermath of the French Revolution and the Latin American independence movements.[13] Instead, his expedition must be seen as forming part of what appears (in retrospect) as the more ambiguous discursive arena of mid-eighteenth-century Europe.

For our purposes, we can think about the ambiguity—or, better, particularity—of this discursive setting in terms of two developments. Following Foucault, we can first see this period as a time when European understandings of the social subject (or the self) were slowly drifting from an inherently historical emphasis on descent and origin to a modern construction of the embodied political subject. As Foucault describes, this transition involved the move from "a concern with genealogy" to "a preoccupation with heredity."[14] The class most clearly affiliated with the genealogical discourse was the aristocracy, whose members defended their privilege as a form of caste distinction based on blood. The class most clearly affiliated with the physiological and sexual discourse was the bourgeoisie—the same class who would most adamantly (and profitably) defend the modern project of the nation. Their understanding of nation, moreover, diverged from older meanings along precisely the same lines that Foucault has described for the shifting discourse of social subjectivity. Whereas the older, aristocratic concept of nation focused on place of origin and descent, the modern concept of nation referred to a mutuality of language, territory, community, and culture.[15] In short, it referred to a sense of community that was compatible, if not synonymous, with the concept of population that would underwrite modern forms of both governance and national identity.

A second contemporary debate of relevance for our interpretation of La Condamine's plate had to do with the anatomical or physiological bases of sensory perception. During the same years in which La Condamine's drama unfolded, France's leading—and most widely read—philosophers and scientists were actively debating the possibility of locating the place where sensory perceptions came in contact with the physiological materiality of the body. This site, known as the "sensorium commune," was thought to form some part of the newly theorized nervous system.[16] As such, it differed radically from the highly localized (and extremely minute) pineal gland, which Descartes had suggested formed the meeting place of sensation and reaction. With its links to the central nervous system, the new concept of the sensorium commune questioned not only Descartes's pineal gland but the whole Cartesian separation that this small (and sometimes absent) gland had helped maintain between European bodies and minds. Instead, the sensorium commune (and the nervous system) blurred the comfortable Cartesian boundaries between body and mind; it also linked them both to an external world of sensations via a more-or-less mechanical model of physical reactions. As the boundary—or, to invoke a more modern word, the interface—between the individual, the body, and the external world, the sensorium commune was "the site at which external objects gave the first internal feelings of themselves, and at which the will was determined."[17] In the words of the leading proponent for the new science of comparative anatomy, Georges Cuvier, the sensorium commune was nothing less than "the seat of the soul."[18]

I will return later to the sensorium commune and its place in the tumultuous epistemic shift that Foucault (and others) have placed at the origins of European modernity—and the modern visual economy. Now, however, let us reexamine what La Condamine's particular project tells us about the relationship of the Andes (and the non-European world in general) to these mid-eighteenth-century quandaries regarding the body, the nation, and perception.

La Condamine tells us that he defines "the Nation" through three agents: the sovereign, his armies, and the academy. The king, of course, defined the nation by giving it a center. His armies fought the wars through which the modern French state—and nation—were formed. Finally, the academicians, like the king's armies, were "national" by virtue of their relation to a particular institution whose royal authority was, in turn, defined by the king. The knowledge they produced served the king and, by implication, the nation that the king defined. Yet both knowledge and the academicians who produced it were also intimately tied to a project and a territory extending well beyond both France and its aristocracy. By traveling to, looking at, and describing a distant part of the globe, La Condamine and his fellow academicians were performing an act of nation building comparable to the one performed by the king's armies. The academician or scientist was thus a representative of the nation and king, and a means through which the interests (and identity) of the nation and king could be extended through the act of perceiving, describing, and studying the world. The academicians provided, in other words, a sort of interface—or sensorium commune—between Science (which we might think of, as did La Condamine, as the mind or soul of the nation) and the King and public who formed the body or bodies of the Nation in its classical and modern senses, respectively.

This reading sheds a different and more nuanced light on La Condamine's decision to privilege the Seniergues incident as the only pictorial plate for his scientific text. I think it is safe to say that neither La Condamine's expedition, nor his subsequent publications, nor his famous frontispiece had as a goal the description—or much less, the (mis)representation—of the inhabitants of Ecuador. This type of representational mission, discussed in the following chapter, would have to await the fundamentally different type of classificatory (and national) thought that would characterize early nineteenth-century science. A reading of this particular engraving as a portrayal of "barbarous" Peruvians would thus somehow miss the point—by at least half a century. Rather, I suggest that La Condamine's (and his readers') interest in the Seniergues scandal had to do with the particularly symbolic or graphic way in which it revealed a violation of the French surgeon's passive—and disembodied—role as an observer of the world. The horror and the fascination that contemporary French readers must have felt at the event and its depiction had to do with the spectacle of a world (whose material form La Condamine was, after all, supposed to be measuring) making intimate, even deadly, physical contact with bodies very much like their own. This sensuous or instinctual identity with the physical plight of the academicians was heightened—if not made possible—by the emergent sense of national community to which La Condamine addresses his *Relation*.

It was also, however, made possible by the related debate regarding perception and anatomy. The assault on the academicians and the murder of Seniergues represented the most dramatic reversal imaginable of the passive Cartesian subject whose mind and senses were to remain separate from the material world of bodies, death, and sex. And because the event occurred in a place that was so different and relatively unknown, it effectively dramatized the extent to which knowledge (or, in the terms of the sensorium commune, perception itself) depended on this "point of contact" between the nation's (or academician's) body and the external and, in this case, non-European world.

As we will see, in the Andes the question of sensuous—and even sexual—contact between French citizen and Andean "other" loomed very large indeed for the eighteenth-century French philosophes.

## ENLIGHTENING THE INCAS

Contemplation of France's relation to the non-European world was, of course, by no means new. French intellectuals had for some time debated the relation between the barbarous customs of savages and the laws, politics, and customs that they sought to reform in "civilized" Europe. During the first decades of the eighteenth century, they looked to the imperial cultures of a largely imaginary Orient for inspiration and ideas.[19] Montesquieu's *Persian Letters* (1721) was one of the most popular of these early works. It presented a critical commentary on European culture and politics as seen through the eyes of a fictionalized royal Persian traveler. Other eighteenth-century writers—most famously Rousseau—resurrected earlier French writings on the Brazilian Tupinambá to fashion the notions of contract and nature through which they would criticize European government, religion, and *moeurs*.[20] On the stage as well, plays such as *L'Arlequin sauvage* (1721), *Le Nouveau monde* (1722), and *La Sauvagesse* (1732) seduced the French public with re-creations of the North American Hurons and Mohawks. Others, such as *Montézume* (1702), portrayed the aristocracies of Central America. With the publicity surrounding La Condamine's expedition, Andean America joined Brazil, North America, and the Orient as a new area for French philosophical and historical speculation. Indeed, for the very brief period of time that elapsed between La Condamine's voyage and the second edition of the *Relation abrégée*, Peru, and especially the Incas, became what can only be described as a minor Paris fashion.

Although La Condamine's mission brought Peru to the attention of a much broader French public, he was by no means the first Frenchman to travel to Andean South America. Throughout the eighteenth century, French smugglers and filibusters plied the Pacific coast of South America. Their accounts—which were eagerly read back home as the adventure stories they were—gave some information on the ports and coastal cities of Peru. Very few of these voyagers, however, ever managed to make it further inland. None made it to the Andean regions of the Peruvian viceroyalty.[21]

During the early eighteenth century, the Spanish Crown allowed several French naturalists to travel and study in its South American colonies. The most influential of these early travel accounts were those of Father Louis Feuillée, the engineer Amadeus Frezier, and the surgeon Bachelier. Feuillée traveled to South America in 1708 as a correspondent of the French Royal Academy of Sciences. His goal was "to make all the necessary observations for the perfection of the Sciences and Arts, the accuracy of Geography, and . . . the security of Navigation."[22] His three-volume *Journal of Physical, Mathematical and Botanical Observations* provided accounts of Valparaiso, Buenos Aires, Lima, and Arica, descriptions of indigenous customs, and 131 maps and plates of the botanical specimens, Indians, animals, and monsters he supposedly encountered on his journey from Buenos Aires to Lima.

Frezier followed closely on Feuillée's heels and virtually along the same route. Although, like Feuillée, Frezier never ventured into the interior of Peru, his 1716 travel account provided detailed descriptions of the economies, cultures, cities, and landscapes of the Andean region. His numerous engravings were arguably the most important source to which eighteenth-century intellectuals turned for visual images of Andean peoples. Like Feuillée's plates,

Figure 2.2. Incas
(1716)

they focused principally on the details of dress and material culture through which his eighteenth-century French readers would have perceived the boundaries of both cultural and "racial" difference. Frezier's famous drawings of Peruvian creoles and Incas, for example, paid considerable attention to details of dress and coiffure (Figure 2.2). Yet from our point of view, the images reveal curiously little interest in registering the physical or phenotypic features that nineteenth-century Europeans would come to think of as distinguishing Europeans and Peruvians. Frezier's famous descriptions of the culture, religion, and civil status of Peru's creoles and Indians reveal a similar eye for the distinctive features of clothing, religion, food, and customs. It was, after all, through just such traits and practices that the aristocracy of France had carved its own idiom of "racial" distinction. Nowhere, however, does Frezier's text refer to the different physical characteristics through which nineteenth-century travelers would construct their "descriptions" of creoles, Indians, and "whites." Instead, his accounts of the Indians' culture and livelihood are very clearly directed toward a denunciation of Spanish governance and its failure to fully exploit the mineral resources of Peru.[23]

In 1720 another French traveler, the surgeon Bachelier, published an illustrated account of the voyage he made several years earlier to Lima and Central America.[24] He described in detail the coastal cities and ports of Lima, Callao, Arica, and Valparaiso and provided copper-plate engravings of a map of Lima,

Figure 2.3. The Potosí Mines (1720)

the mines of Potosí, and the Lima Inquisition (Figure 2.3). Although Bachelier (like Frezier) described the culture of the peoples he observed, he was apparently unconcerned with accounting for physical features, skin color, or appearance. "The Indians in this country," he wrote in Peru, "have in general a subtle and refined spirit. They learn with ease whatever they are shown." To support his statement, he relates a story of an Indian who, after looking only once at an officer's pocket watch, made an exact replica of it. "I swear," writes Bachelier, "that I have never seen a better executed or more delicate work. . . . Yet it is the work of an Indian who has never had any other teacher [maîtres] than his own talents."[25]

Bachelier's fascination for the Indian, however, does not extend to the world of appearances that would dominate nineteenth-century accounts. He gives no description of the Indians' skin color or physical appearance. Nor do the naked Indian miners in his engraving of Potosí appear in the least bit different from the Spanish inquisitors who parade in his representation of Lima's Inquisition. "Race," for Bachelier, Frezier, and others of their time, was an essence that could be traced only over time and through specific lineages of succession. Indeed, Bachelier's sole reference to skin color in Peru fits clearly within the "aristocratic" understanding of "race." The Peruvian creoles, he writes, have "different colors [which] prove only the marriage they have contracted."[26] It was not until the beginning of the nineteenth century and the emergence of a modern scientific discourse of race that physiognomy and phenotype would enter as the principal concerns animating Europe's visual encounter with Andean peoples.

At any rate, the contemporary peoples whom Frezier, Feuillée, and Bachelier might have met in Andean South America were of little interest to the eighteenth-century philosophes. Their imaginations were instead drawn to the moral possibilities of Peruvian history. On the one hand, they were fascinated with the seemingly idyllic—and certainly malleable—past of Inca kings and princesses. On the other, they were drawn to the Spanish conquest as a particularly compelling case of European barbarism.

For information on Inca history and the conquest the philosophes turned to two sources: the writings of the sixteenth-century Dominican priest Bartolomé de Las Casas; and the *Royal Commentaries* of the Inca Garcilaso de la Vega. Las Casas's impassioned defense of the American Indians portrayed the Incas and other native Americans as the all-too-human victims of a conquest in which Christian principles of justice and honor—held to be general to all of Europe—had been betrayed by Spanish lust and greed.[27] Although written as part of a specific debate concerning the role of religion and the Church in the Spanish conquest of the New World, Las Casas's text was taken up by the philosophes as proof of the irrationality and fanaticism that had corrupted Iberian society in general and the Catholic Church in particular. In arguing for a doctrine of tolerance, Las Casas's texts also resonated with many of the same themes occupying Enlightenment thinkers. Not only did Las Casas argue—as would the philosophes—that the American Indians should be considered equal to the Europeans, at least in their capacity for conversion and hence civilization. His specific argument for tolerance also foreshadowed the two concepts most dear to the eighteenth-century humanist: an understanding of rights as a doctrine of equality among individuals; and a concept of difference in which the observed disparities (or inequalities) between groups of people were explained as natural features caused, in the most popular explanation of the day, by the climate in which those people lived.[28] "Cultures" were thus natural, material facts, which had to be "tolerated" (as opposed to valued) because they could be neither changed nor invoked as individual moral agents.

While Las Casas provided support for the philosophes' arguments on tolerance (and their related assumptions about difference), Garcilaso's chronicle provided them with details of an empire that seemed to fulfill their demands for a more egalitarian, just, and benevolent society. Whereas some earlier Spanish chroniclers and administrators had written highly critical accounts of the Incas' political and economic accomplishments, Garcilaso's chronicle of life in Inca Peru provided a compellingly sympathetic portrayal of Inca rule. By the mid-eighteenth century, his nostalgic portrait of Inca society had become favorite reading for those intellectuals on both sides of the Atlantic who were interested in reassessing the pre-Spanish heritage of the Andes and of the New World in general.[29]

The moral histories of Las Casas and Garcilaso, with their emphasis on justice, tolerance, and good government, provided perfect fodder for the Enlightenment. Here, in the distant, and certainly very different, past of the Inca Empire was evidence of both humanity's universal preference for reason and its capacity for generating utopian political and social forms based on justice, benevolence, *and* rank. As inhabitants of an indisputably different time and place, however, the Incas were also of interest for that related set of Enlightenment concerns that involved defining the nature and meaning of difference. The comparative ethnological projects of Montesquieu and Voltaire, for example, included references to Inca culture, law, and religion.[30] Again, however, in these texts, as in those of the travelers, difference for the Americans appears to reside in their morality and culture.[31] In his otherwise detailed account of the Inca conquest, Voltaire—who describes the Incas as the most civilized of the New World empires—is unconcerned with the question of physical appearance. Elsewhere he speculates that the Americans might be divided into two "races" according to the presence or absence of facial hair.[32] This is the only physical trait he mentions in his account of the American Indians.

## THE INCA OPERATIC

This indifference toward the description of American bodies carried over into another, much less studied group of texts in which the Enlightenment concern with difference and tolerance was given an operatic twist. In these works, the Incas—and in particular Inca women—figured not only as examples of reason but as embodiments of the types of perceptual or sensory encounters through which difference itself was to be discovered. Like their companion ethnological works, these texts and images from what I call the "Inca Operatic" drew on Garcilaso, Las Casas, and the contemporary travel accounts of Frezier and Feuillée to construct a romantic and highly sensual portrayal of the Incas, their empire, and above all, their women (Figure 2.4).

Unlike the nineteenth-century texts on which our (post)colonial criticism has more often focused, these texts are less concerned with "inscribing" on other bodies a specific sort of difference than they are in theorizing difference itself through contact with the sensuous and morally superior bodies of Inca women. As such, I suggest that these works reveal an embodied discourse of encounter and sensory perception similar to that which we have seen at work

is race a modern (19th-20th c.) construction; or is race defined in completely different manner in 18th c. (culture based, not biologically/phenotypically based)?

Figure 2.4. Sun virgin
(1790)

*Vierge du Soleil.*

in the sensorium commune. In this metaphor of eighteenth-century approaches to difference and perception, it was the body (or nervous system)
rather than the eye alone that provided the sensory contact between the self
and the world, the self and the other. In the works of the Inca Operatic we find
a similar sense of sensual discovery in the desirable yet aloof, similar yet different figure of the Inca sun virgin.

The first important work to bring the Incas to the Paris stage was Jean-
Philippe Rameau's and Louis Fuzelier's "ballet héroïque," *Les Indes galantes*
(The Gallant Indies), which opened at Paris's Royal Academy of Music on
August 23, 1735—just three months after La Condamine's departure from La
Rochelle (Figure 2.5). As one of the first fashionable works dealing explicitly
with South American themes, *Les Indes galantes* introduced its Inca and Span-
ish characters alongside more familiar characters drawn from the "Orient" and
North America. The first act, entitled "The Generous Turk," involves a love
triangle between a "pasha" named Osman, a Turkish officer named Valère, and

Figure 2.5. Title page
for *Les Indes
galantes* (1735)

a beautiful slave, Emilie, who has been stolen from her lover Valère by one of
Osman's soldiers. Valère is shipwrecked and also enslaved. But after Osman
recognizes him as the man who had once freed him from slavery, Osman
repents, returns Emilie to Valère, and frees all his other (African) slaves as well.

As the curtain rises on the second act, the audience is transported to Peru,
where a very similar love triangle unfolds within an elaborate stage set featuring a large volcano in the "mountain deserts of Peru." This act, entitled simply
"The Incas of Peru," tells the story of a young Inca princess, Phani Palla, who
falls in love with a Spanish officer, Don Carlos. Driven mad by jealousy, the
Inca ruler, Huascar, seeks revenge on the couple by using his telluric powers
to provoke a volcanic eruption during the annual solar feast. Phani and Carlos
escape unscathed, while Huascar is crushed by rocks from his own volcano.

The third act, "The Flowers," constructs a slightly more complicated affair
involving the Persian prince Tacmas and his friend Ali. Tacmas loves Zaire, an
enslaved Circassian princess who belongs to Ali; Ali, in turn, loves Fatima, an
enslaved Georgian princess who belongs to Tacmas. After some dramatic and
nearly tragic misunderstandings, the two men exchange slaves/lovers, and
the foursome rejoices together at a "Feast of Flowers" featuring "pleasant

odalisques from diverse nations in Asia." In the fourth and final act the ballet moves back to the New World, where a French and a Spanish colonial officer vie for the hand of a lovely *sauvagesse* named Zima. Zima, however, rejects both European suitors in favor of her savage lover, Adario. As in the previous act, the four characters become reconciled and celebrate at a "festival of peace."

The combination of exotic spectacle, romantic love, (discreet) political commentary, and a controversial composer quickly turned *Les Indes galantes* into one of the eighteenth century's most successful French ballets.[33] It is difficult to speculate how much of this success can be directly attributed to the play's Inca subjects. Nor do we know what—beyond the possible influence of the well-publicized La Condamine mission—might have compelled Rameau and Fuzelier to include South American characters in their work. The continuities linking the second act of *Les Indes galantes* with those literary and theatrical treatments of Inca subjects that would appear in France over the following decades, however, suggest that there was something about Fuzelier's libretto that went beyond merely applying Oriental themes to South American personalities.

A first motif linking Act II of *Les Indes galantes* to the group of Inca-centered works that would follow is the volcano, which serves—quite literally—to vent Huascar's rage. The opera's original production featured a mechanically staged and flame-filled "eruption" timed to coincide with the Solar Feast and Huascar's final dramatic soliloquy.[34] As a purely mechanical device, this spectacular crowd pleaser was not unusual. Contemporary audiences were accustomed to seeing re-creations of natural phenomena such as floods, thunderstorms, and crashing waves on the opera's stage. These staging conventions, however, formed part of an operatic tradition in which subjects were, more often than not, mythological in nature. This meant that such "natural" forces as floods and volcanoes were viewed on the stage alongside such "supernatural" occurrences as apparitions, divine metamorphoses, and unexplained changes of scenery.[35]

As a harbinger of a more modern European operatic tradition, *Les Indes galantes*, however, represented its volcano in a very different context. In the opera, changes of locale—from Persia to Peru to Turkey and North America—were still largely disruptive and unexplained. But they took place in the very real geography of an expanding colonial world.[36] Similarly, the opera's tale was structured not through the marvelous feats of gods and goddesses, but through the byzantine sexual politics of the libretto's exotic—though still human—characters. The volcano of Act II would have thus been read not merely as a metaphor for either passion or nature in general but, rather, as a feature of a geographically specific landscape in South America. Volcanoes would continue to occupy a central place in future European representations of the Andes.

Religion also figured prominently in eighteenth-century imaginings of the Andes. Anticlerical tendencies within the French Enlightenment found sympathy with religions that had formerly been condemned as pagan.[37] For these intellectuals, Garcilaso offered an image of a benevolent state religion in which individuals seemed to enjoy a more direct, unmediated relationship with the divine. Even for those philosophes who were not quite ready to embrace either paganism or deism, Spanish Catholicism offered an ideal vehicle for voicing relatively safe criticisms of the Church. These critics cited both the historical role played by religion and clergy in Spain's violent conquest of Peru and the all too apparent corruption and enrichment of Spain's actual colonial church.

In Fuzelier's libretto the spectacular Inca solar cults described by Garcilaso became a site within which the sexual politics of opera converged with political debates about the New World and its religions. Far from condemning the Incas' "pagan" religion as idolatrous or barbarian, the triumphal chorus to the sun in Act II of *Les Indes galantes* seems to find sympathy with the Virgins of the Sun, who remain loyal to their god even after his temples have been destroyed.[38] Their loyalty and innocence serve to frame the destructive rage of the male king, Huascar, who betrays both his gods and his people. As the passionate and self-destructive Huascar sings in the opening of the Inca scene in *Indes galantes*, "We obey without question when Heaven commands."[39] Later the ordered submission of the Inca state religion will turn to chaos when Huascar betrays his gods and turns his divine powers to the destruction of his own empire and people:

> The flame rekindles again
> Far from avoiding it, I implore it
> Fiery abysses, I have betrayed the altars
> Let thunder roll
> Avenge the immortals' rights
> Rend the bosom of the earth under my staggering feet,
> Overturn and disperse these arid mountains,
> Hurl your fire on these sad fields,
> Let your burning rocks fall upon me.[40]

For Fuzelier (and presumably for Rameau as well), the dark side of Inca religion lay not with its object of worship but with its total—and hence irrational or "fanatical"—submission to the divine. In striking contrast to Huascar's rage, the jilted European lovers in Act IV end their love affairs in reconciliation and peace.

The final—and arguably most important—theme linking *Les Indes galantes* with the set of works to follow is the Peruvian princess. As spokeswoman for the Incas' lost glory, Phani Palla represents an impulse fundamentally different from that of Huascar. Throughout the act, she distinguishes her own reasoned position from that of the "fierce Incas." "The people," she warns Carlos, "are barbarous and merciless." Nor, however, is hers a position of betrayal. When Carlos attributes her delay in coming to him to her failing love, Phani Palla responds: "Can one that easily break faith with the ties of blood and law? Forgive my uncertainty." In a position that foreshadowed that of other Inca princesses to come, Phani Palla embodies an altogether more reasoned stance than do either her Inca or her Spanish male lovers. Her difference lies in an ability to perceive the good and the bad of each side—unlike both Carlos and Huascar, who remain blinded by their love for her.

Following the success of *Les Indes galantes* other operas and plays took up Inca and Peruvian subjects as vehicles for romantic and moral intrigues. Some, such as *Indes chantantes* (1735), *Amours des Indes* (1735), and *Indes dansantes* (1751), parodied Rameau and Fuzelier's popular ballet, while retaining their largely sympathetic attitude toward New World peoples.[41] Only one parody (*Ballet des romans*) criticized *Les Indes galantes* for its overly romantic view of the Incas. Interestingly, this play was much less popular than were the other, more positive, parodies.[42]

## THE BLACK LEGEND

It is difficult to assess the impact that *Les Indes galantes* and its parodies might have had on public perceptions of either the Incas or the New World in general. When judged by modern standards of realist representation, for example, the work displayed surprisingly little concern with the physical features or even costumes that would signal—to us—that the play's characters were different from their European and Oriental counterparts. Phani Palla, for example, appeared dressed in French "paniers" (hoopskirts), even though information on Inca dress was readily available in Garcilaso's popular chronicle as well as in Frezier's well-known engravings.[43] This disregard for what the nineteenth century would come to know as "local color" (and the twentieth as authenticity) was not unusual. Contemporary operas more often than not were peopled by allegorical characters with names like Wind, Pleasure, or Dream, for whom the concept of a realistic costume simply did not pertain.[44] Nor were the particulars of local color, dress, and custom considered pertinent for the contemporary body of literary works which, though engaging exotic (usually Oriental) subjects, were meant as reflections on universal values and manners. Even in those cases where writers had first-hand knowledge of an Oriental culture, for example, the details of particular customs were considered pedantic.[45] Using an opposite strategy from that advocated by nineteenth-century realism, exotic characters were made to appear credible by locating them within a familiar European system of values. When set within the context of these contemporary literary and operatic traditions, it is not surprising that the Inca characters in *Les Indes galantes* were more prized as allegorical references to contemporary political and philosophical debates than as authentic "representations" of either ancient royalty or contemporary Indians. As with the engravings from Frezier, Feuillée, and Bachelier, "difference" in Rameau's opera had not yet acquired a visual dimension.

Such Inca-based figures as Phani Palla and Huascar did, however, carry a specific set of allegorical possibilities that distinguished them from both Orientals and those American Indians who had not formed recognizable empires or states. Like their Orientalized counterparts, Inca rulers such as Huascar in Fuzelier's libretto were frequently portrayed as overly passionate, hence unpredictable. Both the sun virgins and their colonial counterparts, the *tapadas*, likewise invited constant comparison with the veiled odalisques and harems of an imaginary Orient.[46] The Incas differed, however, from these Oriental subjects in one crucial respect: unlike the rulers who continued to challenge eighteenth-century Europe from Turkey, India, China, and the Middle East, the long-conquered Inca Empire was available as a model of just the type of benevolence that the European imagination routinely denied to the Oriental states. Conversely, as imperial rulers and aristocracy, the Incas could represent neither the innocence nor the barbarism of such celebrated noble savages as the Tupinambá, Hurons, and Mohawks.

Eighteenth-century France was instead interested in the Incas as the victims of a specific sort of European political treachery. As a once-civilized nation steeped in the Garcilasian glories of their solar religion, the Incas had been forcibly destroyed by the fanaticism of Catholic Spain. This focus on the dark side of Spain's misbegotten colonial adventure was known as the "black legend."[47] For the French philosophes, this history of another European monarchy's barbaric past offered a convenient—because relatively inoffensive—avenue through which to extend their critique of the French monarchy and church. In Fuzelier's libretto, good and evil were represented, respectively, by the chaste—though sensuous—sun virgins (identified with, we will recall, the purity of true belief), and an overly passionate male ruler (identified with destruction and unreason). In the more "philosophical" or political works of the black legend, by comparison, all evil was ascribed to Spain as the conqueror of America's enlightened civilizations. The political parables of the black legend, however, shared with Fuzelier's operatic fantasy a fascination with Inca women as the point of sensuous contact through which enlightened Europeans might perceive—and influence—both difference and reason.

The black legend was most fully developed in three eighteenth-century literary works with Inca subjects: Voltaire's *Alzire* (1736), Grafigny's *Lettres d'une péruvienne* (1747), and Marmontel's *Les Incas* (1777). Like *Les Indes galantes*, these works built their basic plot around romantic triangles involving an Inca man, a Spaniard, and an Inca princess or sun virgin. In each of these works too, it is the gendered politics of romance that serve as the medium for political and religious critique.

Voltaire's *Alzire* opened in Paris in 1736, one year after La Condamine's celebrated departure for the New World. Following upon the success of both *Les Indes galantes* and the several earlier plays with New World themes, *Alzire* was the first French tragedy with a specifically Inca setting. It was also one of Voltaire's most popular plays.[48]

Like *Les Indes galantes*, *Alzire* featured a romantic entanglement involving an Inca princess (Alzire), a governor of Peru (Gusman), and an Inca ruler from Potosí (Zamore).[49] The two other main characters are Alzire's father (Montèze) and Gusman's father (Alvarès). Each of the male characters represents opposing positions on the questions of conquest and religious conversion. The two older men (Montèze and Alvarès) advocate methods of peaceful conversion and political alliance between their two peoples. Indeed, it is Alzire's father (Montèze) who convinces her to betray her lover Zamore and to marry Gusman instead, for the good of her people. Alvarès, who was the favored character of both Voltaire and his contemporary audiences, articulates his policy of moderation, alliance, and tolerance in dialogue with the methods of violent conquest and forced conversion advocated by his son, Gusman, whose own commitment to Christianity is presented as hypocritical and insincere.

A similar rift divides the younger and older Inca men. Zamore is imprisoned by Montèze because the insurrection he is leading threatens to prevent Alzire's strategic marriage to Gusman. Voltaire compares Zamore's violence to the intolerant attitudes of his enemy Gusman, yet he clearly also suggests that Zamore's vengeance is justified by the Spaniards' extreme cruelty. Alzire, meanwhile, is portrayed as an obedient, and hence virtuous, daughter. Unlike the male characters, each of whom advocates distinct positions on both Christianity and the politics of conquest, Alzire—as the clearest embodiment of Voltaire's own deist position—accepts that it is possible to embrace some tenets of Christianity while still remaining loyal to her Inca gods. It is God and the sincerity of belief itself, rather than the institutions of an organized religion, that form the basis of Alzire's religion.

The play ends when Zamore mortally wounds the evil Gusman. Alvarès, distraught at the sight of his dying son, condemns both Zamore and Alzire to death unless they convert to Christianity. After much theological discussion, the two lovers refuse, arguing that an insincere conversion would be the worst betrayal. The play then finds an unsuspected resolution in the unlikely figure of the dying Gusman, who enters on a stretcher to declare that he has found true religion. Citing Christ's forgiveness, he pardons his assassin (Zamore) and wife (Alzire) by blessing their union. The two Incas—stunned by the unsuspected benevolence of their European enemy—decide to consider Christianity and are thus spared their lives. Although Voltaire's Incas fare somewhat better than Fuzelier's Huascar, it is still the European man who—notwithstanding his own corrupt and hypocritical past—closes the play as the advocate of tolerance, forgiveness, and reconciliation. The Incas, it is clear, will need European guidance if their capacity for sincerity, passion, and belief is to be sculpted into "universal" reason.

*Alzire* spoke clearly for Voltaire's fascination with both the trappings of Inca royalty and the benign despotism of Garcilaso's Inca state.[50] Here, at a comfortable remove of several centuries and many thousands of miles, was an empire that could stand as a model of the eighteenth century's ideal form of government: an enlightened despotism in which the privilege of royalty did not interfere with the administration of justice, where human weakness had not yet corrupted the principles of true religion, and where pagan religion had not been blackened by the bloody sacrificial cults attributed to the Aztecs and other New World empires.[51] Indeed, Inca Peru offered Voltaire an ideal setting for two of his favorite themes—tolerance and deism. Yet by staging his discussion of these themes in a location—ancient Peru—where the finger of blame would necessarily point away from France and toward Spain, he could do so in a relatively innocuous fashion. In fact, *Alzire* was written largely to appease the censors after the uproar caused the year before by Voltaire's sympathetic account of English Protestantism and government in the *Lettres philosophiques*.[52]

*Alzire* also continues the themes of religion and sex so prominent in the Inca act of *Les Indes galantes*. In Voltaire's script, these themes converge in the body of the play's only female character: Alzire. Alzire is the conduit through which the Spaniards Alvarès and, eventually, Gusman discover reason. She is also, however, the figure through which Voltaire's eighteenth-century audience could most clearly perceive the possibility of a truly radical form of difference. This difference was, for Voltaire, both religious and sexual. Whereas Zamore and Montèze portray elements of a familiar European scepticism, Alzire speaks for the pure form of religious belief (deism), which Voltaire offers as an alternative to the corruption of European belief by both conquest and the Church. It is Alzire's sexuality, however, that makes it possible to imagine such a religious belief as compatible with reason. Politically, her sexuality figures in Voltaire's script as the (potential) conduit for an alliance that might link two peoples—and two cultures. Because Alzire is enough like Gusman to marry him, it becomes possible to imagine her American religious doctrine as one a European might also hold. In the end, however, Voltaire (unlike Rameau and Fuzelier) allows no crossing of the sexual divide separating European from Inca. It is the distinctiveness of their origins—or "nations"—which, in the end, determines the tragic resolution of each character as well as the perhaps equally tragic limitations on Voltaire's ambiguous message about religion. Gusman ends up the rather surprising spokesman for reason; Alzire and Zamore end up married to each other and jointly in awe of Gusman's reason and tolerance. The audience is left guessing about the importance of even imagining a different form of religious belief, and is presumably satisfied with a situation in which no boundaries have been transgressed.

Figure 2.6. "The
Peruvian princess
dragg'd from the
Temple of the Sun"
(1819)

## THE PERUVIAN PRINCESS

Ten years after the first performance of *Alzire*, Madame de Grafigny published
a short epistolary novel with the title of *Letters of a Peruvian Woman* (*Lettres
d'une péruvienne* [1747]). The novel, which was one of the most widely read
books of the eighteenth century, presents the story of Zilia, a Peruvian princess and sun virgin who is first kidnapped from the burning Temple of the Sun
by unscrupulous Spaniards and then rescued by French pirates (Figure 2.6).[53]
In a series of thirty-eight letters to her Peruvian lover, Aza, Zilia recounts her
experiences in Europe, her astonishment at the strangeness of French ways,
and her courtship by the *chevalier* Deterville who sends her treasures looted
from the temple. Assisting Deterville's cause is his friendly, but ultimately
duplicitous sister, Celine (Figure 2.7). By the end of the novel, Zilia has declared her independence from both Aza, who goes to Spain in a failed attempt
to find her, and Deterville, who remains a persistent suitor. Zilia comments
that Europe has made Aza cold. Indeed, both his purity and (American) sensuality have been corrupted by Spain where, Zilia learns, Aza was unfaithful to

Figure 2.7. The
Peruvian princess
(1752)

her. As for the French, Zilia finds them warm yet unsensuous. She feels indebted to Deterville for his friendship and patronage in France, but finds him
an unappealing partner for marriage. The novel closes with Zilia's impassioned plea that Deterville respect her determination to live as a unattached
woman and equal. Deterville then honors her offer of friendship by buying her
a chateau, which he has decorated with portraits of royal Inca women and
treasures hidden in a secret room where Zilia can relive her Peruvian past.

Through Zilia's letters, the recently widowed Madame de Grafigny presents
a bitter commentary on the place of women in contemporary French society.
The princess's Peruvian origins, however, are not coincidental to her feminist
message.[54] Much like Alzire, Zilia offers her readers a radical—and in this case
feminist—vision of what a different society could be. Her European suitor,
like Gusman, is made to see Reason through his contact with her sensuous
(and sexual) being. But this time, Reason is made to bear the feminist message
of true equality, as opposed to simple tolerance. Similarly, for Zilia, it is her

status as an outsider that enables her to perceive the injustices that French society inflicts upon women (such as de Grafigny) who choose to live independently of men. Zilia's combination of independence and sensuality permits her to occupy a position with respect to romantic love that is reminiscent of Alzire's position on religion: just as Alzire represents a deism freed of corruption, material interests, and clergy, Zilia proposes to free romantic love and friendship from the forms of conquest and possession that she sees corrupting relationships between European men and women.

As in other contemporary works discussed here, de Grafigny's *Letters* provides no hint of the physical appearance of its American characters. In the plates that accompany later editions of the novel, the Peruvian princess appears indistiguishable from her European companions. As might be expected, Zilia's own letters describe neither her own nor Aza's features. Nor do they describe any reaction to the strange countenances of her French and Spanish captors. Instead, religion, once again, plays the lead role in marking difference in de Grafigny's book. On her first encounter with Deterville, for example, Zilia wonders at his strange behavior as he kneels beside her bed. "Might not this nation be idolatrous?" Zilia asks Aza in her letter. "I have yet to see him adore the sun: Perhaps they take women as the object of their cult?"[55]

Thirty years after Grafigny's immensely successful novel, Jean François Marmontel published a historical novel entitled *Les Incas, ou la destruction de l'Empire du Pérou* (1777).[56] As a publicist for the black legend, Marmontel's novel was the eighteenth century's single most influential book on Peruvian or Inca subjects. Throughout the book, which Marmontel describes as a tract against fanaticism, he is unrelenting in his criticism of the Spaniards whose greed destroyed the Inca Empire (Figure 2.8). For historical information on the conquest and Inca society, he relied on the usual sources. Garcilaso's detailed history provided a basis for Marmontel's imaginative descriptions of baroque sun festivals and dynastic rituals.[57] But it was, above all, Las Casas whose voice resonated in Marmontel's apocalyptic epic of death and destruction. Indeed, Marmontel dedicated his novel to the memory of Las Casas, whom he described in the preface to the book as "the model of all that I revere."

As with the other works of the Inca Operatic, *Les Incas* develops its arguments about politics, morals, and tolerance through a complex romantic intrigue involving a sun virgin, Cora, and her Spanish lover, Alonzo. "Difference," in turn, is marked by these characters' moral positions rather than by any form of physical difference. Like Alzire and Zilia before her, Cora embodies the purity of religion and sentiment that was violated by the conquest. Her Spanish lover Alonzo is both a soldier and a diplomat. He resembles Voltaire's Alvarès in his advocacy of alliance and reconciliation. Marmontel, however, is much clearer on the ways in which such a peaceful conquest

Figure 2.8. Allegory of conquest (1777)

might have been obtained. Following Montesquieu, he believed that commerce and trade would have brought (and could presumably still bring) both
reason and peace to Peru.[58]

Through the person of Cora, Marmontel compares the fate of the Inca Empire to that of the conquered (or violated) female body. On this point, Marmontel follows along much the same track as his predecessors in the Inca
Operatic: Reason and morality are embodied in the virginal body of the Inca
woman. They are then discovered in their purest—and most different—form
by a European man who becomes romantically (and in this case, sexually)

Figure 2.9. Initiation of Cora as a sun virgin (1777)

involved with the Inca princess. Marmontel adds a new twist to this familiar mode of discovering and realizing difference: he casts the act of conquest as an act of vision.

We first meet Cora as she is about to be initiated as a sun virgin. (Figure 2.9). In a moving (and rather melodramatic) scene, Marmontel describes how Cora first enters the Temple of the Sun. The experience for her is overwhelming. As she utters her vows of chastity, she feels an instinctual foreboding. Her lips tremble and her legs shake. Her very being, we are led to believe, is one of pure sensuous instinct. She engages the world not through reason, but through her body.

These feelings and sensations climax when Cora sees Alonzo for the first time at a ceremony to which the Spaniard had been invited as "a favor of the Inca Monarch."

[Cora] advances, a veil on her head and her forehead crowned with flowers. Her eyes are lowered; yet her long lashes allow their sparkling fire to escape. Her beautiful hands tremble; her lips palpitate; her breast swells, everything in her expresses the emotion of a sensitive heart. How happy [she would have been] had her timid eyes not lifted towards Alonzo! She was lost in a look [un regard]; that single imprudent glance made her see the most formidable enemy of her repose and innocence.[59]

Confused, Cora then looks for solace to the image of her divine husband, the Sun, but what she sees there is none other than the face of Alonzo. Needless to say, Alonzo, too, is caught up in "that rapid and terrible flash [eclair], which embraced at once two hearts made for each other."[60] It is the sense of sight—the perception of the other—that penetrates and alters the physical beings of both Cora and Alonzo. For Cora, the physical sensations are generalized and overwhelming. They effectively transform her from chaste virgin to sensuous woman. For Alonzo, the sensation is localized in the heart; the site—the sensorium commune—from which the sight of Cora penetrates and transforms his body and his being.[61]

The same visual language of flashes, recognition, transformation, and penetration again surfaces in Marmontel's account of the two lovers' next (and final) meeting. This time, however, the setting is the destructive passion of a volcanic eruption. Alonzo, who has not stopped thinking of Cora since the day he first saw her, is wandering in the vicinity of the Temple of the Sun when the volcano begins to erupt. Determined to rescue the beautiful Cora, Alonzo climbs over the crumbling temple walls. The thinly veiled sexual metaphors with which Marmontel (who also wrote erotic poetry) describes Alonzo's entry into the forbidden temple are again expressed in a visual language.[62]

He penetrated into that asylum where no mortal had ever dared to penetrate before him. The shadows favored him. A lugubrious and sombre day had given way to night. The night was lit only by the burning streams thrown out by the mountain; and that frightful light . . . only allowed Alonzo's eyes to see as wandering shadows the alarmed virgins running in the gardens of their palace.[63]

Alonzo is finally able to distinguish Cora among the shadows. He steps forward and announces to the frightened woman that "a god watches over you and cares for your days." Hearing his voice,

Intimidated, Cora stops. At that moment the earth trembles and with a boom the mountain throws out a column of fire, which in the darkness uncovers to the priestess's eyes her lover who extends his arms to her. Whether from a sudden movement of fright [frayeur] or perhaps of love, Cora throws herself and faints in the arms of the young Spaniard.[64]

Alonzo then takes Cora to a palace belonging to a friend of Bartolomé de Las Casas. Later the two lovers consummate their love outside the city walls. Cora warns Alonzo of the horrendous penalty that awaits any sun virgin who violates her vows. Alonzo, however, must reluctantly leave the weeping Cora if he is to carry out his plan to negotiate peace between Inca and Spaniard. Although Alonzo is, in the end, unsuccessful, his efforts are rewarded by the Incas, who offer him a principality in Tumbes.

After many detours and subplots, Marmontel concludes his novel with a scene striking today for its untrammeled melodrama.[65] Cora, who is about to give birth to Alonzo's baby, hears of her lover's death at the hands of his countrymen. As she searches for his grave, columns of vanquished Inca citizens file past, averting their eyes. Finally, the distraught princess finds her lover's grave "in the same place where once stood the Inca's throne." Upon discovering his grave,

> a heart-rending cry burst from the depths of her entrails. She hurls herself to the ground. She falls bewildered on that still moist earth which the grass had not covered and embraces it with the love with which she would have embraced her husband's body. . . . Finally the excess of pain breaks the knots with which nature yet held in her flanks the fruit of an unhappy love, and she expires while giving birth. But that attack of desperation was not fatal to her alone, and the infant which she had brought to this world is also struck. He dies [eteint] without opening his eyes to the light, without having felt its misfortunes.[66]

Far from a melodramatic footnote in the history of the European novel, Cora's tragic demise (Figure 2.10) reveals the extent to which the lessons of the black legend were preached—and learned—through the medium of sentiment, sex, and emotion. If the Spaniards were to be hated, it was as much for the barbarism with which they had destroyed the utopian sexual and sensuous possibilities of the Americas as it was for their shameless cruelty, intolerance, and religious fanaticism. Leaving little to the imagination, Marmontel describes the utopia that the Spaniards destroyed in strikingly sexual terms. In the Americas, the philosopher writes:

> Of all the evils of which humanity complains, only pain [douleur] was known to these people. Not even death was known; they called it the long sleep. . . . Only love could have troubled the harmony and intelligence of such a sweet society. Though peaceful itself, love was subject to the empire of beauty. Sex, made to dominate by the ascendancy of pleasure, had the happy power of varying, of multiplying its conquests, without capturing the favored lover, without commiting oneself. . . . Certain of finding at each instant a sensitive heart and a thousand charms, the forsaken lover did not have time to grieve over his disgrace, or to be jealous of the bliss of the one who had been preferred over him. The ties that bound two spouses was solid or fragile as they wished. Taste [and] desire formed

Figure 2.10. Death of Cora (1819)

it; caprice could break it. Without blushing one stopped loving; without com-
plaining one ceased to please: in their hearts cruel hatred never followed love; all
lovers were rivals; all rivals were friends; each of their female companions saw in
them, without any shame, all the happy men they had made or would make of
them in their turn.[67]

Much like Grafigny, but without her feminist perspective, Marmontel sees
in the Americans and particularly the Incas a means to imagine a form of
sensuous love that is dominated by neither conquest nor possession. For him,
as for Diderot, the triumph of Reason brought with it a nostalgia for the more
"natural" forms of sexual liberty that they imagined preceded both reason and
the social contract. In short, as the privileged vehicle for imagining a sensuous
encounter with the other, sex and romance provided the vehicles through
which these authors could imagine what "difference" truly was. For these men
as for their colleague Madame de Grafigny, it was woman who embodied the
purest means of perceiving that difference. What is striking in Marmontel's
novel as compared with the other works of the Inca Operatic is his use of both
vision and sex as the means of attaining this sensuous encounter. By consum-
mating their love, Alonzo and Cora destroy themselves, their child, the Inca
Empire, and the possibility of realizing a purer form of morality and religion.

## ENVISIONING DESIRE

The image with which we began this chapter, La Condamine's engraving of the "Incident at Cuenca," now has more to tell us. As I suggested earlier, La Condamine's expedition introduced the Andes into French public debate. In the Seniergues incident, moreover, La Condamine was engaging (consciously or unconsciously) two rather specific aspects of this public debate in mid-eighteenth-century France. The first was the shifting semantic registers of self and nation; the second dealt with philosophic and scientific speculation regarding the physiological bases of perception and sensory knowledge. It is now possible to consider how the Andes, of all places, figured in these two arenas of European discursive ferment.

In the decades between La Condamine's original expedition (1735) and the expanded edition of his *Relacion abrégée* (1778), public debate about the Andes in France acquired specific characteristics. Various plays and novels introduced a broader French public to an Inca nobility based partly on fantasy and partly on fact. Others, which we have not considered here, most notably Voltaire's 1759 novel *Candide*, built on this fashionable fascination with both Inca royalty and the El Dorado myth to construct an enduring utopian image of "Le Pérou" as a synonym for wealth and pleasure. In the black legend, popular anti-Spanish sentiment fueled political parables in which these utopian images were pitted against both the very real excesses of Spain's American conquest and the imagined benefits to be reaped by a French civilizing mission based on reason and trade. Finally, the works of the Inca Operatic reveal an interest in the forms of religious and sexual difference embodied in the chaste yet sensuous bodies of the Incas' princesses and sun virgins. As the tragic heroines of the eighteenth century's romance with Peru, Cora, Zilia, Phani Palla, and Alzire speak for the extent to which the "political" message of the black legend was experienced as an aesthetic or sensuous discourse of pleasure and desire. Inscribed within their bodies were both the tragedy of Spain's barbarous conquest and the passion with which Spain's enlightened (northern) neighbors had rediscovered the riches of America.

La Condamine's decision to embellish his scientific account with two letters recounting the more dramatic (or sensational) aspects of his expedition reflects this evolution in public expectations regarding the importance of Peru. First, the Seniergues incident (which, as we recall, becomes more central in the 1778 edition) functions as a thinly veiled attack on the corruption and inefficiency of a colonial government that had become a favorite target of the philosophes.[68] By resurrecting the Seniergues affair, La Condamine sought to increase the visibility of his own expedition by contributing to an emerging eighteenth-century concern with the corrupt and evil nature of Spain's New World empire. In this respect, it is interesting to note the role that both gender and sex played in La Condamine's Andean account. The anonymous confidante to whom La Condamine reveals the details of Seniergues's tragic demise is a Madame * * *; the heroine of his other appendix is a French woman who tramps through the Amazon in various states of wildness (and undress) in search of her scientist-husband. Even La Condamine's martyr, Seniergues, acquires a renewed interest if we consider that his death—like that of Voltaire's Gusman and Marmontel's Alonzo—had everything to do with the sexual jealousies aroused in the "overly passionate" men of Spain's Andean colonies.

Foucault has suggested that by the end of the eighteenth century, sex was becoming "a matter that required the social body as a whole, and virtually all of its individuals, to place themselves under surveillance."[69] The reasons Foucault gives for this are inherently discursive and removed. They are contained within Europe and explained as products of an emergent, developing contradiction between monarchical power and the rule of law. The nostalgia for a purer form of love, which the authors of the Inca Operatic projected on the Incas, may well speak for a certain distrust of these new forms of discipline and sexuality. More important, they also speak eloquently for that "explosion of discourse" about sex that Foucault describes as happening at this time.

The beguiling Inca princesses of Voltaire, de Grafigny, Marmontel, and Fuzelier were, of course, not the only non-European women to attract the attention of eighteenth-century Europe. One need only think of Diderot's Tahitians. The princesses of the Inca Operatic also resemble Diderot's more familiar Polynesians in another respect. Their stories, as told by Voltaire, Marmontel, de Grafigny, and Fuzelier, suggest that one of the reasons their bodies and their sex were so compelling was because of the ways in which they elicited (as women) a more careful scrutiny—or, for Foucault, surveillance—of the (masculine) bourgeois self. Alzire, as we have seen, was the means by which men's "reasoned" principles became embodied or transformed into action. Zilia brings the reason of equality to Deterville. Phani Palla highlights the irrationality of Huascar by her love for Don Carlos. Finally, Cora inspires Alonzo's resolve to secure peace (and commerce) between Inca and Spaniard in part, we might surmise, as a means to secure a future for his unlucky son. For Marmontel, this future was not to be. Nor were the possible fruits of a merger between European and Andean peoples.

By framing reason as the sign of a more disciplined masculine self, the sun virgins of the Inca Operatic could be said to support Foucault's theory of an epistemic shift grounded in new forms of bodily awareness and discipline, or "sexuality." Yet their non-European origin suggests a possible critique of Foucault's theory in another respect. Foucault argues that a European discourse of sexuality developed as a class-based form of self-scrutiny. It was not until the mid- to late nineteenth century, he suggests, that the bourgeoisie began to define the discourse of sexuality with reference to bodies other than their own— specifically, in Foucault's account, those of European working-class men and women.[70] Yet in the Inca Operatic we see clearly that the bourgeois or Enlightenment self constructed its notion of the embodied self at least in part through a sensuous encounter with the non-European other. That this other was not described or conceived as being physically different does not detract from the fact that difference itself came to be constructed through this notion of the sensuous and sexual encounter.

The fact that this encounter with the American other occurred through its women will not surprise most students of European colonial discourse. Women, however, figured in the Inca Operatic not only as what we have now come to recognize as the canonic figures of an already theorized form of "exotic difference." They also figured as the actual sensory contacts through which difference itself could be first perceived and then theorized as a product of a particular sensory relation to the non-European (or "other"). In the Inca Operatic, in other words, women's bodies were the symbolic vehicle for both discovering difference and, as Marmontel's novel makes clear, destroying it. This, in turn, suggests something important about the role that gender played in the emergence in the early nineteenth century of modern racial thought.

In the following chapters we will look more closely at the links among gender, sex, and race in early nineteenth-century theories of race and type. I would like to emphasize here the extent to which the ability to speak about these new forms of embodied difference, which we now think of as "gender" and "race," was itself enabled by a certain shift in European common sense about the senses. This shift was represented by—but not confined to—the debate regarding the sensorium commune. The idea expressed by the sensorium commune was that sensory perceptions shared some physical grounding in the body and that this point of contact was, at least potentially, constitutive of what that body was. To understand what this might have entailed, we need only think of our now familiar trope of "love at first sight." In this trope, vision is conceived as an experience originating in the eye. From there, it goes on to excite the body and transform the self. Through this process, vision—in particular the sight of the other—makes possible that certain awareness of the embodied self which Foucault has referred to as sexuality.

Although this equation of sensuous contact with personal, physical, and moral transformation underlies all the works of the Inca Operatic, it is not until Marmontel's relatively late (1777) novel that the physical or erotic sensations of love are so clearly tied to the sense of sight. Cora is transformed and physically debilitated by the sight of her lover. Similarly, Alonzo's orgasmic entry into the Temple of the Sun is figured as a visual experience in which darkness gives way to flashes of light and the blinding revelation it brings. Finally, the tragic end of the Inca Empire is littered with metaphors of blindness—from the Inca citizens who avert their eyes to the stillborn baby who is deprived of the opportunity to see or feel. He dies "without having opened his eyes to the light, without having felt its misfortunes." Interestingly, Marmontel, who makes the most explicit use of this language of visual sensation, is also the only author to consummate the sexual relations between Inca and Spaniard.

Vision in Marmontel's novel is thus somehow connected with a sense of difference. Yet like the other works of the Inca Operatic, it constructs that difference as a sensuous experience, or contact, between two essentially similar bodies. Difference per se is not yet a visual problem. Both Zilia (in her engravings) and Phani Palla (on stage) wear European clothes. A similar lack of concern with the sort of costume that might distinguish the Inca as "other" surfaces in depictions of Cora in both the 1777 and the 1821 edition of Marmontel's novel. While other Incas are shown in more or less accurate interpretations of real Inca dress, the artists consistently emphasize the sexual nature of the sun virgin's body. The 1777 engravings portray Cora in feathered headdress and skirt similar to the one Voltaire prescribes for Alzire.[71] Her naked body and helplessness convey the innocence and rape of the New World by Spanish lust and barbarism. By 1821 Cora's naked body has become the sole visual motif for Marmontel's history. Three of the four engravings that accompany that edition feature a nude or semi-nude Cora. The fourth shows her Aztec counterpart, the single-breasted Amazili.

Nor do the types of phenotypic or physiognomic differences that we have come to understand as "race" enter in either the descriptive or the graphic languages of the Inca Operatic. Zilia—who literally carries the symbolic burden of the conquest in her body—is portrayed in the engravings that accompany the book's later editions as a fair woman, whose complexion and features make her indistinguishable from her French companions. (In keeping with Grafigny's storyline, Zilia is also fully clothed, even—unlike Cora—at the moment of being dragged from the Temple of the Sun.) In Marmontel's novel, Amazili and Cora stand for the vulnerability of American civilization in the face of Spanish brutality. As graphic icons of the Americas, however, neither Cora nor Amazili bears the physical features or physiognomy that the nineteenth century would come to identify as "Indian." Even in the plates accompanying the more sober accounts of Frezier, Feuillée, Bachelier, and La Condamine, Andean women were pictured as identical to Europeans. Their difference lay not in their bodies but in the degree of their perfection. The Incas, Voltaire reflects, "lack only our vices to be equal in every respect to the Europeans."

As the calculus of "difference" became increasingly visual in the following century, the possibility that a statement such as Voltaire's could easily be made became more and more remote. The sun virgins and utopian agendas of the Inca Operatic would not long survive the languages of sexuality, race, and type through which the nineteenth century would refigure European understandings of both themselves and their "others."

*so, again, does "race" actually exist in 18th c. Fran/Peru (Spain)?*

## CHAPTER THREE

# An Economy of Vision

I began to tire of meeting at each step only Indians
and mestizos, all dressed in the same manner.
*(Alcides d'Orbigny, 1854)*

IN 1739—the same year in which Seniergues was killed in Cuenca, La Condamine finally measured the meridian in Quito, and *Alzire* was entering its second repertory year in Paris—the king of France appointed a new intendant for the Jardin du Roi, or "King's Garden," in Paris.[1] The man he chose for the job was a thirty-two-year-old naturalist named Georges Louis Leclerc, Comte de Buffon. From his position at the Jardin du Roi, this man would reign supreme over French life sciences until his death in 1788, just one year before the beginning of the revolution that would transform French society and European politics forever.

As the King's gardener, Buffon's ambitions were necessarily global. His task, after all, was to articulate a philosophy of nature that could speak for the social order embodied by the king and a method that could further (if not finish) the encyclopedic project through which eighteenth-century philosophers hoped to gain knowledge of the world. As part of his global study of nature, Buffon wasted no time turning his gaze toward distant South America. What he found there was surprising in a time when other Parisians were crowding the ballet halls and theaters to see Voltaire's and Rameau's Incas.

He began, predictably, with climate. Flying defiantly in the face of accounts by travelers such as Feuillée and Frezier, Buffon described the climate of South America as uniformly cool and moist. As evidence for this moist and humid environment, he cited the relative sizes of animals in the Old and New World. The New World tapir, he argued, was smaller than the Old World elephant; American camelids were smaller than Old World camels; the puma was smaller than the lion; and so on. This discrepancy in size was taken as proof of both the overall inferiority of New World animals and the coolness of their climate, since Buffon believed that only warm climates could produce large animals.[2]

Man was no exception to this global law whereby cool, moist climates produced stunted forms of life.

> Although the New World savage be of more or less the same stature as man in our world, this does not suffice to make of him an exception to the general fact of

shrinkage in the living nature of this continent [South America]. The savage is feeble and small in his reproductive organs. He has neither body hair nor beard, and no ardor whatsoever for his woman [*femelle*]. Although lighter than the European, because he is more of the habit of running, he is nonetheless much less strong of body. He is also less sensitive, and yet more cowardly and lazy. He has no vivacity at all, nor spiritual activity. The [activity] of his body is less an exercise, a voluntary movement, than a necessary action caused by need. Take away from him hunger and thirst, and you destroy at the same time the activating principal of all his movement; he will remain stupidly in repose, on his feet or lying down, for days at a time.[3]

Two things stand out about Buffon's description of South American nature and peoples: his interest in size and his concern with what we might broadly think of as vitality. Animals in the Old and New World, he argues, are structurally very much alike. The llama is like the camel; the elephant like the tapir. Where they differ is in size. In the case of humans, size differential is accompanied by lack of sexual and productive "vigor." The type of difference Buffon is concerned with describing is general or systemic, rather than detailed and specific. New World humans are different—and rather repulsively so—because of the very nature of their being. Elsewhere Buffon describes the climate that has produced these aberrant humans in strikingly tactile, even visceral terms: South America is, he writes, damp, slimy, muddy, moldy, vaporous, and cool. In such an environment, only insects and reptiles can prosper. Indeed, he speculates, frogs, toads, snakes, and "other beasts of this type" are "nowhere . . . as large as in the New World."[4]

Consider the very different way in which another Frenchman, Alcides d'Orbigny, would describe the South American Indian some eighty years later. I reproduce his citation in the manner in which it was printed:

### First Race.
#### ANDO-PERUVIAN.
### First Branch.
### Peruvian.

Color: Dark olive-brown. Average height: 1 meter 597 millimeters. Massive forms [*formes massives*]: trunk very long relative to the whole. Receding forehead; large, oval face. Long nose, very aquiline, enlarged at the base. Mouth rather large; medium lips. Horizontal eyes with yellowish cornea. Nonprominent cheekbones. Pronounced features. Physiognomy: serious, reflective, sad.[5]

What we immediately note in this description of the South American is the severe, even ruthless, partitioning of the body. The Indian is made up of a forehead, nose, trunk, and so on. His mouth is large; his eyes yellowish; his skin olive brown. D'Orbigny's language for describing difference is more engaged with a piecemeal inspection or dissection of the Indian's body and less concerned with the sorts of systemic, tactile, and aesthetic modes of plotting difference that occupied Buffon. D'Orbigny's is a language that we have become familiar with as the language of nineteenth-century racial theory.

But what really separates these two modes of describing—and theorizing—the South American Indian? One explanation would see d'Orbigny's account as the product of a general move toward greater precision or accuracy of description, toward what we might think of as visual accountability. In fact, one great difference separating d'Orbigny from Buffon was the fact that d'Orbigny spent eight years in South America. His account carries with it the authority of the "eye witness."

Another explanation would relate Buffon's and d'Orbigny's choice of words to a dramatic historical break or rupture between the qualitatively different sorts of "epistèmes" or epistemological fields that Foucault has described for classical and modern European thought.[6] Rather than seeing a continuous or progressive history that moves toward greater realism, this approach posits a break or rupture between Buffon's eighteenth-century naturalist's gaze and d'Orbigny's nineteenth-century clinical technique.

In reality, of course, the history separating Buffon from d'Orbigny constitutes neither a total break nor a smooth transition. Nowhere is this clearer than in the concept of race that underwrites both men's accounts. If, for example, we were to map the concept of race as an aesthetic hierarchy of difference, we could very easily argue for a continuous lineage connecting Buffon—who, in other texts, was also very concerned with describing human skin color—and d'Orbigny. Similarly, d'Orbigny's description of such things as the texture and smell of the South Americans' skin invokes a sensuous language reminiscent of Buffon, but with an opposite valence. Their skin, he writes, "is smooth, polished, even brilliant, as soft as satin" with a "particular odor different from that of the negro and a bit less strong."[7]

How then are we to explain the dramatic differences between Buffon's and d'Orbigny's modes of describing the body? How are we to relate these different descriptive languages to possible differences—and similarities—in their respective understandings of "race"? In this chapter I explore the historical and methodological issues behind these questions by looking at the work of three authors who made their name writing about South America. First, I examine the relationship between space and perception in the work of Buffon. I then consider the very different spatializing and visualizing techniques used by Buffon's most famous critic, Alexander von Humboldt. Although Humboldt's work is important on a variety of fronts, here I focus on his philosophy of visual perception, his theory of landscape, and the ways in which his "physiognomic gaze" excluded human subjects. Finally, I look at the emergence of a comparative or typological language of equivalencies in d'Orbigny's study of the South American "races." I argue that it is only by looking at this spatializing and statistical language of type that we can understand the dramatic transformation that took place in European understandings of race during the years that separated Buffon from d'Orbigny.

## THE KING'S GARDENER

Any discussion of Buffon must begin with the institution he headed.[8] The Jardin du Roi, which was founded in 1626 as a garden for medicinal plants, had been expanded in the early decades of the eighteenth century into an experimental botanical garden. When Buffon took over the directorship in 1739, the Jardin included, in addition to the horticultural gardens that Buffon would more than double in size, several buildings housing a collection of natural history specimens known as the Cabinet du Roi. Together the gardens and Cabinet offered Buffon and his colleagues an extensive research collection of fauna and flora from all of Europe, as well as a significant—if somewhat more random—selection of living plants and preserved animals from the Middle East, India, Africa, and the Americas.[9]

As one of Europe's leading research centers, the Jardin and its Cabinet spoke for the French state's interest in natural history and the life sciences. Through its patronage of scientific research, the Crown heightened its prestige in Europe. Of even greater importance, however, was the ideological impulse that a science intent on discovering the universal or global laws of nature provided to France's imperial project. By visiting the Cabinet du Roi and by attending classes held at the Jardin, the emerging bourgeois sectors of Paris could participate in the fruits of foreign exploration. In this sense, the Jardin fulfilled a popularizing pedagogical mission whose importance to royal interests equaled that of its status as a research collection.[10]

The large numbers of both amateur enthusiasts and professional scholars who attended classes at the Jardin helped to make Buffon one of the most widely read authors in Europe. His life work was the *Histoire naturelle, générale et particulière* (Natural History: General and Particular).[11] Its forty-four extensively illustrated volumes, published over the course of five decades, offered an encyclopedic survey of the thousands of animals and plants that Buffon had seen at the Jardin and Cabinet du Roi in Paris, the Menagerie du Roi in Versailles, and the numerous traveling sideshows that passed through eighteenth-century France.

If the *Histoire naturelle* was one of the eighteenth century's most popular books, it was so, in part, because it told a relatively simple story. Buffon grounded everything from species differentiation to civilization in a single process: the gradual cooling of the earth, beginning at the poles. As climates became progressively cooler, the very large animals that supposedly thrived in warm regions either became extinct or were forced to migrate south into the tropical zone. Because hotter climates were thought to produce darker skin, this same process could also be invoked to explain variation in human skin color.[12] As evidence for his theories, Buffon pointed to the fossil mammoths in northern Europe and the fact that black people, as well as elephants, giraffes, and other large animals, were found only in tropical regions of the Old World.

Although this explanation of species variation and skin color seemed to hold fairly well for the Old World, it ran into serious problems when applied to the New. Not only were there no "black" people native to the American tropics, but some of the darker-skinned peoples lived in the polar regions of North and South America. Nor did New World animals conform to Buffon's predictions. There was nothing comparable to the elephant or giraffe in the American tropics. Indeed, all of the larger mammals lived in the far north, including the moose whose head Thomas Jefferson sent to Buffon in an effort to debunk his theories.[13]

To accommodate the American evidence, Buffon elaborated his doctrine of South American exceptionalism. This doctrine proposed that, in the New World, all species had originally been born in the north where there was an abundance of "organic molecules." From there, the animals migrated south until they reached the isthmus of Panama where the (supposedly) very cold mountains prevented them from entering South America. Because these more hardy, northern species could not enter, South America was "reduced to its own force [and] only gave birth to weaker and much smaller animals than those that have come from the North to populate our southern regions [contrées du Midi]."[14] Humans—who Buffon believed formed one species originating in the Old World—were not exempt from this general law of shrinkage as they migrated south to the "New Continent."

But how did Buffon explain the mechanism through which climate could make organisms shrink (or grow)? To understand this we need to consider two features of Buffon's theory: his spatial understanding of climate and his theory of generation. For Buffon, the word climat was used interchangeably with contrée, or region, to refer to the latitudinal bands defined by temperature and humidity as well as by distance from the equator.[15] In the later volumes of the Histoire this spatial dimension of Buffon's model moved increasingly toward something very like a modern discourse of nation. Each animal, Buffon wrote in 1761, "has its country [pays], its natural fatherland [patrie naturel] in which it is retained by physical necessity; each [animal] is the son of the land [terre] it inhabits, and it is in this sense that one ought to say that this or that animal is original to this or that climate."[16] In his last major work, written in the years leading up to the French Revolution, Buffon assigns each animal a unique "country of origin" (patrie d'origine).[17]

Buffon explained the fit between these "fatherlands" and the life forms they nurtured through his own, somewhat idiosyncratic, theory of generation. Rejecting popular theories of the homunculus, Buffon instead invoked the action of "molecular organisms" that were present in the environment before life and that combined and recombined according to prevailing climatic conditions. Each life form, he argued, was shaped by the interaction of the embryo with organic particles absorbed from food and hence was specific to the particular environment from which that food originated. To answer the question of how it was that each new generation of a species resembled the last, Buffon posited the existence of an "interior mold" (*moule intérieur*). This mold served as a sort of template for positioning the organic particles that individual members of the species absorbed from their food. However, because Buffon recognized the existence of only two such molds—one suited to the tropics, the other to temperate climates—the mold alone could not account for the appearance assumed by either individuals or species.[18] In the Americas, these two molds were further differentiated by the relative abundance and scarcity of organic molecules in North and South America, respectively.

Within this theory, there was room for divine intervention only in the indirect sense that God determined the universal laws governing the combination of molecular particles around these molds.[19] Nor, it is worth mentioning, was there room in Buffon's world for any mechanism by which the biological makeup of a parent's body could in and of itself effect an arrangement of the "particles" within the embryo such that the offspring would assume the same form or type as the parent. Although his theory of the interior mold indirectly acknowledged the existence in nature of a general prototype for every species, the causal role he assigned to this type or mold was decidedly secondary to that of the environment. In other words, neither God nor heredity nor what the nineteenth century would come to understand as the biological principle of racial inheritance entered into Buffon's theory of reproduction.

The gap separating Buffon from anything resembling our own modern understandings of heredity and race becomes clearer still if we consider his lifelong aversion to the notion of "type." In the *Histoire naturelle*, nature is described as an unbroken continuum or horizontal web (*reseau*) of interrelated beings whose connections could be described but never fixed in time, and where certain species acted as transitional categories or connectors between other larger—and more stable—categories of beings. "Nature advances by unknown gradations," Buffon wrote. It "passes from one species to another, and often from one genus to another, by imperceptible nuances."[20] Nor were any categories in nature immutable. Human skin color, for example, could change with climate, and as a result, "one passes without noticing from white to brown and from brown to black."[21] These changes in skin color were accompanied by corresponding changes in the individual's physiognomy (Figure 3.1). The inherently contingent and mutable detail of individual specimens rendered the very idea of fixed or ideal types a logical impossibility for Buffon.

Given his views on nature and type, it is not surprising that Buffon should dismiss the new science of Linnean taxonomy as "an arbitrary order imposed by the mind."[22] The differences separating the two naturalists resonated with the parallel shift in the meanings of "nation" and "race" that we saw at work in Chapter Two. Linnaeus defined species as ideal types existing in nature. As a simultaneously spatial and statistical concept, his idea of species fore-

Figure 3.1. Skin
color change
(1749)

shadowed the modern concept of population and, more important for our
purposes, a nineteenth-century biological discourse in which human "races"
would be both theorized and observed through the spatial and visual technology of "typification." Objecting that nature contained no such fixed boundaries, Buffon instead defined "species" as the "constant succession of similar
individuals that reproduce themselves."[23] It was the inherently invisible bonds
of blood and history that united individuals into groups, species, or nations,
rather than any criteria of visual or physiological similarity. In accordance
with this aristocratic discourse of lineage or species, he referred to the peoples
inhabiting particular climates as "peoples" (*peuple*) or "nations." Throughout
thousands of pages of writing he only very rarely used the more ambiguous
term "race."[24]

When Buffon is looked at in this way, it becomes somewhat easier for us to
understand the political importance of his Jardin du Roi. From his lectern, the
king's gardener taught more than a theory of nature. He preached a vision of

the world in which species and "races" were defined by the authority of succession. In this sense, the disinterested science of botany practiced at the King's Garden had much to do with the increasingly contested terrain of the eighteenth-century French nation. Indeed, for nearly fifty years, Buffon's *Histoire naturelle* and, by association, the Jardin du Roi, stood as France's most important bulwarks against the cosmological revolution that Linnean science implied.[25]

## THE POLITICS OF DESCRIPTION

I have so far focused on two features of Buffon's natural history. The first concerned the territorial framework through which Buffon conceived of the "material forces" (climate) that cause species variation. Here I suggested that Buffon's language bore a certain affinity to a modern discourse of nation. The second involved his understanding of species and generation. Here I suggested just the opposite: that his "ancien régime" definition of species was both politically and discursively at odds with what we would consider to be a modern understanding of racial identity. Now, I want to look more closely at the perceptual philosophy that, in a sense, impeded Buffon from extending the spatializing and typifying language inherent in his climatological theory to a classification of animals and humans. By looking at the tension between these two aspects of Buffon's work, we can begin to ask a rather different set of questions about the relationship between vision and space in the new sorts of racial discourse that would emerge in the decades following Buffon's death.

For Buffon, the goal of description was to capture the essence—what Buffon called "le tout" or "l'ensemble"—of an animal. This essence, he argued, was best taken from the first impressions we receive of a particular thing. "It is in the first glance [*coup d'oeil*] that we throw toward a thing, that we perceive the essence [*ensemble*] and the totality [*totalité*], before we distinguish the parts."[26] To communicate what had been captured in this "first glance," Buffon preferred drawings to words, because the linear character of verbal description worked against the possibility of capturing the impressionistic quality of the glance. Through words, Buffon argued, it was only possible to see nature in parts.

Such a philosophy of description rested on a particular understanding of sensory perception. Buffon denied an identity between events or objects in the world and our perception or "sensing" of them. Instead, he posited "a Leibnizian parallelism between a proper ordering of ideas and the real succession of events" in the world.[27] The order of ideas, or "sequence of thoughts," provoked within ourselves by this parallelism formed for Buffon "the most real impression upon us and gives us relations with exterior objects that we can look upon as real relations, since they are invariable and always constant *relative to ourselves.*"[28] "Man" thus stood apart from nature as the source of the sensuous perceptions, and hence knowledge, through which nature could be understood at all. And of the senses, it was touch, rather than vision, that Buffon privileged in his definition of man. "It is by virtue of touch alone," Buffon wrote, "that we can acquire complete and real knowledge; it is this sense that rectifies all the others [and] without which all effects would only be illusions."[29]

As the referential center of Buffon's perceptual epistemology, the sensuous body also constituted the necessary starting point for any attempt to classify the natural world.

> One judges the objects of Natural History in terms of the relations they have with him. Those that are the most necessary and useful to him will take the first rank. For example, he will give preference in the order of animals to the horse, the dog, and the cow. . . . Then he will concern himself with those which, while not so familiar to him inhabit the same locales and the same climates, like the deer, rabbit, and all the wild animals. . . . It will be the same for . . . all the other productions of Nature; [man] will study them in proportion to the use that he can make of them.[30]

It was in accordance with "this most natural order" that Buffon and his collaborator Louis Jean Marie Daubenton conceived of the original plan of the *Histoire* as a series of concentric circles moving out from man. Those animals that occupied the innermost circles were those with the closest relationship to humans. Those in the outermost circles were those with little or no usefulness for man.[31]

This concentric structure was replicated in Buffon's descriptive and representational method. In the *Histoire*, the relative distances separating such species as, for example, the llama and the dog from man are described as products of their relative utility to him. In the visual language of the image, "utility" was suggested through the spatial hierarchy moving from man to dog to domesticated beast (Figure 3.2). A similar model of concentric hierarchy animated Buffon's descriptions of individual animals. All animals, wrote Daubenton, "resemble one another in the center and differ at the extremities that are the tail, the hand, the horns, the organs of movement."[32] For Buffon, this technique of description meant that the artist should begin with each animal's heart and "then move progressively to the periphery where all beings differed."[33]

This technique was not only radically different from Linnaeus's competing taxonomy based on the piecemeal description of plant and animal morphology. It was also quite different from the understanding of difference that would come to characterize nineteenth-century thought. Buffon defended a concentric understanding of both space and the way the eye moved through it. In this concentric and tactile ordering of perception, difference was perceived as incremental—whether it be the degrees of "utility" distinguishing

Figure 3.2.
Llamas (1749)

different animals, the nuanced variations differentiating one individual from the next, or the degrees of difference that Daubenton and Buffon assigned to the center and periphery of an animal's body. One shade of variation, skin color, or body surface faded imperceptibly into the next. As we will see, this spatial model for visualizing and representing difference stood at a far remove from the bounded, discrete, and contiguous spaces that Humboldt and other nineteenth-century scientists defended as a means of disciplining the scientific gaze.

## THE GREAT HUMBOLDT

In the early decades of the new century, Buffon's theories of species, climate, and generation came under attack on various fronts. Just a few short years after Buffon's death, Linnean method was enshrined as the official science of the Revolution and the *Histoire naturelle* rewritten to incorporate Linnean terminology. One of Buffon's most influential—and damaging—critics was the celebrated Prussian traveler and geographer Friedrich Heinrich Alexander von Humboldt. Humboldt's assault on Buffon was launched from two related fronts: as someone who had actually traveled to South America, he was able to rally evidence against Buffon's more outrageous claims about South American nature. He also defended a visual methodology based on just that notion of type which Buffon had so assiduously fought against.

Humboldt was born in Berlin in 1769.[34] From his ' Prussian father's side, he inherited his standing as *noblesse de robe*. From his French mother's side, he acquired both social connections within Europe's expanding commercial bourgeoisie and the substantial inheritance that would pay for his travels and publications. Following a brief career as chief engineer and administrator for the Prussian state mines, Humboldt turned to the more romantic art of scientific travel. Inspired by the Pacific journeys of Bougainville and Cook as well as by the Amazonian adventures of La Condamine, whose work he read in 1797, Humboldt initially planned to undertake a journey around the globe.[35] In preparation, he traveled extensively around Europe, crossing the Alps several times on foot. Next he contemplated a journey in the company of English nobility to study the antiquities of Egypt. Finally, together with the botanist Aimé Bonpland, he made several attempts to travel to North Africa. Their first attempt was from Marseilles; their second was from Spain, where Humboldt's imagination was once again diverted, this time from Algiers to America. Having received the necessary blessing of the Spanish Crown, Humboldt and Bonpland finally left Europe in June 1799. They arrived in the Venezuelan town of Cumaná a few weeks later, on July 16.

Following a two-year tour of Venezuela and the Orinoco, Humboldt and Bonpland launched their journey into the interior of South America from the Caribbean coast of New Granada in April 1801. They then worked their way south along the spine of the Andes through Popayán, Pasto, Quito, Cuenca, Loxa, and Cajamarca and on to the coastal cities of Trujillo and Lima (Figure 3.3). After a month in Lima—where Humboldt despaired of creole indifference to Peru's Andean interior and Incan past—the two scientists embarked for Mexico a few days before Christmas in 1803.[36]

On their return from the Americas the following year, Humboldt settled in Paris to lecture and write on his studies in America. His first publication, the *Essay on the Geography of Plants*, appeared in 1805. It was followed three years later by his most popular book, *Views of Nature*. In 1810 he published a two-volume folio of lithographs entitled *Views of the Cordilleras and Monuments of Indigenous Peoples of America* (hereafter *Views*). This was followed by thirty volumes of scientific works published over the next three decades as *Travels to the Equinoctial Regions of the New Continent in 1799, 1800, 1801, 1802, 1803, and 1804*. Finally and in addition to what he considered his more serious scientific work, Humboldt also published a separate three-volume travel account describing his experiences as far as Cartagena.[37]

Figure 3.3. Quindiu Pass in the Andean Cordillera (1810)

It is impossible to overstate the influence of Humboldt's works both in his native Europe and in the new Latin American republics. For French readers accustomed to the fantastic excesses of both Buffon's work and the Inca Operatic, his *Views* provided a fascinating glimpse of what the Americas "really looked like." His work also presented, as we will see, a radically different vision of American history. For those who dreamed of colonial and commercial projects in Spain's restless colonies, the *Travels* provided encyclopedic coverage of the geography, botany, zoology, astronomy, climate, and politics of South and Central America. For the Spanish American creole patriots, his work provided proof of the unique character of their landscape, resources, and history.

Other authors have discussed Humboldt's contributions to Latin American identity, European geography, the life sciences, and travel writing.[38] In agreement with these critics, I understand Humboldt's influence on Americanist thought to be a product of both the breadth of his ambition and the particularities of his method. In the following discussion, however, I focus a somewhat different lens on Humboldt's theories of plant geography and landscape. I argue that his work on South America must be understood as part of a new economy of vision in which the perceptual principles of Buffon's concentric and tactile world would be replaced by a typological or physiognomic discourse of visual experience.


### THE PHYSIOGNOMIC GAZE

Much like Buffon, whose understanding of *climat* carried with it a territorial component, Humboldt considered the world to be made up of regions, each with "its own distinctive character."[39] The similarities with Buffon stopped there, however. For Humboldt, the natural region was an observable, organic whole whose character depended less on such absolute (and ultimately tactile) qualities as temperature and humidity than on the total visual and aesthetic effect that Humboldt referred to as a region's "physiognomy." "As we recognise in distinct organic beings a determinate physiognomy," Humboldt wrote, "so each region of the earth has a natural physiognomy peculiar to itself."[40] For Humboldt, "the great problem of the physical description of the globe [was] the determination of the form of these types [and] the laws of their relations with each other."[41]

No sole element was to be privileged in defining the distinctive physiognomy or "type" of a given place. Certain classes of things, however, were more influential than others in creating what Humboldt repeatedly referred to as the "overall impression" of particular regions and locales. Humboldt considered rock formations, for example, insufficient elements from which to define a region's physiognomy. Because only a limited number of geological formations recurred throughout the world, rocks evoked powerful memories that Humboldt feared could obstruct the scientific task of deciphering the physiognomy or visual character of a place. Animals also proved unsuitable because their mobility prevented the observer from holding them within the visual landscape. Plants, however, elicited precisely the type of stable, replicable visual experience that Humboldt considered necessary to identify the physiognomy of place:

> But if the characteristic aspect of different portions of the earth's surface depends conjointly on all external phenomena—if the contours of the mountains, the physiognomy of plants and animals, the azure of the sky, the forms of the clouds, and the transparency of the atmosphere, all combine in forming that general impression which is the result of the whole, yet it cannot be denied that the vegetable covering with which the whole earth is adorned is the principal element in the impression. Animal forms are deficient in mass, and the individual power of motion that animals possess, as well as often the smallness of their size, withdraw them from our sight. The vegetable forms, on the contrary, produce a greater effect by their magnitude and by their constant presence.[42]

To understand the revolution that the Humboldtian method implied, it is helpful to consider how this focus on *vegetation* differed from the eighteenth-century botanists' interest in plants. For Humboldt, the scientist's task was to gauge the overall or cumulative effect of the whole—and to do so by experiencing nature firsthand. Plants, therefore, were to be studied in their natural settings as part of systemic wholes, rather than ás botanical specimens uprooted from their natural context. To accomplish this, Humboldt argued, the scientist must replace botanical particularism with a holistic (or even artistic) view of the landscape's overall character or "type."[43]

> In determining these leading forms or types . . . we must not follow the march of systems of botany, in which from other motives the parts chiefly regarded are the smaller organs of propagation, the flowers and the fruit; we must, on the contrary, consider solely *that which by its mass stamps a peculiar character on the total impression produced, or on the aspect of the country.* . . . [T]he botanic systematist divides many groups that the physiognomist is obliged to unite.[44]

Humboldt's method resembled Buffon's in its opposition to the particularizing project of Linnean botany. Humboldt, however, was careful to caution against both the botanist's tendency to view a whole through its parts and the eighteenth century's sensuous fascination with the (feminine-gendered) sentiments aroused by the American exotic. In their place, Humboldt urged the traveler to cultivate a (masculine) discipline of both the senses and the intellect. "The unbounded riches of nature," Humboldt writes, "occasion an accumulation of separate images; and accumulation disturbs the repose and the unity of impression which should belong to the picture. . . . [W]hen addressing the feelings and imagination, a firm hand is needed to guard the style from degenerating into an undesirable species of poetic prose."[45] Whereas Buffon saw nature arrayed around man, Humboldt's physiognomic method required a mobile, observing subject whose disciplined senses could perceive the essence or "unity" of the landscapes through which he moved.

The sixty-nine plates in Views speak to the importance of landscape for Humboldt's physiognomic method.[46] His attraction to the Andean landscape was driven, at least in part, by his polemic with the naturalists. For Buffon and other naturalists, mountains formed the structure—or skeleton—underlying the apparent disorder of the earth's surface.[47] Because volcanoes were evidence of the thermodynamic forces through which the earth's surface had been formed, those regions—such as Andean South America—where many active volcanoes were present were taken to be geologically immature and hence unstable environments. In such a hostile environment, Buffon argued, humans could not achieve civilization. Armed with such theories, Buffon only needed to point to the presence of massive mountain ranges and active volcanoes to "prove" that civilized society had never existed in the Americas.

Like nearly every other scholar of his time, Humboldt agreed with Buffon's premise of environmental determination. Where Humboldt disagreed was in his assessment of the particular effects of climate, altitude, and landscape in South America. In Europe, Humboldt reasoned, it had indeed been the benign and temperate qualities of the Grecian Mediterranean that had nurtured civilization. In the New World, however, civilization had found its inspiration not in the temperate valleys but, rather, in precisely those highland areas of South and Central America that Buffon would have considered the least hospitable. "When enterprising races inhabit a land where the form of the ground presents to them difficulties," Humboldt writes, "this contest with nature becomes a means of increasing their strength and power as well as their courage."[48] The architecture and art of the ancient Americans, Humboldt wrote in Views, "bear the imprint of the mountains' savage nature."[49]

Humboldt's appreciation of the wild (or "savage") Andean landscape owed much to contemporary Romantic landscape aesthetics. His method, however, was much more than a simple copy or repetition of these theories.[50] What Humboldt sought to achieve in his descriptions and illustrations of the Andean landscape was a method for translating such emotional or aesthetic "effects" into the material "facts" and forces that shaped human history. To accomplish this Humboldt turned to two related methods: abstraction and comparison. The graphic form in which these methods surface most clearly is the cross section that Humboldt used to depict mountains (Figure 3.4). Across the face of the mountain he inscribed the orderly progression of climatic and ecological zones and their corresponding botanical inventories, from sea level to summit. These drawings condense Humboldt's experience with specific

Figure 3.4. Cross-section of Andes (1805)

peaks into a sort of modal volcano complete with reference markers noting the relative heights of other famous mountains. Much like the tables and maps that figure so prominently in Humboldt's published work, such a drawing translates the disorderly, overwhelming, and even sublime experience he describes feeling in the presence of volcanoes into the ordered abstract space of the map or chart.

A similar abstraction or dissection of both space and perception surfaces in the picturesque landscapes published in *Views*. In a color engraving of the Ecuadorian volcano Chimborazo, for example, Humboldt depicts a snow-capped peak set against a slightly cloudy sky.[51] The mountain's base covers the horizon; its peak pushes toward the limits of the picture's frame. In the middle foreground, Europeans led by Indian guides walk toward the volcano, their backs to the viewer; llamas dispersed in pairs wander off, as if trapped in the spell cast by the volcano's towering bulk. "The plate," Humboldt explains, "shows Chimborazo as we have seen it after the heaviest snowfall, on June 24, 1802, the day immediately following our climb to the peak." He then alludes to the special, transparent light of the Andes. "The extreme rarity of the layers of air through which one sees the Andean peaks," he writes,

> contributes much to the brilliance of the snow and the magical effect of its reflection. In the tropics, at a height of 5,000 meters, the azure vault of the sky acquires an indigo tint. The contours of the mountain become detached from the backdrop of that pure and transparent atmosphere, denuded of vegetation and reflecting back the radiant heat, are vaporous and seem to veil the last planes of the landscape.[52]

The visual problem of high-altitude light crops up again and again in Humboldt's writings on the Andes.[53] At times it is credited with producing greater clarity of vision. At other times it produces something like optical illusions. The high-altitude light, for example, makes Cotopaxi's summit appear to "float" above the earth. As in the Chimborazo plate, Humboldt recognizes this detachment as a visual effect, yet it is an effect from which he can begin to imagine a method for isolating mountains from the landscapes that surround them. On other occasions he attempts to measure the transparency of the light, as if to domesticate its mystery and thereby transform it into the visual method he sought for isolating—and comparing—features of the earth's physiognomy. Elsewhere in *Views*, Humboldt speaks of his project as a "physiognomy of mountains," in which he is driven "to compare the forms of mountains, in the most remote parts of the globe, as one would compare the forms of vegetation under diverse climates."[54] Buffon had looked at mountains much as he looked at difference: as incrementally differentiated links in the single chain of mountains that formed the earth's "skeleton." Humboldt, in contrast, saw mountains as features of the particular "view" or landscape that surrounded them. What was unique about his method is the double sense that such a focus on features gave to the idea of "physiognomy." As features abstracted from a visual whole, such singular forms as mountains could be compared with other mountains as abstract forms in a "physiognomy of mountains." As was more common in *Views*, however, they could also be summoned as the singular features or focal points of a "general impression" which, in turn, formed the essence of the landscape's "natural physiognomy."[55]

## HUMBOLDT'S DILEMMA

Humboldt's physiognomic gaze thus required two related moves: a detaching of vision from the other, more "diffuse" senses characteristic of both Buffon's "glance" and contemporary Romantic aesthetics; and a disciplining of vision through its inscription onto physical (including atmospheric) space. The effect of this inscription was a partitioning or framing of vision, as in the bounded views or natural types through which landscapes were viewed.

This spatializing or framing technique clearly animated Humboldt's theories of plant geography and landscape. Its effects were considerably less evident, however, in his observations of the human subject. In keeping with the iconographic conventions of contemporary landscape painting, most of the nature plates in *Views* include foregrounded figures of either Europeans or Americans. Located for the most part on the margins of the pictorial space, these humans point toward spectacles and ruins, take notes, read books, and converse among themselves. In each case, however, only Europeans are shown reflecting on (or studying) the scene before them. A striking example is the "Pyramide de Cholula," in which two European onlookers discuss the Mexican pyramid, while a half-naked female figure—no doubt intended to allegorize America—is shown reclining and reading a book, her back and eyes turned away from the ruin that the Europeans study. In "Rochers basaltiques et Cascade de Regla" two Europeans point toward the strange rock formations that give the plate its title, while a half-naked American man waits behind them.

In these examples, the European figures—who are clearly meant to refer to Humboldt and Bonpland themselves—bolster both Humboldt's authority to speak for the Americas and his claim that the study of nature must be grounded in subjective, visual experience. But what of the Americans? With the exception of two plates of Mexican costume, the Americans who appear in Humboldt's plates are conventional romantic figures. Nude or draped in loose togalike clothes, they either direct (Figure 3.5) or transport (Figure 3.3) the Europeans through the South American landscape. As in the graphic conventions of the Inca Operatic, they are identical to Europeans. They are of equal or greater stature than the European figures. Their skin color is, in some cases, lighter than that of the Europeans. In only one plate are Americans portrayed as part of a mythic landscape (Figure 3.6). Humboldt's text, however, makes it clear that the rock is the real subject of the engraving. Its rugged, overgrown edges conform to the aesthetic canon of the picturesque. Its surface has been carved into several smoothly worked slab steps. One face bears a pictograph described by Humboldt as "the sun as it is seen represented [*figuré*] at the origins of civilization by people all over the world."[56] The Americans are in the foreground, approaching the shelter of the rock. Their gestures evoke the expulsion from Eden.

At the university in Gottingen, Humboldt had studied with the German naturalist and medical doctor Johann Friedrich Blumenbach.[57] Like Buffon, Blumenbach considered humans a single species. He also agreed that bone structure, melanin, hair form, and expression could change with the influence of both climate and culture. For Buffon, such variation occurred in almost imperceptible stages, and as a result, he argued against the possibility of finding distinctive physical "types." Blumenbach, however, reached a different conclusion: the whole problem was to define the distinctive physical

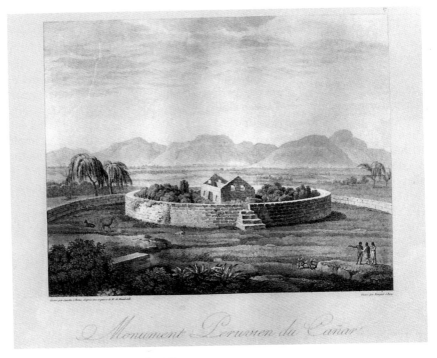

Figure 3.5. Ruins of Cañar (1810)

types into which the human species had been divided through migration. These types corresponded roughly to the "white," "yellow," and "black" races for which Blumenbach popularized the labels Caucasian, Mongol, and Ethiopian.[58]

From Blumenbach, Humboldt acquired an understanding of migration as the historical process that best explained the cultural and physical variation distinguishing different human "races." We might have expected him also to have borrowed an interest in the visual or descriptive language that Blumenbach popularized in European racial thought. Instead, in striking contrast to his teacher, Humboldt's interest in both race and migration was framed in terms of culture and only secondarily as a problem in comparative physiology. If migration was to affect "race" it would be, for Humboldt, less through the darkening of skin or the broadening of noses than through the ways in which culture and art had been altered by different climates, landscapes, and geologies. It was this interest in migration that fueled Humboldt's study of New World archaeology, for it was in the mute stones and hieroglyphs of Andean and Mexican archaeology that he hoped to read America's "racial" history.

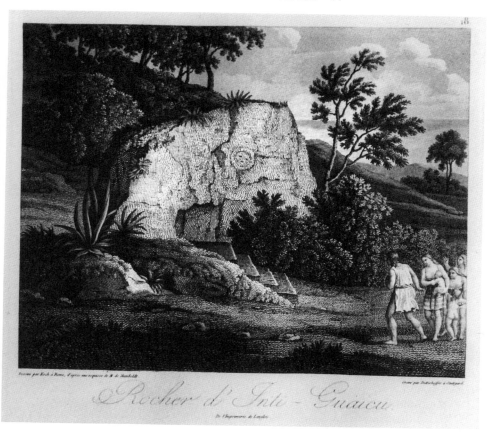

Figure 3.6. Inti-Guaicu Rock (1810)

The Indian peasants, mestizo porters, and lowland native peoples who surrounded Humboldt on his travels, however, provided no such trace of a "racial" or imperial history. They offered no royal genealogies, hieroglyphs, or
masonry—only the mute testimony of bodies and faces; and these bodies provided no visual trace from which Humboldt could read the history that constituted "race." The only extended account that Humboldt gives of an encounter
with an Andean person is of the cacique Astorpilco of Cajamarca. The cacique
(chief) interests Humboldt, however, not as an "Indian" but, rather, as a de-
scendant of the Inca Atawallpa. His tales of "buried splendor and golden trea-
sure" remind Humboldt that "every suppressed nationality looks forward to a
day of change."[59] Of the cacique's appearance, Humboldt notes only that
"traces of beard may perhaps indicate some admixture of Spanish blood."[60] If
"race" was to be studied as a history of migration, it would be studied through

documents or, failing these, through the ruins, artifacts, and stories that Humboldt would read as the racial history of the American Indians.

The contemporary non-noble Indian was not, then, available to Humboldt as an object of racial speculation. Nor was he available as a social individual, for both the tragedy of his history and the savage conditions of his actual existence had colluded to erase those elements of character through which Humboldt was accustomed to read a European face.

> How great is the difference, with respect to mobility of features and variety of physiognomy, between dogs which have again returned to the savage state in the New World, and those whose slightest caprices are indulged in the houses of the opulent! Both in men and animals the emotions of the soul are reflected in the features; and the countenance acquires the habit of mobility, in proportion as the emotions of the mind are frequent, varied and durable. But the Indian of the Missions, being remote from all cultivation, influenced only by his physical wants, satisfying almost without difficulty his desires, in a favoured climate, drags on a dull, monotonous life. The greatest equality prevails among the members of the same community; and this uniformity, this sameness of situation, is pictured on the features of the Indians.[61]

Although other "savages" were also said to register only partial or no expression, Humboldt considered the Americans the most resistant to his gaze.[62] "Immobility of features," Humboldt reflected, "is not peculiar to every race of men of dark complexion. It is much less marked in the African than in the natives of America."[63] On the one hand, this resistance was a product of history and, more particularly, of the "black legend" of Spanish colonialism. If the pre-Columbian civilizations had grown from their struggle with a "savage nature," then how, Humboldt reasoned, were either the mission Indians, who were provided with all their needs, or the highland peasants, who had seen their nation conquered, to develop the character and identity that had transformed their ancestors into kings and "individuals"? On the other hand, however, Humboldt's dilemma in describing the Americans also expressed the ways in which his own visual methodology excluded what he himself dismissed as "mobile" animal forms. Humboldt crafted a typological language for the production of views and landscapes; yet his "physiognomic gaze" did not embrace the physiognomy of man. For Humboldt this remained a separate problem, one addressed by history rather than by the spatial notion of "type."

## THE LANGUAGE OF TYPE

Inspired by Humboldt's inaugural journey, a steady stream of scientists and expeditionaries began to travel to South America in the early decades of the nineteenth century.[64] Among the first was the French zoologist Alcides d'Orbigny. A specialist in mollusks, d'Orbigny was commissioned in 1825 by the

Museum of Natural History in Paris "to investigate thoroughly [*approfondir*] the language and physiological characteristics" of the South American peoples.[65] Through language—and specifically through the vocabularies that were the philologists' stock in trade—he hoped to trace the broad language "stocks" and "families" that could be used to map out South American "nations" and "tribes." The geographic distribution of these families, tribes, and nations would then be used to reconstruct the migratory routes by which the South Americans had arrived at their actual locations. By examining their bodies, d'Orbigny hoped to arrive at a similar sort of map. In this map, physical characteristics such as skin and hair color would be correlated with climatic zones and migration routes.

D'Orbigny's specific "mapping" project was inspired by a gap in the larger map of racial variation. At the time d'Orbigny was asked to travel to South America, European racial theorists had yet to decide on the exact racial status of the Americans.[66] Humboldt's teacher, Blumenbach, for example, had lamented the "quantities of fables . . . spread about the racial characters of this [American] variety" and the lack of reliable depictions.[67] D'Orbigny's own mentor, Georges Cuvier, citing lack of precise physical descriptions, had also refused to pass judgment on the Americans' racial status. D'Orbigny's task was to fill this gap in racial theory.

During the eight years d'Orbigny remained in the New World, he observed the Guaraní, Ona, Mapuche, Aymara, Quechua, and Chiriguano Indians. He learned to speak Guaraní and familiarized himself with several other languages. "Each of these nations," d'Orbigny assures his readers, "was studied with scrupulous attention to all their physiological characteristics, to the smallest details of their manners, customs, religion, language, [and] the changes brought to their primitive state by civilization."[68] He then hoped to compare them in order "to distinguish each group by form, appearance, and complexion [*teinte*]" and "each large division" through its members' corresponding "physiological characteristics."[69]

D'Orbigny first released the results of his investigation in 1839 in a two-volume report entitled *L'Homme américain* (American Man). The book opens with a survey of the geographic, climatological, and physical characteristics of South America. Here d'Orbigny also offers a speculative history of the migrations through which the continent was populated. The remainder of the study is devoted to a description and taxonomy of the continent's three "races" and thirty-nine "nations," each made up of a varying number of "branches" and "tribes." These groupings are, in turn, defined as an amalgam of linguistic and physiological characteristics—as if d'Orbigny did, indeed, wish to merge the study of bodies and words into a single particularizing grid for the comparison and classification of humans. Both "nations" and "tribes" were defined as linguistic groupings. Those languages descended from a common stock were included within a single "nation." Dialects within that stock were then considered to form distinct and identifiable "tribes." "Branches," however, were collections of "nations" grouped on the basis of "either physical or moral traits [*caractères*]." As the most inclusive grouping, "races" were defined by d'Orbigny as "a group of nations based on the identity of their general physical characteristics."[70] In practice, however, d'Orbigny's descriptions of the three racial groups (Ando-Peruvian, Pampian, and Brasilio-Guaranian) slide all too easily from the rigorous language of comparative anatomy—the discipline in which he was trained—to a listing of each group's moral, emotional, and cultural characteristics.

Indeed, what is most striking about d'Orbigny's sometimes contradictory descriptions and style is his apparent distrust of what could be seen on the South Americans' own bodies. Rather than providing a reliable clue to racial identity, skin color, for example, was an incidental—and inconsistent—element in d'Orbigny's system of racial classification. The South Americans, d'Orbigny writes, are "divided into two groups: the brownish olive and the yellow." However, he continues, within these two groups, skin tones vary so widely that both description and classification become problematic. "There are few parts of the world," d'Orbigny notes, "where the color of man varies more in its intensity [and] in the mixture of tints, according to branches and nations."[71] The skin color of the pure Argentine and Peruvian Indian, for example, "resembles very much that of mulatos."[72] In short, as an anatomist, d'Orbigny saw skin color as an infinitely variable surface characteristic, as something that could easily confuse the scientist by causing different races, or mixtures of races, to look alike.

Like Humboldt, d'Orbigny also considered the South Americans' skin color an obstacle to the perception of expression, individuality, and identity. "In all nations the exterior expression of feelings is just as sincere [*naive*] and no less energetic than in the white race; however," d'Orbigny continues, "since the [South American's] tint is deeper, the mechanical effect is less obvious."[73] The uniformity of their facial features also contributed to this effect.   ·

> The Quechua profile forms a very obtuse angle and differs little from our own, except for the jawbones that protrude more than in the Caucasian race; the brow-ridges are prominent; the nose base is very deep. Their physiognomy is almost uniformly serious, thoughtful, even sad, without however showing indifference; it reveals rather a penetration without frankness [*pénétration sans franchise*]. One would say they want to hide their thoughts under the uniform aspect one sees in their features, where feelings only rarely reveal themselves on the exterior [*se peignent à l'extérieur*].[74]

Like Humboldt, d'Orbigny saw Indians as uniform, the same. Indeed, as he laments in the epigraph to this chapter, he was driven to despair by the uniformity, the interchangeability of Peruvian Indians and mestizos "all dressed in the same manner." In d'Orbigny's case, however, his complaints at the similar appearance of the Indians were accompanied by an anatomist's concern for the particular. The uniform aspect that had prevented Humboldt from discerning individuality, became, for d'Orbigny, both a source of ennui and, more important, a basis from which to build the very language of particularization and physical dissection that would be key to his verbal descriptions of "the Indian." This descriptive strategy differed from Buffon's in its emphasis on both vision and type. To think of type at all was to think of uniformity, serialization, and statistical breakdowns from norms to extremes. How else to understand when an individual conformed to "type"? The approach implied, in short, thinking in a way that was simply not possible with Buffon's tactile perceptual philosophy, incremental variation, and species defined as succession over time.

## VISION AND TYPE

As Jonathan Crary has argued, the camera obscura provided the central metaphor and technology organizing vision in the seventeenth and eighteenth centuries.[75] In the camera obscura, a single, stationary, and invisible subject observed an exterior world through a small peephole, or through the inverted reflection of that world cast by a lens on the camera obscura's interior wall. As a statement about the nature of knowledge, vision, and human subjectivity, the camera obscura made two important claims: (1) that all knowledge, or sight, was founded upon a division between an interiorized and stationary subject and an exterior world; and (2) that knowledge itself was organized, like the naturalists' tables, as an extensive field or "unified space of order" that could be observed from a number of exterior and stable positions.[76]

During the first decades of the nineteenth century vision became uprooted from any fixed site or referent. The new science of physiological optics, for example, explained vision by reference to organs of sight and perception. No longer a product of a fixed relationship between interior subject and exterior world (as in the camera obscura), vision became rooted instead in the inherently mobile body of the observer. This rupture with classical models of the observer, Crary argues, took place between 1810 and 1840 as part of the "massive reorganization of knowledge and social practices" that occurred in the late eighteenth and early nineteenth centuries.

Whereas Buffon's philosophy of description and concentric theory of classification conformed quite nicely to the reigning metaphor of the camera obscura, Humboldt and d'Orbigny participated in the construction of a new sense of what constituted both knowledge and the domain of the visual. Humboldt's physiognomic method called for a mobile and sensuous observer and, as such, for a substantive break with the camera obscura's enabling divide between an interior-observing subject and an exterior world. He also introduced the notion of experience and the subject-centered view as the new visual currency through which knowledge of the Americans would be accumulated, archived, exchanged, and compared. As Europeans began to travel to the Americas with greater frequency during the early nineteenth century, their knowledge of South America and its newly independent republics was shaped by this typological and spatializing discourse in which the experience of the New World was structured (and communicated) as a series of visually discrete images—what Humboldt would have referred to as a landscape's "natural physiognomy."

As we have seen, however, this new discourse of type played unevenly across different disciplines and subjects. Bodies and landscapes were differently configured in Humboldt's physiognomic method. Even in d'Orbigny's project of racial classification, the particularizing gaze of the anatomist passed only haltingly over the South American's body. How then are we to think about the relation between race and vision in the new "episteme"? One answer is to look not so much at "race" itself as at the spatial languages and statistical techniques we have seen at work in Buffon, Humboldt, and d'Orbigny.

By comparing Humboldt's and d'Orbigny's work with Buffon's very different sense of vision and description, this chapter has suggested some ways in which the domain of racial discourse was reorganized around what Foucault has described as the "considered politics of spaces" that started "to develop at the end of the eighteenth century."[77] We began by looking at Buffon's spatial model of "concentric description," in which both vision and touch were seen to move out from the body to construct a classification of nature based on proximity or utility to the observer's stationary body. We then looked at Humboldt's very different theory of the "physiognomic gaze" as a *spatial* technology for the description and objectification of "nature" itself. We also saw that Humboldt himself limited his "physiognomic method" of natural description to what he himself described as the "immobile" world of plants and geography.

Here d'Orbigny's much less ambitious—and in many respects less coherent—project is useful for understanding how Humboldt's "physiognomic gaze," despite its reluctance to engage the human subject, did in fact speak to the spatial and visual foundations of a new biologically grounded discourse of race. In his introduction to *L'Homme américain*, d'Orbigny acknowledges his intellectual and personal debt to two men. Like so many others of his time, he cites Humboldt both as his personal inspiration for studying the New World and as Europe's almost exclusive source of information about South American geography, geology, and nature.[78] For guidance in determining how to study and define the humans who inhabited Humboldt's "New Continent," however, d'Orbigny turned to his mentor, Georges Cuvier.

As the principal architect of the new science of zoology and comparative anatomy, Cuvier's influence on d'Orbigny was to be expected. In his writings and classes, Cuvier preached a method based on dissection and taxonomic classification according to type. In this system, organisms were classified not according to their surface characteristics, as in the eighteenth-century naturalist's system, but according to an anatomical structure revealed through dissection. Backbones, nerves, and reproductive systems replaced fur, form, and texture as the organizational framework of an animal kingdom divided into vertebrates and invertebrates, amphibians and mammals. Whereas Buffon and Daubenton described animals as becoming progressively more "different" in the extremities, Cuvier located difference itself in the invisible inner structure of the body. For Cuvier and those who followed, knowledge—and the vision that constituted knowledge—passed, in Foucault's words, through "the thickness of the body," rather than skimming, as had the botanist's gaze, over the tangible surface of individual forms.[79] As a zoologist, d'Orbigny's mission—if not his method—in South America testified to the revolution that Cuvier had helped to bring about in European ways of knowing. Indeed, that the museum in Paris chose to send a zoologist rather than a botanist on a mission to South America would have been unthinkable even twenty years before.

Cuvier's "revolution," however, was not restricted to either dissection as a method or anatomy as an organizational framework for knowledge. Equally important in the zoologist's new regime of knowledge was the resilient and productive notion of "type." Indeed, the concept of type formed the cornerstone of Cuvier's zoological philosophy. Buffon focused his attention on individuals and the "imperceptible nuances" through which individuals were connected in nature. In opposition to Buffon's particularism, Cuvier—like Humboldt—proposed "to relate what nature brings together."[80] In this regime, individuals became specimens of morphologically stable or fixed "types" and variation was explained not, as in modern biology, through principles of evolution and transformation but, rather, through the statistical notion that certain individuals were more (or less) representative of their respective type. Within species, Cuvier focused his dissections and descriptions on those individuals whom he considered most representative of their type. Within genera, he focused on those species that most represented each genus's type.

Cuvier's and d'Orbigny's anatomical understanding of "type" had much in common with Humboldt's overtly Romantic philosophy of landscape and the "general impression." Humboldt isolated specific "physiognomies" within the shifting visual panorama of nature; Cuvier distilled the endless variation of individuals into a stable structural form. Humboldt's method resulted in the concept of the view as a replicable image through which the traveler could encounter nature as a series of interchangeable visual experiences. Cuvier's zoological notion of the stable morphological type contained within it a very similar ideal of replicability or serialization.[81]

Like Humboldt as well, however, Cuvier had difficulties extending the rigor of his typological and visual method to embrace the concept of "race." Within his system, humans formed a single species within which there existed "certain hereditary peculiarities of conformation" or "races."[82] Of these, Cuvier recognized the "Caucasian or white," the "Mongolian or yellow," and the "Ethiopian or black" as distinct races. Three other groups—the Americans, Malays, and Eskimos—were classified as "varieties" rather than "races" because, Cuvier argued, too little was known to allow for an accurate classification. "The Americans," Cuvier argued in the *Animal Kingdom*, "have no precise or constant [physiological] character that can entitle them to be considered a particular race."[83]

The plates that illustrate these varieties in the atlas for the *Animal Kingdom* convey something of Cuvier's dilemma. In the first plate, Cuvier illustrates the principal "races" with drawings of their distinctive skull forms. In the plates that follow, he provides drawings of faces based on travelers' and artists' sketches.[84] In these faces, culture, clothing, and hairstyle mask the skull shape that serves to group the individuals portrayed into a single "race." As in d'Orbigny's study of the South American races, physiognomy and phenotype clouded the accuracy of racial groupings based on invisible skeletal and tissue structure. To correct this problem, Cuvier instructed artists who accompanied scientific missions to "represent all the heads [they drew] with the same hairstyle," to eliminate any body ornaments, deformations or tattoos, and to draw them with "a geometric precision obtainable only in certain positions of the head." Foreshadowing the art of the mugshot, Cuvier then advised that, to achieve true comparability between specimens, the drawings "must always juxtapose a true profile with a frontal portrait."[85] Only in this way, he cautioned, would it be possible to construct a scientific classification based on the careful study and comparison of individual specimens.

By grounding a theory of visual observation and description in the spatial and statistical regime of "type" Humboldt and d'Orbigny, each in his own way, helped to lay the groundwork for the comparative "rigor" that Cuvier envisioned—but did not achieve—as necessary for a precise definition of "race." I have argued that to understand the logic and, to a certain extent, the origin of a modern understanding of "race" we must look to the spatializing regimes, typological discourses, and comparative practices through which, to again cite Foucault, visibility was "isolated" and the gaze "inscribed in social space."[86] These practices and discourses may not always speak directly of "race," yet they hold the key to understanding what was, in fact, new about the nineteenth-century meaning of that very old word.

## CHAPTER FOUR

# A One-Eyed Gaze

[The women of Lima] are generally beautiful enough,
of a sprightly Mien, and more engaging than in other
Places: tho' perhaps their Beauty is in Part owing to
the hideous Faces of the Mulattos, Blacks, and
Indians, which serve as Foils to them.
*(Anonymous, 1748)*

IN THE DECADES following Humboldt's and d'Orbigny's forays to the New World, French interest in the Andes grew with European curiosity about the economies, markets, resources, and politics of the newly independent South American republics.[1] As economic and diplomatic relations with Latin America became more pressing, increasing numbers of scientists, artists, and just plain travelers were recruited to the work of empire. Through their labors, a more defined repertoire of images began to emerge of the Andes and Andean peoples.

As in other parts of the non-European world, the first icon to emerge from this early nineteenth-century encounter with the new Andean republics took the shape of a woman's body. This option was in many respects an overdetermined move. In European art in general, the category "woman" provided a seductive and familiar vehicle for male creative expression—one well sanctioned by centuries of European artistic tradition. This legacy acquired particular meaning in the case of the Peruvian sun virgins and princesses of the eighteenth-century Inca Operatic; the bodies of these imagined Andean women served certain philosophes as imaginary contact points for their century's (re)discovery of Andean South America.

For the men who would actually go to the Andes in the early decades of the new century, however, it was another kind of woman who captured their imaginations. This woman was worldly rather than imaginary; coquettish rather than demure; ambivalent rather than principled; and, above all, of a recognizably European, rather than Inca or "Indian," extraction. This woman was the famous Limeña *tapada* or "covered woman," so-called after the custom of holding a shawl drawn around and over the head and face such that only one eye could usually be seen (Figure 4.1). Anonymity—and thus an escape from surveillance by families and husbands—was the purpose of the shawl. The effect, however, was one of seduction. This use of the shawl, which had

Figure 4.1. Tapadas

been a custom during the period of Spanish colonial rule, went out of fashion in Lima shortly after Peru achieved its independence in 1821. Nevertheless, for the French, English, and North American men who arrived in the wake of Peru's new-found political and economic autonomy from Spain, it was Lima's disappearing veiled women who came to symbolize both the availability of Peru as a postcolonial market and its timeless nature as another world where customs never changed.[2]

This chapter explores representations of tapadas and other Peruvian women in the work of two early nineteenth-century European artists. The first, Johann Moritz Rugendas, was a German illustrator and painter who visited Lima between 1842 and 1845. Prior to visiting Peru, he had spent time in Brazil, Mexico, and Chile. In each country, he compiled a vast portfolio of drawings, watercolors, and oil paintings depicting social customs and landscapes.[3] These works were intended for sale, and several were published in the popular Parisian publications *L'Illustration* and *Le Tour du monde*.

The second artist was Léonce Angrand, a French diplomat who arrived in Lima in 1833. Like Rugendas, Angrand's work fits broadly within the nineteenth-century literary and artistic tradition of *costumbrismo*, a term derived from the Spanish word for the popular customs (*costumbres*) that the *costumbristas* sought to describe in their work. During his six years in Peru, Angrand traveled throughout the country painting popular religious practices, costumes, and characters. His drawings and watercolors were done largely to satisfy a personal desire to understand and record the social customs and personalities he had observed. Angrand's collected work provides one of the most informative pictorial compilations of what might be thought of as the "local color" of nineteenth-century Peruvian society and culture.[4] His reliance on the academic traditions of European art, however, also reveals the ways in which this "local color" was toned and hued to fit categories of an illustrative "other" fashioned by European colonial adventures in India, Africa, and the Middle East. These "colonial others" were, in turn, shaped by the visual economy of "type" whose emergence in Americanist studies we traced through the work of Humboldt and d'Orbigny.

In examining the work of Angrand and Rugendas, I look into their fascination with three Peruvian female types: the criollo tapada, the *mulata* or black woman, and the native or Indian woman.[5] These three female types spoke for the prevailing racial and cultural divisions within contemporary Peru: on the one hand, coastal Lima, as the Spanish-speaking capital of Peru, was home to both the criollo tapadas and the mulata market women of African descent. The Indian women, on the other hand, came from—and represented—the remote Andean highlands, where Quechua-speaking Indians supposedly carried on the ancient traditions of their Inca ancestors. These three racially and nationally defined female types took shape at a moment when the eighteenth century's ethereal sexual fantasies and disembodied notions of race as a historically mutable essence were giving way to a modern—and more visual—understanding of race as fixed biological or physical "types." As such, they speak for the important place of gender in the consolidation of a nineteenth-century visual economy based on the notion of racial and national types.

## FROM BETHLEHEM TO BEAUTY

The tapadas were "white" women from Peru's criollo landholding and merchant classes.[6] Their distinguishing costume consisted of a full skirt called a *saya* (or *saya picada*, if the saya was old and worn) and two plain dark shawls called *mantos*.[7] One manto was worn draped over the tapada's shoulders and breasts. The other was held to cover all of her face except the eyes. Far from being an enforced gesture of religiosity, chastity, and shame, as is often the case with the Islamic veil, the tapada's manto was a voluntary or self-imposed veil. Under this cover, the otherwise tightly managed women of the upper classes could escape, albeit briefly, the scrutiny and surveillance of husbands and other relatives. That the custom survived into the Republican period at all was a tribute to the women's determination to flaunt the restrictions imposed by the conservative upper-class culture of Lima. During the colonial period, the tapada's costume had been repeatedly and unsuccessfully prohibited by

Figure 4.2. Announcement of a cockfight

order of the Spanish monarchs Felipe II, Felipe III, Felipe IV, and Carlos III, by the Third (ecclesiastical) Council of Lima (1583), and by the Peruvian vice-regal governments of Francisco de Toledo (1571), the Marqués de Montesclaros (1609), and the Marqués de Guadalcazar (1624).[8]

The second defining element of the tapada's costume was the skirt, or saya. Until roughly the 1820s—or until Peruvian independence—the saya was gathered tightly just above the knees (Figure 4.2). The effect was to highlight the woman's buttocks (and restrict her movements). Although at the time both Angrand and Rugendas arrived in Lima the gathered saya was no longer in fashion, it continued to be worn by some women.[9] More important, its figurative effect continued to capture the eye of European travelers and artists. Thus even when drawing the more fashionably loose or ungathered skirts of the day, both Angrand and Rugendas consistently exaggerated the size of the buttocks in their drawings of tapadas (see, for example, Figure 4.3).[10] Indeed, their preference for drawing tapadas viewed from behind suggests that the large buttocks served (in their minds) as a sort of extension of the veil. Like the veil, the posterior focus allowed them more easily to erase a woman's individual identity and to view her as an exclusively physiological or sexual form. And it did so without at the same time destroying the abstracted or fetishized mystery of the tapada as a secluded and anonymous upper-class woman, since the face remained discreetly hidden, this time by the back and rear of the woman herself.

Figure 4.3. Nuns and clergy with tapadas

The distinctive dynamic characterizing the tapada as a type emerges in part from this paradoxical juxtaposition of her hidden upper-class social identity (the face), and the prominent, even defining, emphasis given in the drawings and paintings to her publicly displayed sexuality (buttocks). This dynamic, moreover, was not entirely created by the European artist. It functioned as well as part of the tapada's projected image. As members of a relatively small urban elite, the tapadas capitalized upon the intrigue of their costume. This intrigue rested, at least in part, on the assurance that the tapada's personal or family identity would be instantly recognized should she let down her "veil." The lines of her tightly gathered skirt were accordingly meant to emphasize her figure, highlight her anonymity, and play upon prevailing standards of feminine sexuality. In this respect, one might say that fashion followed function by drawing the eyes of the observing male away from the woman's individual social identity and toward the anonymity of her sexuality.

Such is not to say, however, that the European's fascination with the tapada's derrière was merely a case of nineteenth-century realism. In the tapada's fashion strategy the shapely saya formed part of a strategically thought-out whole. By reducing the tapada to her buttocks, the Europeans displaced this vision of the whole with a metonymic logic informed by contemporary racial and gynecological theories. These theories traced female sexual deviancy to perceived similarities between the genitalia and buttocks of African women and European prostitutes.[11] In her unsolicited representation by the European male artist, the upper-class white woman of Lima thus acquired those racially marked attributes of promiscuity and deviancy that her own aristocratic ideology would have vehemently rejected.

This perception of the tapada's sexuality was derived not only from the tapada's provocative dress but also from European men's opinions of her scandalous freedom and aggressive behavior.[12] They were fascinated by the tapada's willingness to initiate conversations with men. "It is ordinarily the tapadas who take the initiative" in conversations, observed the French traveler Maximilian Radiquet. "Their saya and manto, which were originally destined to serve the ideals of chastity and jealousy, have thus ended," he continues, "in protecting habits that are diametrically opposed [to these ideals]."[13] Angrand too was entranced by the charms of these "shameless hussies" (*agresoras desvergonzadas*) who by

> hiding their provocative graces under the folds of ragged skirts, and veiling their fine smiles behind the tapada's shawl, . . . either mingle with the [male] strollers or line the walkways where they pass, inviting them to do battle with that look which is theirs alone; and driven by their whims, they choose the victim whom they wish to sacrifice or enchain.[14]

According to these same French observers, it was due to just such perilous charms that the tapada became transformed by her helpless male victims into the object of what Angrand describes as a "public cult," and Lima itself into a city where Radiquet claims "women ruled as veritable sovereign queens."[15]

The tapada's feminine charms were all the more threatening because of her disturbing resemblance to European fantasies of Arab women. "At first glance," wrote d'Orbigny, "they could be taken for those phantoms of invisible women that travelers to the Orient find in Constantinople and all the Muslim cities."[16] An Orientalist influence also colors much of the nineteenth-century visual imagery of the Peruvian tapadas. These Orientalist overtones surface, for example, in the artists' rendering of the veil itself, their fascination with the tapadas' "prayer rug," and in their tendency to depict tapadas in pairs (see, for example, Figures 4.1, 4.2, 4.3, 4.4, and 4.9).[17]

Europeans also compared the tapada to the unlikely figure of the Catholic nun. Both Angrand and Rugendas were visually intrigued by a certain shadowy religiosity that they assigned to the tapada. In both men's drawings, the tapada's cowled form is often explicitly associated, or contrasted, with that of the habited nun (Figure 4.3). Both artists also tended to depict tapadas in and around churches, in religious processions, or as alms collectors.[18] In other scenes Angrand assigns an even more overt sensuality to the tapada's religion, by suggesting that they flirt with men during such solemn religious events as masses and processions.[19]

This same alluring mixture of sensuality and devotion surfaces in the comparison that nearly every French observer made between the tapadas and Saint Rose. Saint Rose of Lima was a seventeenth-century Limeña known for her severe forms of physical chastisement and her mystical visions. Radiquet— who was perhaps the most enthusiastic, and certainly the most flowery, of the

Figure 4.4. Tapadas

tapadas' many French admirers—was also a fervent devotée of Saint Rose and a frequent visitor of Melchor Caffa's sculpture of the dying saint in Lima. His description of the sculpture reveals the extent to which sensuality and mysticism overlapped in what he calls Saint Rose's "double beauty":

> The saint is bedded [couchée] on a rock; her parted lips exhale their last breath; her right hand hangs, as if to find again the rosary which she has let fall. There is at once in her the angel's ecstasy and the woman's sleep. Her face is resplendent with a double beauty: a plastic and precise beauty which determines an adorable purity of line [and] an ideal beauty which reflects all the divine perfections of an equally exceptional nature.[20]

Radiquet first met Rugendas in front of Saint Rose's sculpture. As Radiquet explains, they would later become close friends largely owing to their shared admiration for both the saint and her statue.[21] Rugendas's sketch of Caffa's sculpture seems to confirm the sensuous bond that the two men shared with regard to Santa Rosa. In it the reclining figure of Caffa's saint is shifted toward the viewer, so as to strike a markedly Maja-like pose. Her breasts and legs are more clearly outlined than in the discreetly robed sculpture, and the guardian angel hovering over her in Caffa's original has been strategically removed in order to emphasize the woman's physical solitude.[22]

For men like Radiquet and Rugendas, the ambivalent seductions of Saint Rose's mystic figure revolved around the polar attractions of the chaste and the bold. Like the tapada, Saint Rose was perceived to have quested aggressively after the male Christ she served, while retaining a paradoxical (and highly "feminine") concern with both sensuous purity and physical perfection. Radiquet equates this "double beauty" with the power of the tapada as a double woman. The Limeña, he writes,

> is passionate, spiritual, playful, sensitive, with no more pressing need than to charm . . . ; she moves, without the least difficulty [and] with an incredible elasticity of conscience, from the burdens of her illicit tendencies to the practices of her religion; you will see her by turns assume the ecstatic mask of the saint and the ardent expression of the courtesan, and pass from the holy sacraments to maddening sensualities.[23]

To capture the idea of the tapada as a woman willingly torn between devotion and sin, other French observers referred to the Limeña's "double personality."[24] One of these personalities was the chaste yet sensuous Saint Rose. The other was Mariquita Villegas, a well-known and dark-skinned actress known as La Perricholi, whose romantic intrigues made her colonial Lima's most famous public woman. For the tapadas' French admirers, La Perricholi captured the sensuality, the availability—and the racial enigmas—of Lima's veiled women.

The danger embedded in the tapada's enigmatic gaze was thus, in the words of one contemporary observer, that of drawing a man's "attention . . . from the spiritual to the temporal, from the Virgin Mother of the past to the virgin daughters of the present, from Bethlehem to beauty."[25] Her ambivalences confused men by diverting sensuous pleasure from a contemplation of ideal woman to a confrontation with the seductive, physical realities of the female body. One pole of the tapada's sexuality was judged against a constellation of ideal women ranging from the nun to Saint Rose to the eighteenth century's (unseen) Inca princesses. The other pole was defined by the racially informed connections that her buttocks and veil suggested with other colonial realities. These connections facilitated the European's appropriation of the tapada as a symbol for the troubled identity of Peru as a postcolonial nation in need of European guidance and investment. But before exploring this political dimension of the tapada's identity (and derrière), we must consider her relationship to the African and Andean women who surrounded her in Lima's public spaces.

## WHITE FEET, BLACK BREASTS

If the chaste and feminine side of the tapada's elusive persona was constructed against a backdrop of churches and saints, it was in the streets, plazas, and bullrings of Lima that her other, more devious, face came into play. Each of

the Europeans who wrote about the tapada remarked on her seemingly ubiquitous presence in the city streets. Some describe the urban space of Lima as
a landscape of tapadas. For these men, it was the tapada who graced Lima's
fiestas with beauty and color, who gave the Plaza Mayor its "piquant attraction," and who "encarnated the city itself."[26] Part of this charm was due, of
course, to the fact that it was only in public that the tapada became both
dangerous and worthy of intrigue, since it was only in public that she put on
her veil. Like other French travelers of the time, Radiquet was appalled by
Lima's domestic life—and its effect on the women. Inside their homes, he
wrote, the women wore elegant yet (for this Frenchman) boring Parisian fashions and presided over tedious meals. But outside, these same women could
intrigue him with their anonymous seductions.[27] For Radiquet, the women
are literally transformed from mythic being to mortal when they remove their
sayas and mantos at the doors of their homes. As the dark saya "drops
down around her feet [and] the shawl slips loose in a similar manner," writes
Radiquet, "the angel sheds her wings, but in her place remains a charming
mortal."[28]

The pictorial construction of the tapada as type played upon this divide
between the public and private domains of permissible sexuality. Indeed, the
tapada's intrigue as a sexual object depended on a violation (or veiling) of the
woman's domestic identity as daughter and wife. This intrigue is heightened
in European art by depicting the tapada against the backdrop of Lima's public,
and above all peopled, streets. Her "unnatural" aggressiveness emerges from
these public spaces and from the act of masking, which allowed her access
to them.

Of particular importance in the pictorial construction of the tapada's mystique was the way that the racial dynamic of Lima's public spaces shaped her
ambivalent charms. Toward the end of the colonial period, Peru registered
a population of more than one million inhabitants (1,076,997), of which
80 percent were classified as Indians (609,000) and mestizo (244,000). Of the
remaining population, 41,000 were counted as *pardos* (person of mixed European and African descent), 40,000 as black slaves (not emancipated until
1854), and only 136,000 as white or criollo.[29]

European fantasies of the tapada often focused on a man's fear that a seemingly perfect veiled woman would, once unveiled, turn out to be less than
perfect, less than white. Willis Baxley, the U.S. envoy to Peru, for example,
describes his fear that the woman behind "Mokanna's veil" might be less white
than her "white-gloved arms and whitened eyelids" had led him to believe.[30]
Radiquet was similarly disturbed by the idea that beneath the shawls he so
admired, there lurked not Saint Rose, but "une Africaine."

One is never sure how to overcome the extreme severity with which the shawl is
held closed, above all if, contrary to the Limeña's custom of going bare armed, a
long sleeve goes just up to the glove in such a way that it does not allow [one] to

guess the color of the skin. Have no doubt, the treacherous shawl conceals an African, black as the night [and] flat-nosed as death, before whom it would be superfluous to sow the pearls of gallantry. As one can see, the saya and manto has afforded women only advantages [and] men only with discomforts [*desagréments*].[31]

The shawl hid more than the tapada's face. It concealed as well the perils of a public sphere in a city where whites accounted for only a very small percentage of the total population. The tapada, as rebellious woman, depended for her limited liberty on this public space; and therefore, in the eyes of those men who surveyed her, she came to incorporate as well the racial dangers inherent to public life in Lima.

A number of Angrand's and Rugendas's drawings are set up to emphasize the contrast between the tapada's delicate features, small waist, and dainty feet, and the mulatas' voluptuous—and somewhat disheveled—bodies. Mulatas appear as fleshy, strong, assertive women, who drink, dance, ride horses, and cavort openly with men. Frequently a solitary breast heaves, as if uncontrollably, from the top of their distinctive low-slung dresses. This image is derived in part from the highly sexualized European stereotypes of the Caribbean mulata, and is repeated in Rugendas's drawings from Brazil and the Caribbean area.

In Lima, however, the disorder of the "mulato element"—and more particularly of mulata women—is constituted through their negative qualities as "what the upper classes are not." In Rugendas's painting of the "Fiesta de San Juan in Amancaes," for example, the public arena is clearly divided between the competing spheres of upper-class whites and the decidedly more tumultuous activities of the "lower orders" (Figure 4.5). In Rugendas's interpretation of this division, he chooses the overtly theatrical context of the public feast to emphasize the extent to which each group is constituted by the other's gaze. In the painting, a small group of refined white onlookers maintains a guarded distance from the surrounding melée that is slightly below them. Those few tapadas and white women who have penetrated into the more festive plane of the event are assigned a morally dubious character in keeping with contemporary painterly and literary tropes of the fallen or wayward woman.

Rugendas's paintings of Lima's central market repeat this structuring of public space as a stage on which different racial groups and social classes occupy distinct—and clearly delineated—positions. Another Rugendas painting, for example, shows two upper-class women with hats on horseback in one of Lima's several markets.[32] From their elevated station at center frame, they appear to survey the crowd below. Their removed presence draws the eye to several tapadas who promenade in highly visible pairs amid the crowd itself. Other tapadas converse with the market women around them. Unlike the mounted women, these tapadas' faces, and identities, are securely veiled. Their anonymity guarantees their ability to mix with the market rabble.

Figure 4.5. Popular Rejoicing outside Lima (1843)

This image of tapadas conversing with women of the lower orders was very much a part of their mystique. It was through such transactions that the tapada situated herself squarely in the midst of a public life that was seen by Europeans to be perilous precisely because of its proximity to the mulatas and market women, with their disorderly nursing children and dark, exposed bodies.

Many of the disorderly aspects of the mulata's image were derived from the commercial realm of the market. The public market (and to a lesser extent, the public feast) was seen as an exact opposite of the traveler's other romanticized space in Lima: the private gardens. One of Angrand's few writings about Lima is a letter describing these gardens, which he—like other Europeans of his time—compares to Oriental gardens, largely because of their seemingly guarded character as an "inner sanctum." In the same letter, he compares the "orderly wildness" of the gardens with the sublime, chaotic force of the desert surrounding Lima and the rivers that descend from the Andes to irrigate the coast.[33] In direct contrast with these peaceful gardens was the raucous public market where mulatas sold their goods and raised their children. European and North American men who visited Lima, including Angrand and Rugendas, frequently remarked upon their public nursing.[34] Writing some thirty years later, when public hygiene had become, if anything, an even greater worry to foreign observers, the U.S. consul Baxley commented that

> All sellers in the Lima market are women, generally *cholos* [*sic*]. . . . The dainty stranger should not visit the market before breakfast; his appetite will not be strengthened by seeing a saleswoman fleahunting in her dog's hairy tegument . . . ; or by seeing another crack between her fingernails less agile insects taken from the head of her child. . . . Women may sometimes be seen riding astride a mule with an infant in the arms taking its primitive meal, or asleep with the pendant breast exposed to the public gaze. In fact it is rarely the case that one walks in any part of the city during the day or night, without being shocked by sights of indecency, immodesty, and immorality, too gross even to be hinted at.[35]

Some years later, another U.S. traveler, the archaeologist Ephraim George Squier, was able to admit that "the Central Market of Lima [was] better, in many respects, and more commodious than any existing in New York." He nevertheless advised travelers to leave their shopping "to a confidential majordomo possessed of a strong stomach," since

> the mass of venders, who are women that squat on the pavement at the edges of the galleries or in the open spaces . . . chatter and "chaff" with each other and their customers, nursing children perhaps, or performing some other less pleasing maternal duty, at the same time. These children, when they have attained the requisite strength, tumble and sprawl about in a very promiscuous way, not at all appetizing to purchasers.[36]

Tapadas are separated from this disorderly maternal mess by virtue of their distinctive physical shape and, above all, by their decidedly nondomestic, nonmaternal attributes. Tapadas are never shown with their breasts exposed and are never shown with children. Instead, in both Angrand's and Rugendas's characterizations of them, the torso, like the face, is kept suggestively covered by the shawl which, in its ornamental drapery, converts maternal breast into sculptured bosom. The tapada's distinctive figural icon is instead transferred to the unnaturally restricted waists, the large buttocks, and the tiny feet with which all tapadas were supposedly endowed.[37] This dissection of the tapada's body is particularly striking when compared with Rugendas's few portraits (mostly pencil sketches) of unveiled upper-class women. In these portraits, the female subjects assume the bourgeois individuality characteristic of the portrait genre. They wear European hats and French fashions. They have recognizable and—above all—uncovered faces. They are, in short, whole, domestic women, with social (or at least family) identities of their own. Tapadas, in contrast, are never drawn as portraits. Their representation occurs exclusively as types—dissected, restrained, confined to that status of icon which had come to constitute their pictorial selves.

The tapada's fetishized physical traits thus served to differentiate the domestically discreet woman from the publicly viewed and publicly consumed tapada. As signs of her status as an upper-class public woman, however, these same sequestered body parts also served to distinguish the tapada's physical constitution as woman from that of the mulatas who surround her in the urban streets. Her sheltered distance from these other classes of women is further enhanced by the fact that tapadas are nearly always pictured in pairs or accompanied by their maidservant or chola. In Rugendas's paintings, the pairing of these one-eyed women establishes their equivalence with a whole, two-eyed woman (Figure 4.4). The pairing of black market women, though also frequent, tends to occur in scenes of public revelry and drinking or in images of the powerful black male (whose breast is often exposed as well) accompanied by his two female consorts.[38] Both forms of doubling imagery draw from popular Orientalist fantasies of the Islamic harem or the husband with two wives.[39]

### INCA VIRGINS REBORN

In comparison with the mysterious tapada and the disorderly mulata, the Indian women in Angrand's and Rugendas's drawings are chaste, retiring, and simple. As with the tapada, the Indian woman's type is elaborated against the backdrop of other women who differ from her in both class and race. In one Angrand sketch, for example, an Indian woman confronts a mestiza who is carrying firewood, presumably to sell (Figure 4.6). The two women are

Figure 4.6. Mestiza and Indian

Figure 4.7. Coastal Indians

Figure 4.8.
Indian women

differentiated by their forms of dress (and undress). Depiction of the indigenous or rural woman as a virtuous or passive female type recurs throughout
both artists' work. Angrand tends to purify and idealize the world of Indian
women as one accompanying, yet clearly separate from, the masculine public
sphere through which they move relatively unnoticed (see, for example, Figures 4.7 and 4.9). This idealization of indigenous women was undoubtably
informed by the enduring fantasies surrounding the sun virgins and princesses of the eighteenth-century Inca Operatic.

Angrand's and Rugendas's fascination for the indigenous woman, however,
is more than just a nostalgic exoticism. In their drawings and sketchbooks,
female Indian subjects are routinely dissected into the component parts of
their dress, each of which is minutely detailed and labeled. (Figure 4.8).[40] This
mode of piecemeal representation had the effect of virtually eclipsing the existence of the body or woman inside the costume. Whereas the tapada was
fetishized as singular body parts (the buttocks, a hand, an eye, or a foot) and
the mulata through a focus on the "unclean" body parts associated with mater-
nity, the Indian woman is fetishized as surface, as gloss, as the clothing that
masks her body and sex. For the artist interested in capturing a "picturesque"

Peru, this folkloric costume, or ethnic marker, was the surface form and shape constitutive of the individual under scrutiny by the artist. Its recurrent dissection and labeling is therefore of double interest as a reflection of both the artist's attempts to homogenize real Indian women into an idealized folkloric type and his desire to reduce this female subject into a scientifically constituted image or "type."

The dissection of the Indian woman into the surface elements of her costume or disguise also rendered her effectively invisible as a sexual being. In striking contrast to the tapada and the mulata, the Indian women seen in Angrand's and Rugendas's work exhibit neither positive nor negative signs of female sexuality. In this respect, their pictorial role is often to provide a context or backdrop to these other forms of womanhood. In the drawings and paintings that show tapadas and Indians together, the Indian women are figured as pictorial forms, included because their presence is necessary to the formal compositional balance of a well-done Romantic drawing. The Rugendas oil painting shown in Figure 4.9, for example, constructs a hierarchy of female subjects defined by the intersecting lines of four different gazes. First, the tapadas gaze outward toward the viewer of the painting. Their gaze, however, is itself intersected by a second one coming from the monk and gentleman, whose eyes are directed so as to see, in effect, only the two tapadas before them. Excluded from this masculine gaze is the tapadas' retinue of mulata servants. One of these maids directs her gaze (the third one) toward an unidentified subject. As a sidewise glance, this gaze is deviously uninhibited, and as such invokes popular conceptions of mulata sexual morals. Finally, the two Indian women on the left exchange a gaze whose radius is restricted to themselves. Neither their presence nor their gaze engages in any way those of the other subjects of the composition. Their presence is meant, instead, to mark the picture's frame, to complete the triangle that is the public, racial context in which the tapadas promenade. Another Rugendas watercolor places an Indian woman next to a tapada engaged, apparently, in seducing a man.[41] The Indian woman huddles, faceless in the right-hand margin opposite to the shadowy tapadas. Her ethnicity and race are marked by her hat and, more specifically, by the distinctive triangular form of her skirt as she sits. It is the clothing, and not the body, that marks the racial identity or type of the indigenous woman.

In these paintings, as in others by Rugendas and Angrand, the Indian woman is the "context." She is the defining opposite for the real subject of the piece—the sexually alluring, mysterious, and (it is hoped) white tapada. In no case where Indian women are included in a composition with other types of women do the Indians appear as the subject of the picture. Rather, they assume a form of sexual nonidentity that serves to contextualize or accentuate the sexually intentioned invisibility of the white tapada.

Figure 4.9. Tapadas in the plaza

## EMBODYING TYPES

The nineteenth century brought striking changes to the comfortable sensuality fueling both the Inca Operatic and the picturesque metaphysics of Humboldt's inaugural voyage. Throughout the eighteenth century, Spanish protectionism held the places and peoples of the Americas at a convenient distance from both European politics and the naturalists' gaze. Spanish protectionist measures were strictly enforced. Commerce with foreigners was punishable by confiscation of possessions and death. All ships entering Spanish harbors in the New World were to be treated as ships of war. Although these regulations loosened toward the end of the colonial period, and naturalists such as Frezier, La Condamine, and Humboldt were allowed to travel with relative freedom in Spain's American colonies, independence still marked a significant and unprecedented opening of South American ports to European commercial interests—and European eyes. As a result, Spain's colonial dependents began to acquire a new, more active presence in the European imagination.

This presence was further heightened by the political activities of the Americans themselves. Inspired by the principles of the French and U.S. revolutions, creole patriots throughout Latin America turned to Britain and France for the moral and material support necessary to launch their campaigns of national liberation. In the fashionable drawing rooms of Paris, the names of Bolivar, San Martín, and Sucre became common currency. Their moral and political causes converged nicely with European speculation about Spain's American markets and a long-brewing liberal skepticism about the legitimacy of its colonial pretensions. With the independence of the Andean republics in the early 1820s, speculation turned to diplomacy and trade wars as European powers vied with the United States for the commercial favors of the continent's new creole elites. The sudden prospect of accessible landscapes, open markets, tradeable goods, and Indian labor also put a premium on compiling new, more precise descriptions of the Andes. Resources, rivers, mines, roads, and climates needed to be specified, itemized, and counted. Populations needed to be scrutinized, landscapes explored, rivers navigated, resources inventoried, jungles tamed. Angrand and Rugendas were the first tier of this army of Europeans who would, in the decades ahead, come to observe, describe, and represent the Andes for the publics back home.

Like the work of most of these early travelers, that of Angrand and Rugendas was restricted in its scope. They confined themselves, for the most part, to a description of cities. They were also more concerned with people than with the landscapes and nature that had captured Humboldt's imagination. The flesh-and-blood Peruvians with which these nineteenth-century artists, travelers, and diplomats would replace the Enlightenment's gilded Incas were of a decidedly different cast. As residents of the New World, the exotic cachet and tragedy ascribed to their royal ancestors lingered about them. Yet, unlike their ghostly forebears, they demanded, by virtue of their very contemporaneity, a more material existence. This physical, embodied presence would be the concern of the new European discourses of race, biology, and anatomy that emerged together with Latin American independence in the early decades of the nineteenth century. With the dawn of this new era of science, modernity, and race, the arena in which European debate on the Americas was waged would be displaced from the diffuse realm of New World nature to the more focused site of the American body.

Angrand's and Rugendas's pictorial pursuit of the elusive tapada occurred within this broader arena of political and scientific debate about the new Latin American republics and the meaning of both race and type. As we have seen in the work of Humboldt and d'Orbigny, the notion of "type" as a visual and physiognomic construct with an essence or object-status of its own emerged independently of—and prior to—the full-blown taxonomic and biological discourse that would later become associated with "scientific" theories of race. The transformation in racial thinking that took place during the early decades of the nineteenth century from a genealogical or historical paradigm of racial identity to the objectifying discourse of biologically determined racial types was conditioned by this visual discourse of type. As in Humboldt's case, type was a strategy for disciplining the scientific gaze. Through the notion of type and the "physiognomic gaze" Humboldt and others of his time struggled with a new visual economy defined by the agency of a mobile, sensuous observer and the serial production of images and image-objects.

The work of Angrand and Rugendas differs, however, in one fundamental respect from the pictorial traditions in Humboldt's engravings. Because Humboldt's concern was to establish the mobile, sensuous observer as the cornerstone of a visual, scientific method, he included the European subject in many if not all of the Andean landscapes published in *Vues*. For Angrand and Rugendas, by comparison, the observing European subject is excluded from the pictorial frame. One goal of this strategy of deletion was to lead the observer to believe in the precision or transparency of the medium through which the figures were portrayed.[42] Deleting the observer, however, also allowed the artist to isolate the represented figure from any specifically narrative frame and to make it speak—as it were—for itself. The represented, visual type acquired a materiality and existence of its own. Like race, the notion of "type" acquired a physical—and physiological—dimension that it had not had in Humboldt's work.

The tapada's appeal for this new visual economy of (race and) type derived from both her gender and her nationality. For northern European artists such as Rugendas and Angrand, the Andes formed a virgin terrain—one whose attractions had much to do with the growing market for travel literature and illustration. Within this market, ideas about what South Americans were had not yet jelled. Their "types" were still in the process of emergence; the meaning of their particular forms of "exotic intrigue" had not yet been resolved. The Inca Operatic had left no pictorial traditions of what Peruvians looked like. Nor did there exist a good inventory of travel illustrations or even descriptions of the inhabitants of Humboldt's New Continent. In short, neither the artists nor the writers who described South Americans had at hand the vast repertoire of stereotypes and picturesque types available to, for example, the Orientalist painter or the traveler to Africa. Unlike either the "Oriental" or African woman for whom clear stereotypes already existed, the South American woman was, in a sense, more actively scrutinized.

What drew the Europeans to the tapada—and made her a symbol of Peru— was her apparent mission of *self*-representation. The tapada was a real woman who purposely held her veil over her face as a gesture of both rebellion and sexual flirtation. As a woman stripped of her social or individual identity, moreover, the tapada (like the Oriental odalisque) offered the European observer the seductive vision of a woman reduced to the pure material essence of her body. As the product of a masculine empowering gaze, the tapada functioned as fetish precisely because of this cutting-off from the social. As a one-eyed woman, the tapada invited reduction: as a woman, she could nevertheless be embodied in the single (small) foot, (large) buttocks, or (small) "white gloved hand."

Equally important, however, for the women involved, the veil was also held as a bulwark separating her from the dark-skinned classes who dominated Lima's urban streets. Ironically, the Europeans who observed her act of racial segregation saw the tapada's sexuality as necessarily derivative of these other, more visible types of women. The Indian and black contributions to this reconstitution of the fantasized, hidden woman were, moreover, strikingly complementary: the black woman served to highlight the physical sexuality of the tapada as the rebellious, and hence available, woman. The Indian, through her association with the Andean highlands, highlighted the chastity and reticence of the discretely veiled religious woman idealized in the Marian cultures of Lima and Catholic Europe.

As Peruvians, however, the tapadas had an importance for Angrand and Rugendas involving many more dimensions than that formed by the comparatively simple dualities of the heterosexual contract. Peru was a recently liberated republic, whose ruling criollo elites were struggling to forge new identities and, above all, new ties with the European countries who had supported the Latin American republics' political—and economic—independence from Spain. The dominant "gaze" informing European impressions of Peru—and its women—would, therefore, have been the alternately welcoming and suspicious gaze exchanged between European colonial interests and the controlling elites of Peru.

Lima's creole tapadas projected an image in keeping with the troubling cultural, racial, and political uncertainties of the new republic. Whereas the country's large African and Indian population had little relevance for the political intrigues and caudillo wars that occupied Peru's criollo men, women often had very intimate relationships with their Indian and black servants.[43] The image of women, therefore, unlike that of their husbands, fathers, and brothers, necessarily included—and thereby framed—that other, "nonwhite" world of republican Peru.

This context meant that Peru's tapadas were simultaneously more inscrutable and less easily confined to the single dimension of sexual difference than many of the women these artists might have placed before their easels in, say, Paris, London, or New York. They were less easily inserted into any of the available narratives of (male) empowerment and (female) disempowerment from which Western art drew in constructing its discourse of representation.[44] Lima's creole women were not immediately accessible as Cassandras or Pandoras, Virgin Mothers or Victorian dames. Rather, their social and representational identities had to be simultaneously negotiated and reinvented through novel combinations of these established strategies of feminine emplacement.

In navigating through this relatively new terrain of the South American other, it was the idea of type that oriented the artist. Narrative forms of painting were in certain respects inappropriate, because—as a New World country—Peru was not easily inserted into either the biblical or classical narratives that underwrote much of the Orientalist imagery through which nineteenth-century Europe situated its geographically (and historiographically) contiguous colonies to the East. Whereas North Africa, Egypt, Arabia, and India could be incorporated (to differing degrees) into an established canon of history painting, the dominant pictorial genre in postcolonial South America came to be the non-narrative illustrative type. In Angrand's and other artists' representations of nineteenth-century Peru, figures are set apart from their surroundings. Backgrounds and street scenes, when portrayed, provide a setting establishing the parameters of a given "type." Those axes of differentiation that constitute each type are then set up as lines of contrast or opposition with the other human types considered native to Peru.

This representational dynamic was not, however, one-sided. The case of the tapada is interesting not simply for what it reveals about European ideas and representations of non-European women. It is also useful for thinking about how local constructions of gender and race helped to shape the particular forms of representation and typification that would come to characterize the images that Europeans assigned to particular regions of the world. The elaborately constructed sexual and racial identities with which the tapadas caught and held the European gaze contributed to a concretization of the visual types that came to signify "Peru" in the European visual imagination. As the visual,

moral, and sexual foils for the tapadas' deceptive beauty, the mulata and Indian entered the nineteenth-century European visual imagination as icons of
the sort of embodied, physical difference that would constitute the modern
notion of "race." We will next look at the photographic technology—and indeed industry—through which these racial types were commodified and
transformed in the decades that followed Rugendas's and Angrand's adventures in Lima.

## CHAPTER FIVE

# Equivalent Images

People will form collections of all kinds.
*(Louis Jacques Mandé Daguerre, 1839)*

IN NOVEMBER 1854 André Adolphe Eugène Disdéri patented a new photographic format that would revolutionize the art of photography. The specific advantages of the new 6 × 10 cm format, which Disdéri proposed to call the *carte de visite*, or "calling card" photo, were its small size, ease of manipulation and printing, and possibilities for mass production. For the consumer, the size brought with it the advantages of novelty, portability, and price.[1] For the photographer, the small size meant eliminating the time-consuming and expensive retouching and spotting operations necessary to polish large-format portrait prints. And for the sluggish photography business, the carte de visite would mean a boom of extraordinary proportions. By opening the market in photographic portraits to include what Disdéri referred to as the "public masses," cartes de visite marked the threshold between photography's early artisanal years, in which the very concept of the photographic image remained tied to art, and its later development as an industrial technology for the reproduction of visual images as capitalist commodities.[2]

In this chapter I examine the forms of objectification and exchange associated with the carte de visite as both a representational technology and a social practice. Because of the carte de visite's peculiar characteristics as an icon of exchange, I argue that the two most important categories of Andean carte-de-visite photography—photographs of "types" and bourgeois portraiture (Figure 5.1)—must be analyzed not as simple representations but as commodities whose value and meaning were accrued through specific forms of exchange.

## CIRCULATING IMAGES

Although cartes de visite were used for a wide range of representational tasks, their most common (and economically significant) use was as personal calling cards (Figure 5.2). Often, the person offering her carte would dedicate the photograph to a friend, relative, or lover with a personal note or dedication inscribed across the top or backside of the portrait. In addition, most cartes carried an embossed logo on the back indicating the photographic studio

Figure 5.1. Cholas

Figure 5.2. Upper-class portrait from Lima

where the portrait was made. Like today's designer labels, the logos confirmed the taste and social standing of the purchaser of the portrait.

As the European carte-de-visite fashion of the 1860s caught on, the practice of exchanging pictures as sentimental keepsakes among friends and relatives rapidly evolved into a social obligation in which visitors were more or less expected to proffer a portrait of themselves as "payment" for visiting a particular home or *salon*. Cartes de visite were collected in albums, exchanged among friends, and shown off as evidence of the breadth—and quality—of an individual's circle of acquaintances. As tokens of status and prestige, the cartes de visite circulated through middle-class society as a form of symbolic capital or social currency, immortalized by a contemporary American observer as "the sentimental green-backs of civilization."[3] As a visible, iconic trace of social relationships, cartes de visite penetrated to the very heart of nineteenth-century bourgeois culture.

In part because of the highly ritualized role assigned to them as items of exchange, cartes de visite soon acquired a ritualistic connotation in the realm of production as well. For the subject, the decision to pose for a carte-de-visite portrait was a momentous one. The image that would be captured and immortalized through the lens—and circulated through society—would remain as unalterable testimony to his or her moral, spiritual, and material achievements. It was an image in which the individual was expected to transcend her worldly self and to reconfirm the moral and physical beauty that would stand as evidence of her soul's unique, immortal essence. For such a subject, the photography studio was more than a commercial establishment. It was, in many respects, a place of ritual transcendence and self-contemplation.[4]

Photographers capitalized on the ritualistic connotations of these moral images. Disdéri counseled photographers to isolate the studio setting from any sights and sounds that might remind the subject of the world outside the studio. The posing areas within the studio were set up as stages, with floor spaces visually segregated from the rest of the room by a carpet and three enclosing walls. Each "posing salon," instructed Disdéri,

> must be entirely separated from laboratories, sheltered from all noise; it must be a peaceful and silent workshop [atelier] . . . preferably built on the top of a house so that no reflection from neighboring objects might inadvertently trouble the artist's chosen effect. . . . The atelier, cleared of all miscellaneous objects, must offer the eyes a calm and agreeable space.[5]

Once ensconced in the ritualized space of the posing salon, the client and photographer could capture the subject's inner moral character. Here the photographers—and to a lesser extent, the subjects—were called upon to utilize their knowledge of physiognomy, the popular science in which specific facial features and postures were read as signs of the innate moral or ethical qualities of an individual. During the 1840s and 1850s, physiognomy had become a virtual obsession in Paris and other European cities.[6] Building on Giambattista della Porta's seventeenth-century theories regarding the meaning and nature of human-animal resemblances and Johann Caspar Lavater's late eighteenth-century analysis of human facial features, popular physiognomic handbooks flooded Europe in the mid-nineteenth century. These manuals offered their readers easy guidelines and rules with which to discern the true inner character of a new acquaintance, old friend, or prospective employee. Other books, known as *physiologies*, offered a guide to the diversity of human types that could be encountered in Paris or other European cities. In these, the major calculus was neither character nor moral quality per se, but rather class. They offered their readers a technique for distinguishing a person's class origins on the basis of physical appearance.

Disdéri's invention coincided with the peak of the physiognomy craze. By the time cartes de visite were in wide demand in the 1860s, physiognomy had passed from being a fashionably new and "scientific" pastime to forming part of every Parisian's inventory of commonsense knowledge. Lavater's *Essays on Physiognomy* had gone through hundreds of editions, priced to suit every pocketbook, and Porta's quasi-totemic calculus for correlating animal and human countenances had become the subject of renewed interest as physiognomists sought to give a more systematic quality to their "science's" admittedly random mode of deciphering hidden personality traits. Through its emphasis on physical appearances as the clue to an invisible inner worth, physiognomy offered a ready-made vocabulary for interpreting the popular new photographic portraits. Ever the good entrepreneur, Disdéri capitalized on the natural affinity between photography and physiognomy by including a medallion portrait of della Porta alongside those of the founding fathers of photography in the reception hall of his luxurious "Palace of Photography."[7]

Historians of U.S. and European photography have frequently pointed out the ways in which the portrait aesthetic that developed along with the market for cartes de visite reflected the needs and aspirations of the bourgeois clients who flocked to Disdéri's and other photographers' studios to purchase the new portrait cards.[8] The first requirement of these clients was that the portrait stand as testimony to their social standing and material achievements. A second demand was that the portraits reflect their personal achievements as individuals whose moral qualities, personality, and character spoke for an inner essence free from the societal bounds of status and rank. Of these two, somewhat contradictory, demands, it was the latter that Disdéri—who set the global standard for carte-de-visite style—chose to emphasize in his public discourse and writings on the new portrait form, and the former that surfaced most clearly in the finished cartes de visite. The photographer, Disdéri wrote, must first carefully observe the client "to unravel the true character that lies underneath the attitudes and borrowed looks." Then, through skillful placement of light and shadow and considered choice of studio backdrop, pose, attire, and accessories, the photographer must chart "the subject's essence [fond] . . . his intimate and profound appearance" and, through them, make "the soul itself" speak.[9] The photographic portrait, wrote Disdéri, "must not be only a facsimile of the face; besides a material likeness it must also be a moral likeness."[10]

The contrast between Disdéri's lofty prose and the thousands of nearly identical images that were churned out daily by his and other carte-de-visite studios could not be greater. To capture the essence of each individual, the studios relied on a limited inventory of props, poses, and backdrops. Their repetition in the thousands of cartes de visite produced each year gave the portraits a formulaic quality entirely absent in Disdéri's seductive paeans to individualism.

What is perhaps most striking about the uniformity of feeling, pose, and expression that became institutionalized in the carte de visite is the extent to which cartes de visite from all over the world look very much the same. Barring the very few cartes that make use of national themes, costumes, or symbols as part of the studio props, a historian would be hard pressed to differentiate portrait cards from Boston, Paris, New York, Vienna, Mexico City, Buenos Aires, or Lima, to name just a few of the cities in which cartes de visite were actively produced and marketed from the late 1850s on. The similarities are not casual. Almost immediately after Disdéri announced the new format in 1854, the carte-de-visite trade began to spread throughout the world. Disdéri opened up studios in Madrid and London in 1865. Fascinated by the new possibilities for profit, other photographers quickly adopted Disdéri's guidelines to enter the industrial world of small-format, multiple-exposure, portrait photography. They lured new clients by advertising the modern technology and the dream of being photographed with the latest airs, postures, carriage, demeanor, and props used in the European cartes de visite.

The worldwide rush to purchase carte-de-visite photographs during the 1860s reflects the extent to which these small, circulating images of self answered the shared desires and sentiments of what was rapidly emerging as a global class. As a form of social currency—or "sentimental greenback"—the carte de visite circulated through channels much broader than the immediate network of friends and acquaintances through which any single portrait card traveled. As models of the self, the millions of small pocket images produced during the 1860s, 1870s, and 1880s also served to disseminate the particular canon of aesthetic value, moral judgment, taste, and distinction that would come to constitute nineteenth-century bourgeois culture. Here the carte de visite's double character as both commodity form and representation (or image) came into play. As a mass-produced and interchangeable commodity form, the cartes' standardized poses, airs, and demeanors bridged distances, languages, and national boundaries. As such, the very sameness of the cartes' images helped to shape the specific forms of self-imagining, the personal aesthetics, and the elements of style that would come to characterize bourgeoisies (or "bourgeois cultures") in different parts of the globe. Much as the "print capitalism" described by Benedict Anderson helped to articulate the shared interests of class sectors within emergent national (and linguistic) territories, the expanding cartes-de-visite market helped to shape feelings of community or sameness among metropolitan bourgeoisies, aspiring provincial merchants, and upper- and middle-class colonials scattered around the globe.

The cartes' importance, however, went beyond the functional act of community formation implied by Anderson's print capitalism. In exchanging cartes de visite, friends or acquaintances were offering not just things with a detached symbolic value or an arbitrarily defined monetary or exchange value. As emotionally invested images of the self these cartes contributed to the formation of a diffuse and powerful cultural and sentimental identity more appropriately discussed as what Raymond Williams has called "structures of feeling." As defined by Williams, structures of feeling are "characteristic elements of impulse, restraint, and tone; specifically affective elements of consciousness and relationships." As modes of affect and feeling attendant on such emergent social processes as class formation, they are "social experiences in solution, as distinct from other social semantic formations that have been precipitated and are more evidently and more immediately available."[11]

The explosive global popularity of the portrait carte de visite is explained by the ways in which both its affect-laden poses and ritualized forms of production and exchange distilled many of the economic and moral dispositions that remained unsettled in the new structures of feeling that would eventually form what we might think of as a mature, international bourgeois culture. The carte de visite, with its morally charged images of exemplary (bourgeois) citizens, was destined to fulfill what Disdéri himself referred to as the "civilizing mission of photography."[12] While Disdéri clearly conceived this mission in terms of the European masses, the carte was to have equally important repercussions in that other "civilizing mission" of European colonialism.

## IMAGE AS OBJECT

Although Disdéri initially imagined the portrait as the motor force driving the carte de visite's civilizing mission, other subjects were also quickly enlisted in the cause. Disdéri himself followed the announcement of his new patent with proposals to photograph every object in the Louvre, to make a carte-de-visite inventory of the Universal Exposition and the Palace of Industry, and to establish a photography department for the French Ministry of War.[13] Soon Disdéri and nearly every other photographer in Paris were offering cartes de visite of monuments, street scenes, public buildings, works of art, and celebrities. These images were either sold individually or in thematically defined packages and albums.[14]

Although large-format photographic landscapes and travel scenes had been marketed in Europe by photographers such as Gustave Le Gray and Francis Frith since the 1840s, the more immediate precedent for the mass-produced cartes de visite of scenes and views was the stereograph (Figure 5.3).[15] When viewed through a special apparatus called a stereoscope, the double images of the stereograph merged to create a three-dimensional effect. Like carte-de-visite views, stereographs were often prepackaged and marketed under themes such as monuments, city views, works of arts, history, and culture. Other packages were organized as series in which a play, humorous story, or erotic scene would unfold through a sequential viewing of the stereo cards.

In many ways, the stereograph prefigured the market and public demand for nonportrait cartes de visite. Both stereographs and cartes offered their respective publics photographs that were relatively inexpensive.[16] Both, too, built their markets around the seductive promise of a small, novel, and constantly updated commodity whose enjoyment came from the prospect of owning it in quantity or from collecting all its many varieties. No longer were

Figure 5.3. Stereograph of Cusco: "The fort where native chiefs held off sixteenth-century Spaniards"

images singular, artistic works to be admired from afar. With the carte de visite and the stereograph, the visual image attained the status of an object to be owned, hoarded, bought, and sold like any other industrially produced commodity.

The stereograph shaped—and to a certain extent revolutionized—an understanding of photographic images as material artifacts, or commodities, in several important ways. First, the stereograph's hand held viewing apparatus or stereoscope and its illusion of depth colluded to create a unique relationship between the image and the viewer. The sense of newness and wonder that stereographs aroused in their nineteenth-century viewers was best described by the American critic Oliver Wendell Holmes in an 1859 article published in the *Atlantic Monthly*.[17] The principal innovation of the stereoscope, Holmes explained, was to confer solidity to the image. "The stereoscope," he wrote, "is an instrument which makes surfaces look solid" and allows "the mind [to] feel its way into the very depth of the picture."[18] For this nineteenth-century critic, the stereoscope displaced the notion of the two-dimensional "representation" with the illusory tangibility of objects that appeared to bear a concrete, even threatening, spatial and physical relation to the viewer.

The stereograph's second innovation lay in the perception—created by the same sense of solidity and immersion described by Holmes—that the image itself had acquired an independent physical or material existence of its own. Holmes refers to a Greek theory of imagery to explain this seemingly miraculous transformation of image into matter. Vision, the Greeks taught, was produced by material "bodies [that] were continually throwing off certain images like themselves, which subtle emanations, striking on our bodily organs, give rise to our sensations." Whereas the Greeks had taught that such effluvia were transitory and nonmaterial, Holmes speculated that the photograph, and particularly the stereograph with its sensation of depth, tangibility, and solidity, had enabled the "forms, effigies, membranes or films" shed by material bodies to acquire a "real existence, separable from their illuminated source." "Form," he continued,

> is henceforth divorced from matter. In fact matter as a visible object is of no great use any longer, except as the mould on which form is shaped. Give us a few negatives of a thing worth seeing, taken from different points of view, and that is all we want of it. Pull it down or burn it up if you please. . . . Matter in large masses must always be fixed and dear; form is cheap and transportable.[19]

Once this "divorce of form and substance" had been realized, Holmes imagined that the "skins" could then be stored, inventoried, and studied in a way that nature and material objects with their transient "effluvia" could not. "The time will come," Holmes prophesied, "when a man who wishes to see any object, natural or artificial, will go to the Imperial, National, or City Stereographic Library, and call for its skin or form, as he would for a book at any common library." Stereographs, he reasoned, would facilitate study of the skins or forms drawn from these libraries by making possible an exact equivalency or comparability between objects. If taken through lenses of the exact same focal length, if posed at the exact same distance from the camera, and if viewed through a standardized stereoviewer, such naturally dissimilar objects as an elm tree and a cathedral, Holmes concludes, would be transformed into what he describes as equivalent, and hence comparable, images.[20]

In this final innovation, then, the stereograph introduced the principle of equivalency or comparability between images (or "skins") of otherwise quite disparate and incomparable objects. Because images were rendered as tangible or solid objects, and because they were viewed in groups or collections, they appeared to form their own set of objects separate and distinct from the objects they portrayed. The enjoyment of viewing stereo-photographs was not derived from the pleasure of comparing their realistic image with the original reality they portrayed—as in other forms of large-format, two-dimensional photographic prints—but from the almost corporeal experience of immersion in an image that had acquired its own spatial and temporal coordinates.

As objects produced for sale to collectors and curiosity seekers, Disdéri's cartes de visite replicated, on another scale, this fascination felt by the viewer of stereographs with the materiality of the visual image. What cartes de visite lacked in three-dimensionality, they made up in portability and tangibility. Unlike other photographs, they were neither fragile nor difficult to handle. Mounted on firm cardboard backings and printed on the most durable paper and finish available, these were images that could be fondled, caressed, possessed, displayed, and secreted away in a manner that stereographs—whose illusory tangibility ultimately relied on a mechanical viewing apparatus—could not. As objects, the cartes de visite accrued value through the social facts of ownership and display, rather than through the solitary act of experiencing a stereoscopic view.

The range of subjects portrayed in the cartes de visite reflected the relative advantages and limitations of the format's unique mode of objectifying the image. Early attempts to sculpt a market for nonportrait cartes de visite by Disdéri and other photographic entrepreneurs replicated the subject matter and style of the already popular stereographs. Cartes de visite depicting rural landscapes, urban street scenes, monuments, and historical buildings were sold both singly and in thematic groups. Theatrical or erotic scenes were also marketed. In portraying such subjects, however, the carte de visite's small size proved more a liability than an advantage. The stereoscope offered its viewers a visual experience in which monuments, landscapes, and erotic scenes took on a depth and scale that were physically or corporeally experienced; the carte de visite's representations of such scenes remained static and distant. Nor could the carte de visite successfully profit from the seductive appeals of the miniature, which had so fascinated nineteenth-century observers of both daguerreotypes and large-format prints.[21] The printing technology and materials necessary to keep costs down in carte-de-visite production gave the smaller format a distinct disadvantage when compared with the high resolution and realistic detail of these older photographic forms. The same small size that had given the carte de visite its competitive advantage in the portrait market would thus prove a liability in marketing landscapes, monuments, and scenes.

The one area in which the carte de visite could outpace the stereograph as a form of collectible photographic object was in the representation of human curiosities and types. Although the stereoscope delivered a unique sensory experience in the viewing of landscapes and scenes, it afforded few advantages for viewing human faces and bodies. When viewed through a stereoscope, studio portraits retained much of their original flatness. The face and body took on some perceptual bulk, form, and texture. Unless subject(s) were posed in a natural setting or landscape that offered receding perspective and depth (as, for example, in the stereograph shown in Figure 5.3), however, the human figure offered very little to heighten the sensations of immersion and incorporation that the public sought in its stereographs.

The shallow studio settings and theatrical artifice of the cartes de visite were situated at an opposite extreme from the stereoscopic experience. Posed in the unreal planar space of the studio, the human body acquired a flatness that heightened the effect of objectification inherent to the photographic image. Deprived of the weight, substance, movements, smells, and warmth that form the sensuous contours and space around a human body, and visually isolated from the contexts and activities that normally bring bodies to life, the body as

Figure 5.4. "Terèse Capac, 41 years old, of very pure race, taken to Paris by the Mariscal Santa Cruz" (Paris, 1864)

portrayed in the tiny carte-de-visite studio portrait offered itself up for both scrutiny and possession in a singularly powerful way. Women's dresses were often foregrounded or displayed in horizontal "trains" to increase the effect of this flatness. In the compelling portrait of Teresa Capac, for example, the arm and back of the ornate chair on which she sits serve to draw our attention to her awkwardly placed arm and hand (Figure 5.4). In this and other portrait cartes, studio props served to call attention to the model's body and gestures rather than to pull the eye away from the body with the distracting detail and perspective planes that so mesmerized contemporary viewers of the stereograph.

The carte de visite's flattening effect also proved perfect for caricaturing physiognomic traits. Just as artificial lighting could be used—as the business-conscious Disdéri wisely counseled—to downplay clients' more undesirable

*almost look like mugshots...*

Figure 5.5. "Indian brigands"

facial features, so too could it be made to emphasize the "deviant" or "lower-class" features of criminals, peasants, beggars, prostitutes, and "freaks" portrayed in the commercial cartes de visite. Harsh or direct lighting, for example, could be used to emphasize the high cheekbones and to broaden the noses of Andean Indians. Through such lighting effects, and by removing the subjects' hats and caps to reveal unkempt hair and phrenological contours, it was possible to suggest conformance with ruling physiognomic definitions of "bandits" and other "criminal types" (Figure 5.5).[22]

Public fascination for cartes of curious or exotic human types grew steadily in the 1860s and 1870s, along with a general interest in travel literature and the exercise of European colonialism itself. As advances in photographic technology made photography more portable and practical, increasing numbers of photographers began to travel abroad with the specific intent of compiling carte-de-visite photographs of "exotic" or "native" types. Other photographers turned their lenses toward exotic types closer to home. Among the favorite European subjects were peasants from France, eastern Europe, Italy, and Russia as well as urban street vendors and artisans.

## AESTHETICS OF THE SAME

In the Andes, cartes de visite were produced by both national and foreign photographers. The favored nonbourgeois subjects were tapadas, mulatas, and picturesque or rustic workers such as water carriers, candle makers, and fruit sellers. The trades depicted in most early cartes were directly modeled on the *métiers* (trades or crafts) described in the popular Parisian physiologies, as well as on the writings and artwork of early nineteenth-century costumbrista painters such as Angrand and Rugendas, or the Peruvian writer Ricardo Palma.

In Peru, photographers who produced cartes de visite for the foreign market began to specialize in a subject that had been left relatively unexplored by the earlier, urban costumbristas of Lima.[23] This subject was the highland or Andean Indian. Inspired by the European market for exotic images and métiers, photographers throughout the Andean area began to search out Indians who could model for the cartes de visite. Although little is known about the procedures through which Indians were made to pose for the photographs, the cartes themselves leave little doubt regarding the relations of power separating the photographer from his subject. A majority of the Indians in the cartes appear distrustful and, at best, reluctant models. Others, made to pose as lice-pickers or with the tools of some trade they probably did not themselves practice, stare with suspicion into the camera lens (Figures 5.5–5.8). Perhaps they were paid for their time with a small amount of coca leaves or alcohol. It is unlikely that they would have been given a copy of the completed photograph. Others modeled in return for money. The same model will often turn up under varying guises and captions in different cartes de visite.

Although some cartes de visite of indigenous subjects were bought and treasured as individual objects, most were inserted into albums alongside other cartes of natives, peasants, and "exotic types" from other parts of the world. Other albums were organized around national or geographic units. Photographs of Peruvian, Bolivian, and Ecuadorian Indians, for example, were frequently mounted together with those of other South American "person-

Figure 5.6. Water carriers

alities" to create a sort of additive image of the "American type." One such album, now owned by the Bibliothèque Nationale of France, contains over seventy cartes de visite of South American characters and types.[24] Among the pages of uncaptioned and anonymous military and political figures, bull-fighters, gauchos, soldiers, and just plain people who make up the bulk of the album, the collector has included some half-dozen cartes of Andean subjects: a peasant girl from Peru's central highlands, an Andean Indian in ragged cloth-ing, a lowland Indian, a Chinese coolie, and, finally, a puzzling portrait of a seated naked man adorned with ornate body paint.[25] In this and other similar albums, the indigenous subjects of the Peruvian cartes stand out in a continent seemingly peopled by Spanish politicians, mestizo soldiers, and the ubiqui-tous—and strangely denationalized—gaucho.[26]

Another contemporary album unites eighty cartes de visite in a sweeping inventory entitled "The Indigenous Types of America."[27] As the viewer moves through the pages of uncaptioned images, Mexican, Peruvian, Ecuadorian, Paraguayan, and Guatemalan Indians parade in relentlessly anonymous suc-cession. With a heightened effect of sameness produced by the cartes' identi-cal size and standardized poses, the images seem to merge into a uniform "American Type." As equivalent or interchangeable icons of America, the cartes' only salient markers of difference are the familiar tools and studio props that signify the subjects' supposed trades or métiers.

In creating this composite or additive image of the American type, aesthetic factors often outweighed the sociological. An album of two hundred carte-sized albumen prints, now owned by the George Eastman House, provides a striking example of the importance of aesthetics to both the manufacturers and the purchasers of cartes. This beautifully preserved leather-bound album contains nearly the full range of types available to collectors of Andean cartes: Indian couples, porters, soldiers, cholas, merchants, beggars, lice-pickers, muleteers, and *rabonas* (the women and wives who accompanied Indian soldiers).[28] Other, more unusual selections include elaborately staged scenes in which Indian children "confess" to other children dressed as priests, or upper-class Bolivians pose as Indians playing flutes. Lowland Indians are also included, as are a smattering of Africans and one Aymara of African descent who is identified with the intriguingly arithmetic label of "Noir + Indien." The range and breadth of occupational and racial types contained in the album, as well as the fact that the carte-size albumen prints were not mounted on the cardboard backings used to manufacture individual cartes, indicate that the album may have served as a sampler for a photography studio, probably in La Paz.[29]

This use is also suggested by the highly formal or patterned arrangement of the photographs. We may speculate that a photographer's eye went into its creation, for the album does not respond—as one might perhaps expect—to categories of occupational type, ethnicity, or even gender. Instead the photographs, which are mounted two to a page and viewed in sets of four (that is, two on each facing page), are clearly arranged to convey a sense of both symmetry and balance (Figure 5.7). If, for example, the two images on the right-hand page each portray two seated subjects facing toward the right, the two prints on the opposite page portray two seated subjects facing to the left. If the right-hand page holds two photographs each showing two Indians, the left one seated and the right one standing (Figure 5.8), their poses and scale are precisely mirrored on the facing page where the right ones stand and the left ones sit. Full-body portraits are classed together, as are facial portraits and medium-distance half-body shots. In each case, principles of symmetry override any consideration of occupation, ethnicity, or general type. The album's aim was to convey not only the range of sociological types available to the studio's customers but also the range of compositional formats, poses, and moods that could be obtained from its archive of images. Indeed, the formal aesthetic behind the album's classificatory logic leads one to imagine a prospective customer stepping up to the counter to order not "two porters and one lice-picker" but, rather, "two standing medium shots and one left-reclining long shot." By drawing on this inventory of poses, moods, and angles the collector could use the formal qualities of the print to provide a sense of finish or balance to his or her own collection.[30]

Figure 5.7. "Lice-pickers"

Figure 5.8. Seated men and standing boys

## COLUMNS AND ROWS

The arithmetic logic of the cartes-de-visite collector surfaces even more clearly in an album donated to the Geographic Society of Paris on June 27, 1885, by Dr. L. C. Thibon, the Bolivian consul in Brussels.[31] Like other contemporary albums, Thibon's moves from large views to smaller-format scenes and finally to the tiny cartes de visite of types. The decreasing image size in Thibon's neatly arrayed album coincides with a thematic ordering that roughly parallels that found in the albums kept by most bourgeois European families as well as by many upper-class Peruvians, Bolivians, and Ecuadorians. In Europe, these albums typically opened with several pages of carte-de-visite portraits of the royal or imperial family. The ensuing pages contained carte portraits of political and public celebrities. The album then closed with numerous cartes de visite of family and friends.[32]

Though focused on a country rather than on a family, Thibon's album replicates the same orderly progression from genus (royal family/nation) to species (class/political affiliations/taste) to subspecies or type (family/friends). The opening images, which show the election and nomination of Bolivia's president, Gregorio Pacheco, provide a republican version of the royal family por-

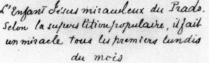

L'Enfant Jésus miraculeux du Prado.
Selon la superstition populaire, il fait
un miracle tous les premiers lundis
du mois

Grand saurien à trois têtes
de 11™50 de longueur
tué dans le Beni après avoir reçu
23 balles de carabine
(?)

Figure 5.9. "The Miraculous Baby Jesus" and "Large dragon with Three heads"

trait. The album then moves into six pages of smaller-format pictures that could be thought of as the "species" section. These include photographs of the cemetery in Potosí, the mining town of Colquechaca, the luxurious country home of President Pacheco, some men standing outside a mining camp, a street in Sucre, and a llama troop (which, for added emphasis—or perhaps as an announcement of things to come—is repeated on pages 3v and 4 of the album). The next four images in this section are more surprising. The first is a carte de visite of "the Miraculous Baby Jesus of Prado," who, Thibon notes, "performs a miracle on the first Monday of each month" (Figure 5.9). The young Christ child shares the page with a dragonlike beast that Thibon identifies as a "large saurian with three heads and 11.5 meters long slain in the [lowland Bolivian region of] Beni after having received 23 carbine rifle bullets (?)." It is unclear whether the question mark signals Thibon's skepticism regarding the dragon's existence or the number of bullets that killed him. In any case, the modern viewer is struck by the obvious fact that the photograph has been made from a painting. For us, the dragon's unlikely image is a jarring intrusion into the domain of photographic realism, suggesting a different view of what photographic images are meant to convey.

On the next page, the viewer's gaze—only recently recovered from Thibon's saurian sphinx—encounters an oval cabinet-card portrait of President Pacheco, attired in an elegant suit. Below the image, Thibon writes: "G.regorio [*sic*] Pacheco former horse tamer, current President of the Republic of Bolivia, Mixed blood, uneducated, wealthy miner, and gentleman." Facing him on the same page is a much smaller carte de visite of a modestly attired and pleasant-faced woman who rests her hands on the back of an ornately fringed studio chair. Although her hat, with its flowers, elegantly upturned brim, and long, flowing train, alludes to her familiarity with Parisian fashion, her jacket suggests a strategic compromise between European fashion and the ornately ruffled blouses or waistcoats worn by Bolivian mestizas, marketwomen, and *cholas*. Hanging several inches below her skirt is the trademark lace petticoat of the Bolivian chola. Her photograph is captioned: "Mariquita, President Pacheco's mistress." (*Chola* refers to a woman of indigenous origins who has adopted urban or "Spanish" clothes and who may or may not be of "mixed race.")[33]

Mariquita's hybrid image serves as both commentary on the "former horse tamer and wealthy miner" whose mistress she is, and preface for the following fourteen pages of Bolivian types. The seventy-eight cartes de visite that make up this section are arranged five or six to a page. Their tidy arrangement and identical size suggest that a logic of interchangeability or sameness shaped Thibon's fascination with Bolivia's diverse national types. The section opens on page 7 with cartes of the men most often included in albums of South American types. The first is an "Argentine Gaucho." The second is an indigenous Andean soldier, in this case captioned "Infantry bugler." Thibon then shifts mid-page to the Europeans' favorite Bolivian type—the chola (Figure 5.10). The women in Thibon's thirty-two cartes of cholas are portrayed in nearly identical poses. Some stand with their hands gripping the back of a fringed or upright chair. Others lean on a wooden podium or pillar. The reappearance of the same fringed chair and podium in one after another of the cartes suggests that Thibon bought the cartes de visite from the same photography studio.

But were the women known to Thibon? Thibon suggests a certain intimacy with the women through the captions and names he assigns them. Indeed, in the initial sequence of cholas the captions are applied with an almost compulsive thoroughness. A "young four-year-old Chola" initiates the sequence. After her, in rapid succession, come:

"Cook from a bourgeois household"
"Servant from a rich household"
[An uncaptioned chola]
"A *Cocotte du peuple* [darling or tart of the people] from Sucre"
"The Beautiful Rosine"
"*Cocotte en négligé*" [she appears in clothes identical to those worn by the other cholas]
"*Cocotte* of the upper crust of Sucre"
"Doña Juana Vidaure, arch-millionaire who sometimes wears more than 2,000,000 jewels"

[Two uncaptioned cartes of cholas]

"Young chola"

"Young Chola recently married" [two copies]

"Chola reknowned for the enormous quantity of jewels that she wears on her fingers" [This is the same woman in different dress that appears in the previous carte.]

"Spanish woman born in Bolivia"

Following the guitar-strumming Spanish woman, Thibon seems to abandon his project of providing an identity for every woman. Of the eleven women who follow, only one —"Farmer's wife from around Sucre"—is assigned an identity. It is not until the last two cartes of cholas that Thibon, as if to provide closure to the section, identifies the next-to-last carte in the series as portraying "A woman who cut her husband's throat and was consequently ex-communicated for three years and exiled to the frontier." The final woman in the series is then captioned simply—and somewhat anticlimactically—as "Serious merchant woman."

Could Thibon have known all these women whose images he so confidently labels? Or are the captions his attempt to provide order to the long sequence of identically posed and similarly attired women who stared at him from the orderly rows of his albums? Thibon, like other contemporary European travelers to the Andes, appears fascinated with the Bolivian chola. This fascination operated on two levels. As sexual objects the assertive and economically independent cholas, who ran most of the inns, markets, and businesses that catered to travelers in Bolivia, seduced the Europeans with a tantalizing blend of feminine availability and female domination. The ambivalent appeals of their sexuality were reinforced by their mixed ethnic and cultural heritage. As "cholas," they eluded, by definition, description as white, Indian, or mestizo. They confronted the race and class-conscious travelers with an interstitial racial identity—or, even more horrifying to the nineteenth-century European mind, with no discernible racial identity at all. Bound by the conventions and moeurs of no single culture or race, associated with no single trade or métier, and bearing clothing and jewelry suggestive of surreptitious wealth, the chola—like the equally intangible Peruvian tapada—existed as a pure woman, unfettered by the rules of either bourgeois class society or the traditional (and presumably racially pure, or Indian) Andean world. As such the chola's body and her image were available in singular ways for inscribing European fantasies of power and possession.

Thibon's cholas affirm the workings of this triple calculus of race, class, and gender. As in other contemporary albums, mestizo men—on whose bodies a mixed racial status wore less well—are entirely absent. Instead, it is woman who embodies this neither-here-nor-there racial category of the hybrid Andean citizen. Miniaturized, objectified, and distanced in the planar space of the carte de visite's fetish-sized surface and arranged in even, tidy rows and

Figure 5.10. Thibon's cholas

columns on the album's many pages, the cholas' portraits invite the viewer to label, classify, order, and reorder their essentially equivalent images. The inscription below each woman's image seems to suggest that Thibon himself succumbed to this urge to label, classify, and possess their images.

In the eight pages that follow the cholas (pages 13–20), Thibon continues his calculus of type with forty-four carte-de-visite images of Indian types (Figure 5.11). Here, too, the consul captions nearly every image. Some captions—such as "Woman who sells stew prepared with hot pepper" or "Man who sells corn beer"—allude to the pots and jars with which the Indians have been posed in the photographer's studio. Others, like "Milkmaid from La Paz," "Indian fiancée," or "Family of gold seekers," contain no clue why Thibon might have chosen those captions. Captions in Spanish and French describing trades such as "agriculturalist," "bearer," or "stevedore" predominate. Other captions are intended to shock. Above the simple caption of "worker" (*ouvrier*), for example, an Indian man reclines awkwardly on the studio floor staring guardedly at the camera while pouring himself a large drink from a wine bottle. On the opposite corner of the same page, a carte of a young woman, who stands above a huddled child, bears the improbable caption: "Young fourteen-year-old girl with her five-year-old baby." Two cartes of the popular lice-grooming scenes that surface in posed type photography from all parts of the colonial world as well as in cartes of European peasants are here spiced up with labels such as "*La toilette*. The women eat the lice which they find." In another carte a group of kneeling Indians stares out at the viewer above an alarming caption that identifies them as "A Family of Poisoners" (*Famille des empoisoneurs* [sic]).

The degrading quality of many of the captions will come as no surprise—and may even seem mild—to anyone familiar with nineteenth-century European representations of non-European or colonized peoples. For contemporary viewers as well, the captions would have served to pull the far-off—and technically speaking, not colonized— Andean people into the familiar sphere of "colonial other." The specific histories and cultures of the Andes are submerged within rubrics defined by the same poses, trades, and degrading and dangerous acts used to depict colonized, working-class, and peasant peoples throughout the world. Unlike the bourgeois subjects, for whom cartes de visite helped to consolidate a uniform demeanor and style, the indigenous subjects portrayed in Thibon's album were, in all likelihood, not paying clients or even willing subjects. Most often they were paid models. In several cases, the same model appears twice in different cartes. In others, photographs of stiffly posed Indians are assigned captions implying that their subjects were just caught in the act of performing their trade. For example, a man posing in profile with a water or alcohol tin on his back bears the unlikely caption "Cargador after having sold his coca." Another image of four Indian men standing akwardly around a table filled with bags is titled "Merchants counting their money" (Figure 5.11). Here again, as with the cholas, the photo-

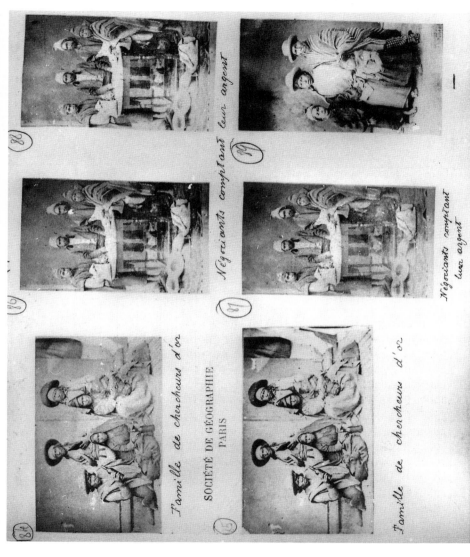

Figure 5.11.
Thibon's Indians

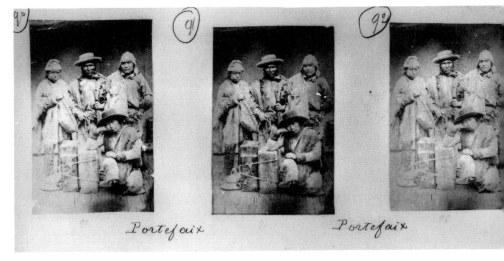

Figure 5.12. "Porters"

graphs' lack of authenticity and obvious artifice do not detract from their value
to the collector as images of "types."

Thibon's goal seems to be to represent Bolivia by a sheer accumulation of
essentially similar images, the sum total of which might then add up to something called "Bolivia." The arithmetic logic is accentuated by the cartes' uniform size, similar poses, neat rows, and tidy columns as well as by Thibon's
disarming tendency to mount multiple images of the exact same carte on
a single page. On the first page devoted to Indian types, a "Marchand de
Chicha" is repeated twice. On the following page a carte of a small boy is
included twice, and both times left uncaptioned. Flipping the page, we encounter two likenesses of the same "Aymara Indian family." On page 16, a
carte of two *cargadores* is included twice along with, on the same page, three
copies of thrice-captioned "Mule drivers." On the next page, a carte of "Agriculturalists" is included twice; on page 19, we find two copies of the same
"Family of gold seekers" and three of the elaborately posed "Merchants counting their money" (Figure 5.11). On the album's final page Thibon abandons all
pretense of diversity and aligns three identical cartes in the center of the page,
creating the effect—for modern viewers—of a strip of movie film in which the
single frames are bridged by Thibon's two final captions: "Portefaix" (stevedores or porters) (Figure 5.12). These repetitions heighten the effect of sameness created by the uniform dimensions, tones, and expressions of the neatly
aligned cartes. Perhaps Thibon's goal in assembling his album was simply to
fill the rows and columns of the empty sheets, as in a game or crossword
puzzle. Diversity—indeed, Bolivia itself—has been sacrificed to the force the
cartes acquire as objects in need of arrangement and display.

Figure 5.13. Wiener's "guilds"

A similar aesthetic motivates other contemporary Andean carte-de-visite collections. Of those brought back to France, one of the most important was the collection of nearly one hundred cartes de visite purchased by Charles Wiener in his travels through Peru and Bolivia (Figure 5.13; see also Figure 5.5). Wiener's cartes provided material for the hundreds of engravings that appeared in his published accounts of travel in Peru and Bolivia.[34] The originals were later donated to the Musée d'Ethnographie, which Wiener himself helped to found from the exhibits at the 1877 Palais d'Industrie.[35] The classificatory arrangement of Wiener's cartes avoids the more sensational captions favored by Thibon. As part of a scientific collection, the photographs have instead been assigned the task of portraying the *corps de métiers* (guilds) of

Bolivia and Peru. The titles or labels cover roughly nine broad categories of occupations: (1) market vendors (*marchands*), (2) *médecins* ("doctors" or curers), (3) coal sellers (*charboniers*), (4) brigands, (5) porters and stevedores, (6) miners, (7) agriculturalists and farm hands, (8) muletiers and drivers, and (9) domestic servants.[36]

As in the Thibon album, the captions and the images they label are at best precariously related. Here, assembled on the museum *fiches*, appear row after row of Indian faces. Most stare into the camera with a startled or even frightened look. A few smile cautiously. Others glare in seeming anger. Some clutch the tools of their trade: a ponchoed "butcher" sits smiling, ax held loosely in his hand. Two "ropemakers" pose with ropes slung over their shoulders, in the same manner—and probably with the same ropes—as the "porters" who appear in other cartes de visite. In other of Wiener's cartes, the photographer has made no attempt to insinuate any trade at all. In these cartes the models were intended to represent not trades, but "Indians" pure and simple. Their lack of identifying tools or other signs of a particular occupation highlights the distance separating Wiener's captions from the actual content of most of the cartes. In two instances, Wiener assigns trades ("fishermen" and "domestic servants") to photographs in which Indian models have been made to pose as if gathering lice off each other's heads. In other cases different photographs of the same person are assigned different occupations.[37]

By assigning labels, occupations, and trades to these images produced for another purpose, Wiener transformed the Indian bodies reproduced in the miniature cartes de visite into equivalent and interchangeable images, which could then be classified, hierarchized, and serialized to portray the corps de metiers through which contemporary sociological discourse defined societal structure. With the cartes in hand, there would no longer be any need to scrutinize the real objects (or persons) the forms once portrayed. Rather, as in the library of "skins or forms" called for by Holmes some twenty years earlier, the images in Wiener's, Thibon's, and other collectors' systems assume a life of their own as objects whose meanings are derived not from their fidelity (as "realistic" photographs) to an original but from the systems of accumulation, classification, and exchange through which they circulate as image-objects divorced from the substance they once portrayed.

## THE FINAL INDEX

With the carte de visite the Holmsian ideal of constructing an archive of images in which "form could be henceforth divorced from matter" had been at least partially realized. The bourgeois portrait-card granted the photograph a commodity status previously denied it by the artisanal techniques that had produced singular or "artistic" images. As mass-produced icons of exchange, cartes acquired value by circulating through society and among people. Like other currencies, their value as exchange objects within this social network had little to do with the specific images portrayed on any one carte (what might be thought of as the carte's use value). Although the standardized poses, props, and airs portrayed on the cards did play a role in articulating the structures of style, taste, and feeling through which the bourgeoisie would come to define themselves as a global class, the cartes' resulting homogeneity reinforced the symmetry by virtue of which they could become truly equivalent objects of exchange.

Because the carte-de-visite genre was so closely associated with the bourgeois portrait-card (and its status as an icon of exchange), images of nonbourgeois subjects and types produced in the same format were necessarily read within the system of values already established for the bourgeois carte de visite. As individual images, the photographs of awkwardly posed and exotically attired "natives" and "tradesmen" were judged by the same canons of beauty, propriety, and physiognomy used to evaluate the bourgeois portraits. Such images appealed to the nineteenth-century bourgeois consumer of visual exotica precisely because of the ways in which the types marshaled the indexical truth of photographic realism as evidence for the legitimacy of these class-based canons of taste and distinction.

As a class of objects or images, the type cartes were also shaped by the logic of equivalence or exchange of the portrait calling cards. Like the portrait cartes, the cartes de visite of types were collected, classified, and displayed in (their own) albums. Unlike the portrait cartes, however, the photographs of Indians, cholas, and métiers were not items of reciprocal exchange given by the individual portrayed, but mute and anonymous images of "types." Because the reality of the person portrayed in the carte was so distant from the familiar world of the photograph's viewer and owner, the carte's content acquired an added irrelevancy to the systems of classification and display in which it was assembled with other similar cartes. What difference did it make to a viewer in Paris if the Indian portrayed in his carte was North or South American, Bolivian or Peruvian, Quechua or Aymara, a mule driver or a domestic servant? As a carte de visite the Indian's likeness acquired its meaning as part of an archive made up of all the other equivalent images of types. By standardizing the size, format, and style of the image and by framing each subject's person and body in the universally identical and ritually charged space of the bourgeois photography studio, the carte de visite produced a system of representation in which even the most dissimilar objects could, in Holmes's words, be "transformed into equivalent, and hence comparable, images." For collectors, the attraction of such a system of interchangeable and equivalent images resided in its potential for accumulation, display, and arrangement in albums and archives as diverse as those of Wiener and Thibon.

The implications of the carte-de-visite system of equivalencies, however, went beyond the personal whims and fetishes of the casual voyeur or collector. As a technology of representation that combined the notion of equivalency or comparability with the principle (founded on the idea of photographic realism) that the image could replace its original, the carte de visite dovetailed nicely with the quantitative turn in racial theories that occurred in the late nineteenth century. Building on Cuvier's theory of fixed morphological types and the foundational theories of Camper and Blumenbach regarding the relation of "facial angles" and cranial configuration to racial identification, biologists and anthropologists in Europe and the United States began in the mid- to late nineteenth century to develop new systems for measuring and quantifying the illusive specter of "race."[38] In general terms, these biologists and anthropologists proposed to delineate the boundaries separating distinct races within the human species by mapping cranial measurements onto statistical curves that would define the normal cranial conformation for a particular race. By compiling measurements of Aymara crania and comparing them with measurements of Quechua crania, for example, the scientists hoped to settle once and for all the question of whether Quechua and Aymara speakers formed distinct races. Although the scientists disagreed among themselves as to which measurements should be taken and how they should be plotted into curves, all agreed on the fundamental principle that racial identity could be best discerned through careful, quantitative study of the human skull. Much like the phrenologists and physiognomists, who read an individual's moral character and personality from the visible surface of the body, the scientists proposed to decipher an individual's race by looking at visible (and measurable) cranial coordinates.

As the most inexpensive, numerous, and widely circulated images of colonial and non-European people, cartes de visite were soon enlisted to service the new racial studies. The notorious and little traveled Harvard polygenist, Louis Agassiz collected cartes de visite of types from throughout the world as evidence for his theories of separate racial origins.[39] The British zoologist and ethnologist Alfred Haddon also worked with a collection of cartes de visite that included at least some Andean Indians.[40] As neutral or equivalent images, the cartes de visite lent themselves with equal facility to the imaginative construction of racial hierarchies and classification, the formation of voyeurist albums, and the imagination of national types. Indeed, some of the same cartes collected by Agassiz from La Paz and identified with the simple—but, for Agassiz's purposes, sufficient—"racial" label of "Aymara" appear as well in the Eastman House album and the Wiener archive.

Cartes de visite were also used by the French physical anthropologist Arthur Chervin to study the "racial physiology" of Bolivian Indians, cholos, and mestizos. As a member of the 1903 Mission Scientifique de Créqui-Montfort et Sénéchal de la Grange to study the Bolivian ruins at Tiawanaku, Chervin was responsible for analyzing the racial composition of both the archaeological skulls uncovered in the mission's excavations and the contemporary peoples whom they encountered in Bolivia. Through study of these two sample populations, Chervin hoped to accomplish two specific tasks. First, he believed that the five hundred anatomical specimens collected by the mission could provide clues to the prehistoric migration routes of the Quechua and Aymara peoples. Second, he believed that a study of Bolivia's actual racial composition would shed light on the country's future prospects for development (and colonization). On the first point he concluded that the Quechua and Aymara formed "two distinct brachycephalic peoples" and therefore came in two distinct migrations. With regard to the second, he concluded that Bolivia's strength and "originality" lay with its "most useful social class," the mestizos.[41] Bolivians would therefore need more, not less, racial mixture if they hoped to achieve "progress."

The relevance for our purposes of Chervin's authoritative recommendations for Bolivia's national development lies in the fact that he arrived at them without ever setting foot in Bolivia. When the other members of the mission left Paris in April 1903, Chervin remained behind. Considering it unnecessary to travel in person to view Bolivia, its peoples, and its skulls *in situ*, he instead dispatched an assistant, Julien Guillaume, a specialist in anthropometric photography from Alphonse Bertillon's Service Anthropométrique de la Ville de Paris.[42] Guillaume's task was to collect photographs, especially cartes de visite, of Bolivia's indigenous peoples, and to make his own "scientific" photographs of Andean peoples. Chervin would then complement this collection with other Bolivian cartes de visite that had been brought back to Paris by travelers. It was through comparative study and measurement of these photographic images that Chervin arrived at his conclusions regarding the racial identity and national future of the Bolivians.

The photographs upon which Chervin bases his analysis fall into two categories: "photographies pittoresques" and "portraits parlés." The first category includes a selection of photographs by E. Sénéchal de la Grange, M. Saumier, and J.-B. Vaudry, all presumably members of the mission.[43] It also includes a number of cartes de visite given to Chervin by L. Galland and M. Wolff, both of whom remain unidentified in the text. The larger-format photographs taken by mission members are assigned explanatory captions detailing the provenience, occupation, and, at times, name of the subject(s). The cartes de visite, however, are displayed in Chervin's publications in rows and columns, much as in the albums and archives of men such as Thibon and Wiener. Several of the cartes are the same as those contained in the Wiener collection and in the Eastman House album. Predictably, however, they bear different captions, more in line with Chervin's racial interests.

With his "portrait parlé," Chervin sought to improve on the carte de visite's principle of comparability by complementing the information contained in the photographic image with a set of verbal and statistical descriptions. The concept of *portrait parlé* (speaking portrait) was originally developed by Chervin's collaborator, Alphonse Bertillon. As conceived by Bertillon, the portrait

Fig. 22. — Photographie au 1/7ᵉ obtenue directement et qui a servi pour faire les épreuves en demi-grandeur des pages suivantes par agrandissement de 3 diamètres 1/2.

Figure 5.14. *Portrait parlé*: "M. Sandibal, Quéchua Indian from Cochabamba (Bolivia)—Right profile and front"

*now this is a mugshot!*

parlé included a frontal and profile portrait of an individual (Figure 5.14) with an archive fiche containing measurements of nine physiognomic features. Bertillon further prescribed that the portraits be taken at a precisely measured distance, using the standardized focal length, camera, measurement devices, and posing chair (called the "Bertillon apparatus") developed by his Service Anthropométrique de la Ville de Paris, and put to use in the criminal archive of the Paris Prefecture (Figure 5.15).[44] In this way, photographic images would acquire an exact indexical relationship to their (criminal or anthropological) subjects as well as a precise comparability, or equivalency, with other similar images. To enhance their comparability, Chervin prescribed that each Bolivian portrait be accompanied by a set of anthropometric measurements of the individual's head, body, limbs, chest, and other physical features. To prove the precision of his method, Chervin compared photographs of subjects naked and in their traditional "Indian" clothes. It was the exact equivalency or comparability of the photographs, Chervin argued, that enabled him to identify the images as representing the same individual.[45]

The appeal of Bertillon's system for Chervin, however, lay not in its ability to identify the individuals that interested criminologists, but rather in its potential for constructing a statistical portrait of the range of both actual phenotypical variation and historical anatomical variation in far-off Bolivia. First, by quantifying individual photographic images into comparable numerical sets, the portrait parlé measurements allowed Chervin to conceive of the subjects in his photographic archive as part of a single, statistically defined population.

Fig. 20. — Installation de photographie anthropométrique en plein air, dans la cour de la maison de la Mission française, à Pulacayo (Bolivie).

Figure 5.15. The Bertillon apparatus in use in Bolivia

In accordance with the goal of assessing Bolivia's racial future, Chervin was less interested in defining discrete racial types (Quechua, Aymara, or white) than in discovering a way to encompass the broad range of physiologies and countenances recorded by the camera into a single population group composed of all Bolivians. "It is not the mean [*moyenne*] that is of importance to us," Chervin wrote. "[I]t is the variation that will enable us to judge the homogeneity of the people under study."[46]

Second, the portraits parlés permitted Chervin to effect an exact equivalence between cartes de visite, photographies pittoresques, and the more than five hundred Bolivian and Peruvian skulls that made up the other, larger, portion of the collection brought back by the mission (Figure 5.16). To accomplish this equivalence between living and dead Bolivians, Chervin cited the "fundamental rule" of the portrait parlé: "the analytic separation of the two primordial elements that make up the portrait: form and dimension."[47] "Form" was defined by facial lines, profiles, and distinctive physiological features. As such, it varied considerably from one individual to the next (and thus offered an important basis for Bertillon's project of identifying criminal individuals). It was of virtually no use, however, in describing the featureless skulls that constituted at least half of Chervin's racial sample. Rather, as both

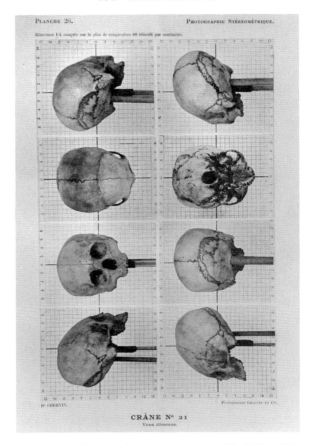

Figure 5.16. Photographie stéreométrique: "Skull No. 21"

Chervin and his mentor, Paul Broca, acknowledged, the skulls presented two special problems for the system of photographic equivalencies. First, as Chervin explains, it was necessary "to transform the physiological plan [fundamental to live portraits] into an anatomical plan."[48] Second, and most crucial, to do this it was necessary to locate the subject's gaze. "Can one recognize the gaze, there where there is no longer any gaze?" wondered Chervin.[49] Drawing on writings of his teacher Broca, Chervin argued that it was indeed possible both to find the skull's absent "gaze" and to reconstruct it as a physiological (as opposed to simply anatomical) subject. He proposed to do this by allowing Bertillon's second and more quantitative principle of "dimension" to supersede "form" as the axis along which equivalencies could be wrought between images of live subjects and images of archaeological crania.

Taken in his laboratory in Paris, and under the guidance of Bertillon himself, the hundreds of cranial photographs enabled Chervin to construct the ultimate system of photographic equivalencies. By quantifying the features recorded in individual portraits in sets of anthropometric measurements and skin tones, Chervin's system effectively enabled photographs to acquire an infinite range of comparability not only within races and national types but among all races and nationalities.[50] As visual support for his system of equivalencies, Chervin provided outlines of the skulls on orange-tinted tissue overlays. Armed with these removable transparencies, the reader could then compare the dimensions and forms of each skull illustrated in Volume III of Chervin's *Anthropologie bolivienne*. Chervin saw the tissue overlays as the final proof that his system of anthropometric photography provided an improvement over the stereoscopes prescribed by his mentor Broca for the study of skulls. Whereas it was impossible to conduct a systematic comparison of different skulls using stereoscopic images, Chervin argued that his two-dimensional photographs did allow for just such an archive to be built.[51]

## RACE AND PHOTOGRAPHY

The seemingly immense aesthetic and conceptual distance traveled from Disdéri's morally charged carte de visite portraits to Chervin's scientific system of anatomical equivalencies was covered in a little more than three decades. Although the obvious differences between the two genres might at first appear to surmount their similarities, study of their uses in the Andes suggests that the carte de visite laid the groundwork for conceptualizing the very principles of equivalency and difference that would inform both Bertillon's police archive and Chervin's system for measuring racial populations. Bertillon is widely credited with inventing modern systems of criminal photography and criminological identification. The principle of equivalency or comparability upon which his "signaletic system" rested was first introduced, however, in the extensive archives of criminal cartes de visite compiled by the Parisian police in the decades prior to Bertillon's employment at the Paris Prefecture.[52] The importance of the colonial or type carte in consolidating the archival system of exchanges and equivalencies that would be fundamental to Bertillon's system is perhaps signaled as well by the fact that Bertillon—who was himself a member of Broca's Société d'Anthropologie de Paris—used cartes de visite as illustrations for his first professional publication, *Les Races sauvages*.[53]

The historical and discursive genealogies connecting cartes de visite with Bertillon's more well studied signaletic (or criminal) photography have been largely erased by photography critics who persist in approaching photography as an exclusively European discourse and technology. In his study of

European and North American criminal photography, Alan Sekula points out the important relationship between bourgeois portraiture and the criminal archive as two opposing ends of the practice and discourse we know as "photography." "Every proper portrait," Sekula writes, "has its lurking, objectifying inverse in the files of the police."[54] He then concludes that it was by virtue of this polarized moral field separating (and connecting) the bourgeois portrait and the criminal mugshot that "photography came to establish and delimit the terrain of the *other*, to define both the *generalized look*—the typology—and the *contingent instance* of deviance and social pathology."[55] Missing from Sekula's account, however, is any mention of either colonialism and its racial ideologies or the thousands of native and colonial cartes de visite that joined—and indeed anticipated—criminal photography in delimiting what Sekula aptly refers to as the "terrain of the *other*." Indeed, the non-European world and its images have been oddly elided from virtually all the photographic histories that attempt to link photography with the history of disciplinary and ideological systems forged during the height of Europe's colonial era.[56]

Andean cartes de visite, and other colonial (or non-European) cartes can help us to rethink both the history of photography and the parallel histories of colonialism and racial ideologies in several ways. First, I suggest that it was not "photography" per se that came to define Sekula's "terrain of the *other*," but a specific conceptual linkage among race, photography, and the systems of commodification and exchange associated with capitalism. This conceptual linkage was in turn embodied in a specific form of photography: the carte de visite. As an image-object, the carte de visite was, as we have seen, valued not for the intrinsic aesthetic content of its image, as was the case with many of the larger-format "artistic" prints. Rather, the uniform size, poses, backdrops, and props used in the bourgeois portrait-card enhanced the carte's allure as a modern, industrially produced commodity to be accumulated and displayed like any other of the numerous collectibles found in nineteenth-century bourgeois drawing rooms. In short, value accrued to the carte de visite as an object to be owned, collected, displayed, and arranged. It was this form of value production that enabled the carte de visite, and not other forms of photography, to accommodate the classificatory ideology underlying both racial typologies and the criminal archive.

Second, although what Sekula called the "honorific function" of the bourgeois portrait may well define the ideal against—and for—which the criminal archive was formed, it was the *colonial* carte de visite that defined the possibilities of constructing an archive at all. Accumulated as anonymous images in private albums and public archives, the cartes of colonial natives' anonymous faces and bodies distilled the forms of value and signification found in the bourgeois cartes. Unlike the bourgeois cartes, whose imagery retained a residual "use value" as likenesses of friends and relatives, the colonial or "native" cartes de visite portrayed anonymous and historyless subjects. As a result, the colonial cartes—unlike their bourgeois counterparts—were emptied of what we might think of as the "photographic use value" of representing reality. Value accrued to the colonial carte solely through the acts of ownership, collection, accumulation, and exchange. The urgency with which Thibon filled the pages of his album with neatly arrayed and, at times, identical images speaks for this form of value production, as does the equally compulsive archival impulse behind Wiener's "scientific" arrangement of his aptly named "corps de métiers." In arranging the photographs, it was clearly neither the photos' subjects nor their referentiality with respect to the reality of Bolivia and Peru that motivated Thibon or Wiener. It was, instead, what Baudrillard has called "the passion for the code . . . the ambivalent fascination for a form [that is the] logic of the commodity or system of exchange."[57]

Closer examination of such linkages among the colonial image, European photography, and the class formations and ideologies that have accompanied the spread of capitalism outside of Europe reveals the importance of both colonial photography and racial discourse to the history of photography itself. Equally important, the historical formation of the carte de visite as a commodity form also tells us much about the ways in which race itself—as a discourse of visual difference—developed in tandem with a specific sort of visual economy. As the work of Humboldt, d'Orbigny, Angrand, and Rugendas suggests, this visual economy rearticulated the place of the human subject within a highly mobile or fluid field of vision. It also reorganized, as we have seen, the forms of value placed on the image-objects that circulated both within Europe and, more important, between Europe and the non-European world. In the following chapters we turn to look at various uses of cartes de visite, racial photographs, photographic portraits, and picturesque "types" in two Peruvian national and cultural projects. These projects set out to contest, in different ways and to differing degrees, the unequal ties that bound Peruvian and European cultures. They did so, however, in terms that reveal a very clear understanding of the historical linkages among photography, race, and European-dominated economies and cultures.

## CHAPTER SIX

# The Face of a Nation

Lima is more distant from Peru than London.
*(Alexander von Humboldt, 1803)*

IN JULY 1866 the Peruvian statistician, lawyer, satirist, and journalist Manuel Atanasio Fuentes put the finishing touches to a book that he hoped would rectify some of the strange ideas that "certain fanciful" European travelers had written about the "fairyland" (*pays féerique*) of Peru.[1] Worldly enough to know that the majority of Europeans could care less about Peru and its reputation abroad, Fuentes introduces his book with some examples of how travel writers had represented their European neighbors. "One French traveler," he points out in the first lines of his Spanish manuscript, "arrived in Madrid at the precise moment in which two bloodied youth were fighting, knives in hand. The traveler immediately took out his travel diary and wrote, 'Each day at twelve noon all the Spaniards slash each other with pocket knives.'" Fuentes next cites the case of an English traveler who witnessed an incident in which a carriage ran down an elderly pedestrian on the streets of Paris. "The cruelty of Frenchmen," the Englishman noted in his travel journal, "is so extreme that on Thursdays at 6:00 P.M. they kill the old ladies . . . with municipal carriages that first chase them through the streets." If Europe's most "distinguished travelers" commit such atrocities in representing even their closest neighbors, "with what ease," inquired Fuentes, "will they not slander far-off countries, and especially the South Americans?"[2]

In response to this question, Fuentes offers his own country as an example. In Peru, he argues, European fascination with Andean geography and the pre-Columbian past had caused many travelers to mistake the highlands for the whole of Peru. By doing so they had not only mistaken the part for the whole. They had also conflated distinct historical periods. "When in recent years, travelers of diverse nationalities have written something about Peru," complains Fuentes,

it would seem they had proposed to describe what Peru must have been years before the [Spanish] conquest. Right now in Paris a travel account is being published in which, if one were to judge truth by what it reports about different peoples in the world, from what this book has to say about Peru you might think

Figure 6.1.
Father Plaza

that the authors had set out to write a novel whose characters should have all the gross type of the savage.[3]

To drive home the implications of this exoticizing process, Fuentes points toward the powerful politics of visual representation. Three woodcuts from a recent French travel account serve as his examples.[4] The first depicts Father José Manuel Plaza, whom Fuentes describes as "an inexhaustible worker in the great enterprise of civilizing ignorant tribes" (Figure 6.1). Although Fuentes is willing to concede that Father Plaza was "without doubt not a model of masculine beauty," he nevertheless feels that the French artist's portrayal does an injustice to the man's "agreeable exterior appearance, and his intelligent, modest physiognomy" by portraying the priest "with the vulgar figure of a muletier."[5] The second and third drawings are of a theology student and a rabona.[6] The first, Fuentes complains, is shown "under the guise of a pile of straw, upon which has been placed a grotesque mask crowned by a hat, and the second as a fury with Medusa's head, who carries not only all her own household articles, but her soldier's weapons as well."[7] Why, Fuentes inquires of his readers, must the traveler look toward "his own fantasies rather than the truth? If in reality there exists a gross or slovenly person, why pretend to represent him as the type of a family, a race, or a guild?"[8]

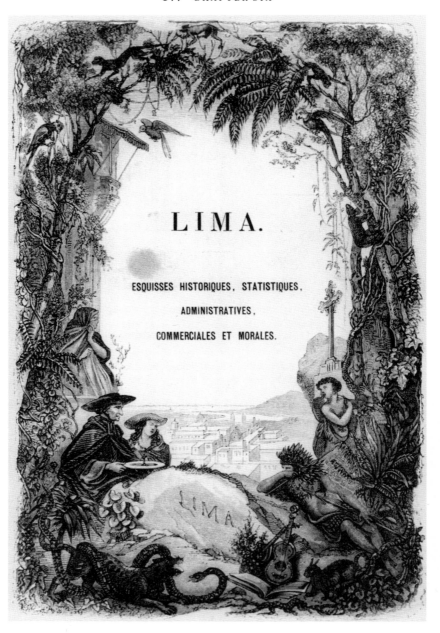

Figure 6.2. Title page of *Lima*

With this question, Fuentes centers his interrogation of European travel literature on the thorny issue of type. As a Peruvian, he objects to the ways in which Europeans have gone about constructing their notions—and images—of types. He does not, however, question the philosophical possibility of the existence of types. Nor does he phrase his objections in the scientific or realist language of representational method. Instead, this Peruvian author objects to the images on both aesthetic and statistical grounds. The Europeans, he argues, have erred statistically by deriving "type" from only a limited range of experience with (or viewings of) Peruvians. Their types thus fail the statistical tests of representativeness and sampling. Aesthetically, as well, their focus on the exotic and gruesome had led them to present the most extreme examples as representative types. True types, he implies, necessarily exist in opposition to the unrepresentative or marginal extremes of the "gross" and "slovenly." These norms correspond statistically to the average or mean, and aesthetically to the balance and harmony that defined "beauty" in nineteenth-century aesthetics.

In his introduction, Fuentes thus carves out the simultaneously statistical and aesthetic terrain through which his book—*Lima*—would contest the Europeans' "fanciful" impressions of Peru. Published in Paris in simultaneous French, English, and Spanish editions, the book proclaimed its aesthetic agenda with the numerous, costly illustrations that appeared on nearly every page.[9] Its statistical agenda was announced by the descriptive subtitle—*Historical, Statistical, Administrative, Commercial and Moral Sketches*—that identified it to contemporary readers as a study in social statistics (Figure 6.2).

This chapter explores the organization and logic of Fuentes's *Lima* as a means to understand two of the larger issues with which this book is concerned. The first concerns the relationship of nineteenth-century visual technologies to their attendant ideologies of realism and science. Whereas in the preceding chapters, I have explored how visual technologies and ideologies inflected European understandings of modernity and race, here I will be particularly concerned with asking how one South American intellectual appropriated descriptive technologies such as photography and statistics to construct his own project for modernity. In the next chapter, we return to this theme with a discussion of the highland Peruvian intellectuals who, at a slightly later date, blended photography and European romanticism to defend a quite different intellectual and political project.

A second issue that emerges from Fuentes's book concerns our continuing interrogation of the relationship between modernity and the visual discourse of race. Whereas in examining d'Orbigny's incipient racial system, the Orientalizing magic of Lima's tapadas, and the fetishistic qualities of the cartes de visite we have been concerned with race as a discourse of objectification and commodification, in this chapter I explore how race works as an aesthetic discourse of taste and distinction—or as what I will refer to as the "gut aesthetics" of Peruvian nationalism.

## RACE AND NATION IN NINETEENTH-CENTURY PERU

Like other Peruvians of his time, Fuentes's racial beliefs and nationalist sentiments were shaped more by the tumultuous decades that followed independence than by any ill feelings toward Peru's former European colonial master. Born one year before Peruvian independence, Fuentes grew up in a city in which class divisions mapped very closely onto lines of racial difference. At the bottom of the social hierarchy were the slaves and freed blacks who worked as domestic servants, street vendors, field hands, and artisans. By some estimates, this group accounted for up to 30 percent of the total population of Lima.[10] Sharing the lowest ranks with the blacks was a smaller urban population of indigenous peoples, many of whom worked as domestic servants. Other Indians lived just outside the city's colonial walls. Ruling over this urban population was a small creole elite who identified themselves as "white." Given the concrete benefits this elite had reaped from Spain's centralized administration and trade monopoly, a majority of them did not support the move toward independence that began to shake Spain's American colonies in the early decades of the nineteenth century. Indeed, it was fear rather than conviction that finally convinced the Lima elite to embrace the inevitability of the new republic formed in 1821. As Spanish troops prepared to withdraw from Lima, the Limeños found themselves caught between their distrust of Simón Bolívar's liberal nationalism and the disturbing thought that the mestizo, Indian, and African soldiers who made up the liberators' army might be tempted to seek revenge on Lima's royalist creoles for the abuses they had suffered under Spanish rule.[11]

Ironically, following the Spanish defeat, members of Lima's elite seized on nationalism as a means to enforce the protectionist measures that would ensure their continuing monopoly on trade. The British, French, and U.S. merchants who had backed independence were held at bay through severe import tariffs, property restrictions, and naturalization laws. Very few European shops were allowed to open in Lima, and those foreign merchants who did enter the city were frequently intimidated by the mestizo and African-American artisan guilds, who also opposed free trade.[12]

The more serious challenge to Lima's power and protectionist principles, however, came not from abroad but from within Peru itself. Elites from the southern city of Arequipa and the northern coast had supported independence as a means to break loose from the administrative and commercial stranglehold that Spanish colonialism had placed on their own regional economies. For these provincial planters and merchants, free trade doctrines provided an appealing weapon with which to dispute the colonial privilege that had kept their economies subordinated to the demands of Lima's commercial and bureaucratic elites.

For the first decades following Peruvian independence, the battles for control of the Peruvian state and its economic policies were fought between Lima and these rival regional elites to the north and south.[13] The Limeños, on the whole, continued throughout the 1820s and 1830s to favor strong central government and protectionist policies. Their power was periodically challenged, however, by a series of southern caudillos, who used their brief terms of office to implement more liberal economic policies. It was not until the mid-1840s that the Lima elites, under the leadership of General Ramón Castilla, were finally able to wrest permanent control of the Peruvian state. Under Castilla, Lima entered a period of relative prosperity in which discussions about Peru's national character and economic future took on increased importance.

The idea of nation and nationhood were, of course, not new to either Peru or Latin America. It was the discourse of nation that had enabled the creole liberators such as Simón Bolivar to imagine a community of Latin Americans united by their opposition to the metropolis and by their shared identity as "Americans."[14] In Peru itself the concept of an imagined community of Peruvians had been bandied about since at least the 1780s, when the mestizo muleteer and self-proclaimed Inca heir, José Gabriel Tupac Amaru, had rallied hundreds of thousands of highland Indians and mestizos in a violent rebellion to protest Spanish economic privilege. Shortly thereafter, the Inca kings—whose public representation had been banned by the Spanish Crown following Tupac Amaru's defeat—were resurrected in both literature and the popular imagination as evidence for Peru's historical identity as a nation.[15]

As the prospects of an independent Peruvian republic took shape, poets and writers such as Mariano Melgar, José Joaquin de Olmedo, Hipólito Unanue, and José Faustino Sánchez Carrión began to refer to the Andes, Incas, and the pre-Columbian past as arguments for the unified or national character of Peru's historical and territorial identity. As was also true in many other parts of the world, these early poets and writers who championed liberal concepts of the nation were, almost without exception, men who had come to Lima from the provinces. Their provincial experience provided them with an understanding of not only the territorial integrity and diversity of Peru as a nation incorporating south and north, highlands and coast, but also the importance of Peru's precolonial or Inca past. For these early provincial nationalists, the task of recovering Peru's Inca or Andean heritage did not conflict with the European legacy of Spanish rule. "My nation," wrote Melgar, "is the entire globe, I am brother of the Indian and the Spaniard."[16]

The possibility of imagining a national culture that could incorporate both Spaniard and Indian had effectively disappeared by the time Castilla took on the task of rebuilding Lima's central state in the mid- to late 1840s. Following years of civil wars and rivalries between Lima and the provinces, little was left of the emancipationists' dream of a unified national territory in which, in Melgar's utopian words, "The Indian and the wise man in fond union, will govern you from now on [El indio (y) el sabio de la union amante, Os han de gobernar en adelante]."[17] In its place, Lima's intellectuals and politicians sculpted a discourse of national community that would perpetuate—rather than heal—the racial and political divides separating Lima and the provinces. As historical support for their vision of the nation, they looked to the aristocratic traditions of Lima's colonial past.

Leading this effort to reinforce Lima's historical privilege was a conservative intelligentsia headed by the priest and congressional deputy Bartolomé Herrera. On July 28, 1846, the twenty-fifth anniversary of Peru's independence and the first year of Castilla's government, Herrera set the terms of Peru's new national debate in an unexpectedly dramatic sermon in Lima's cathedral. In the sermon, Herrera invoked biology, race, and history to argue that European ideas of popular sovereignty were inappropriate for Peru. Inverting the emancipationists' romanticized image of the Inca past, Herrera argued that, although the Incas had begun to unify Peru's savage Indians into a single national territory, they had sacrificed their historical mission of nation building by succumbing to the dynastic disputes that had led to civil war between the last Inca princes. The Spaniards, however, were able to continue the job of nation building owing to the unifying and sovereign principles of Catholicism and the monarchy. Independence was but a brief—and divinely ordained— parenthesis in Peru's national history. To continue with the task of reconstructing Peru's national identity, it was necessary, Herrera concluded, to respect this Iberian, monarchical, and Catholic heritage. Peru must have a strong central government positioned in Lima, invested by God (that is, the Catholic Church) with absolute sovereignty, and in which "the right to dictate laws [would] belong to . . . an aristocracy of knowledge created by nature."[18] Suffrage was to be selective. Indians in particular were to be prohibited from voting because what Herrera referred to as their "natural incapacity" for intelligent reasoning made them ineligible for full citizenship.

Herrera's conservative doctrines were refuted by an expanding circle of liberal, anticlerical intellectuals. Many of Herrera's most vocal critics, such as Francisco de Paula González Vigil from Tacna and Benito Laso from Puno and Cusco, introduced a strident provincial—or in the case of Laso, Andean— voice of opposition to the new intellectual and political sovereignty of Lima. On the whole, however, intellectual life in Peru remained remarkably centralized in Lima. Castilla's open trade policies and the oligarchy's renewed prosperity brought a sudden influx of European books and ideas to Lima. Journalism also flourished during Castilla's regime.[19] In the extensive and ill-defined national territory of nineteenth-century Peru, however, the "print capitalism" that helped to unite many other national communities served primarily to reinforce the parochial nature of the country's many competing national projects.[20] In the southern highland city of Cusco, for example, it was more common to find Argentine and French periodicals than any of Lima's five major newspapers. Among Lima's liberal intellectuals, none envisioned a national project that would incorporate the vast majority of the country's citizens and territory that lay beyond Lima's city walls. Even liberal romantics such as Ricardo Palma celebrated an alternative national identity based in the colonial traditions of Lima. It was a coastal, creole, and urban popular culture they celebrated, and not that of the rural, indigenous Andes.[21]

Fuentes's position within the cultural and political debates of his day ranged from youthful rebel to secular conservative. In many respects, his career mirrors the precarious state of both personal loyalties and ideological allegiances in early republican Peru. Sometime between 1841 and 1844, he left Lima and joined ranks with Manuel Ignacio Vivanco, a southern free-trade caudillo who fought a prolonged and bitter campaign against Ramon Castilla.[22] After Castilla's rise to power, Fuentes, along with Vivanco and others of his supporters, was exiled to Chile for his participation in the revolt. There Fuentes began his career as a journalist and satirist with a series of attacks on Castilla. In 1856 he wrote a satirical biography of Castilla that helped to incite Vivanco's third attempted revolution against Castilla—this time at the head of a motley crew of conservatives and southern regionalists united by their shared hatred of both Castilla and his Lima-centered regime.[23]

Picking up where he had left off in Chile, Fuentes resumed work in Lima as a journalist, satirist, and political cartoonist. His work, which was published under the penname "The Bat" (El Murciélago), drew on a tradition of satirical journalism existing in Peru since at least the late colonial period. Fuentes's cartoons also relied on the physiognomic conventions of European—in particular Parisian—political caricature art, in which facial features were read as signs of an individual's moral character.[24]

Fuentes's political activities were not limited to journalism. He also practiced and taught law, legal medicine, and statistics. In 1858 he published the *Estadística general de Lima*, a work from which he draws most of the facts and figures in *Lima*. In 1866 he published an internationally distributed memoir on the coca plant and its commercial possibilities.[25] Ten years later, as head of Peru's Department of Statistics, he directed Peru's first successful National Census. In 1877 he wrote Peru's official economics textbook. The following year he published two guidebooks to Lima. As the author of Peru's first self-conscious political guide, architect of its first census, and Peru's most famous cartoonist, satirist, legal theorist, and public critic, Fuentes was not merely a representative upper-class Limeño. He was, in the words of the historian Paul Gootenberg, quite "literally the social constructor of Limeño reality."[26]

Of all his works it is, perhaps, *Lima* that provides us with the best example of how Fuentes went about constructing this "reality." *Lima* was Fuentes's most accessible publication—and certainly his most lavishly illustrated one. The volume's Parisian imprint, simultaneous English, French, and Spanish editions, and polemical introduction meant that it would have been read, or at least perused, by representatives of the bourgeoisie on both sides of the Atlantic.[27] As his introduction makes clear, he was concerned on some level to correct European misperceptions of his country. Yet he was also—and perhaps principally—interested in reaching the small but politically vital audience made up of Peru's own creole elite. Fuentes wished to convince this particular audience of the viability of his own, politically situated, national project.

To convince the Europeans, however, Fuentes needed to move away from the particularizing language of nation. For these readers—for whom, as we will recall, a rather negative image of the Peruvian national type already loomed large—Fuentes instead needed to invoke the more neutral languages of authenticity and aesthetic taste. He needed to prove that, as a Peruvian, his own experiences provided a better statistical basis upon which to describe Peru and the Peruvians than did the haphazard or casual experience of the passing traveler. He also, however, needed to convince his European readers that his voice was to be trusted because, at heart, he and his fellow Peruvians were not so different after all. He needed to prove that Peruvians, despite their different origins and language, spoke the same language of beauty, taste, and distinction as the cultivated French or British citizen.

It was Fuentes's skillful negotiation of the visual and descriptive technologies of statistics, photography, lithography, and satire that enabled him to construct an image of national community that would appeal to his Peruvian public, without at the same time alienating his European readers. The visual format of *Lima* allows Fuentes to invoke the discourse of community and belonging constitutive of the idea of nation without actually using the contested language of "nation" itself. In fact, once the reader has gone past the introduction—in which Fuentes sets up his book as a polemic against Europeans—the word "nation" does not appear. Isolated from the political language of nationalist polemic and grounded in the realist languages of statistics and photography, Fuentes's encyclopedic tour of Lima presents the racial and cultural dichotomies of Peruvian nationalist discourse as objective, natural facts. Such is not to say, however, that Fuentes's account is itself neutral or objective. By presenting these racial "facts" in the highly aestheticized formats of portraiture, engraving, and lithography, Fuentes inscribes them within a particular discourse of aesthetic or class distinction. It is through this visual and racial discourse of distinction that Fuentes gives voice to his particular project for Peru's modern national identity. More specifically, Fuentes relied on the same transnational aesthetic of distinction and identity that we have seen at work in the carte-de-visite portraits that were so popular at the time.

## A FIELD OF FLOWERS

In *Lima*, Fuentes constructs what we might think of as a "physiognomy of Lima." In this physiognomic method, the city's material surfaces and people are offered as transparent or self-evident signs of the interior essence or worth of the city and its inhabitants. These "transparent" or objective images are then subjected—as would be an individual's face in a real *physiognomie*—to a rigorous discourse of racial and aesthetic distinction.

The text itself is divided into six well-ordered sections. In sections 1 through 5—approximately the first third of the book—Fuentes inventories Lima's administrative, ecclesiastical, military, educational, economic, and cultural institutions.[28] Presented as a register of the city's physical infrastructure, the text in these sections is strikingly nondiscursive. Narrative argument, definitive conclusions, paragraph structure, and even complete sentences are the exception rather than the rule. Instead, each building, church, school, and public place is provided with a separate entry. Below each heading, Fuentes lists such facts as the building's date of creation, measurements, physical organization, and principal uses. For occupied buildings such as convents and monasteries, he also provides a census of their inhabitants.

Two types of visual images accompany this statistical text. On the one hand, many small, uncredited wood engravings of public plazas, streets, government buildings, churches, nuns, *beatas* (lay nuns), and priests are interspersed between the descriptive entries (Figure 6.3). Another series of full-page inset lithographs contrast with these small wood engravings in both detail and size. Fifteen of these lithographs show buildings, churches, monuments, and prominent public men, including President Castilla and the railroad entrepreneur Candamo. Another thirty-one lithographs show portraits of upper-class Limeña women (Figure 6.4). While the numerous small woodcuts are placed to illustrate specific sections of Fuentes's text, the lithographs are interspersed, at regular—seemingly random—intervals. With few exceptions, the lithographs have no direct or illustrative relation to the accompanying text. They instead function as an independent and overarching commentary on Lima's civic culture. These lithographs of buildings and women provide visual evidence of the city's well-ordered public administration, religious institutions, military governance, and white or European racial makeup: they provide evidence, in short, of Lima's "modernity."

doña Tomasa de la Cruz et doña Bernarda de la Madre de Dios, qui
avaient déjà créé auparavant une maison de cet ordre.
**Santa Rosa (Sainte-Rose).** — Ce fut à la sollicitation de plu-

Figure 6.3. Nuns

In the sixth and final section of the book—entitled "Brushstrokes and
Sketches"—Fuentes switches descriptive regime. Whereas in the earlier sections he passively presents and documents the statistical and visual "facts" of
Lima, here he supplements the engravings and lithographs with satirical and
editorial descriptions. Together, the visuals and the text introduce the reader
to the full range of characters, customs, and manners that make up the picturesque underbelly of modern Lima. This section accounts for two-thirds of the
book's length. It opens with a mildly sarcastic essay entitled "What Colors!" in
which Fuentes compares the variations in skin color found among Lima's inhabitants to a "field of flowers." If, he argues, the field is "totally covered with
white flowers," its effect on the viewer is "a monotonous sameness that tires
the senses." By contrast, a multicolored field is "neither uniform, nor monotonous, nor tiring for the eyes."[29] Because "Lima's inhabitants present a range of
shades [*teintes*] from the most fine and brilliant black to white and from that
color on to yellow," the effect, Fuentes reasoned, must be similarly pleasing to
the senses.

Figure 6.4.
Limeña

Fuentes then describes the racial groups that make up this "field of flowers." Beginning with the black descendants of African slaves, he moves on to describe first the Chinese and then the Indians.[30] Curiously, the racial stereotypes that Fuentes rallies for his descriptions of these races differ little from those of the contemporary European accounts which he so severely attacks in the book's introduction. He describes the black African slave, for example, as "the most submissive, loyal, and humble servant one could hope for."[31] Like others of his time, he laments the harsh punishments and cruel treatment slaves had received, and extols the paternalism of the white masters who had baptized and cared for them. He nevertheless attributes their "humility" and servility to the stupidity that marks them as a "race." The Chinese—who were brought in to replace slave labor on the plantations—are described as good cooks who are "neither as robust nor vigorous for hard work, nor as long-suffering [sufridos] and submissive" as the Africans.[32]

Indians receive the shortest treatment in Fuentes's racial inventory—a decision intended, no doubt, to deflect both the Europeans' fascination with Peru's

Figure 6.5.
"Zamba"

Andean heritage and the concerns of those few liberals in Peru who still considered Indians to be potential citizens. He observes that, as individuals, the
Indians' physical types vary according to climate. Peru's coastal Indians therefore differ from those found in the highlands. Of their "racial" qualities, he
notes only that the Indians are stubborn and hardworking.[33] Finally, to divert
any residual liberal sympathies toward the Indian on the part of his fellow
countrymen (as well as, perhaps, the popular image of the indigenous soldier
and rabona found in nearly all European carte-de-visite collections), he de-
rides the Indians' potential as modern citizens. The Indian soldier, he notes,
"serves and fights without knowing what he serves, nor why he sheds his
blood, without any other thought than to fulfill a duty that is imposed on him,
neither reflection, nor conscience, nor patriotism, only fear alone; he follows
the flag or he betrays it, as his leaders follow or betray it."[34] Clearly there is
little room—other than as a laborer and follower—for the Indian in Fuentes's
vision of the nation.

Nor, argues Fuentes, are there historical grounds for considering Indians as
part of the modern nation. The pure *nonwhite* races of Peru are, for Fuentes, a
phenomenon of both the past and of that part of Peru (the Andes) which still

Figure 6.6. "Indian woman from the mountains"

embodies the dubious virtues of that past. As the center of modern Peru—and thus of the nation—Lima, Fuentes argues, has a declining number of pure racial types. Of the "black Africans," he writes, "there would hardly be one or two old negroes to represent them."[35] To drive home his point, he consistently employs the past tense when speaking of Lima's "black Africans." Visually, he provides only small caricatures of African types. By contrast, he includes two inset photoengravings of the mixed-race women who, as we saw in Chapter Four, had come to occupy such a special place in the European sexual imagination (Figure 6.5).[36]

A similar logic informs Fuentes's portrayal of Lima's "very scant" indigenous population.[37] Their types are shown in two plates of an Indian woman (Figure 6.6) and male *arriero* or muledriver. Fuentes is careful to label the indigenous woman as "from the mountains," and thus as a foreigner to Lima. The muledriver (which Fuentes later argues is the principal occupation of Lima's Indians) provides similar proof of the Indians' transient presence in Lima— and hence in the modern nation.[38] By denying that pure racial extremes can still be found in Lima, Fuentes simultaneously extracts his city from its colonial past of slaves and Indians and brings it closer to the type of racial and cultural homogeneity considered constitutive of a modern nation-state. Fuentes's agenda here, however, is also aesthetic. If Lima's citizenry cannot be totally "whitened" and homogeneized, then they might at least be made to occupy a tasteful middle range where the more jarring extremes of skin color have been tactfully removed.

Fuentes's following section on "the Limeños' moral, intellectual, and physical qualities" provides clues as to how he hoped to transform this tasteful middle range into a Peruvian national type. Here Fuentes focuses in particular on the details of culture and religion that distinguish Lima's collective (that is, national) culture. As in the section on race, the emphasis is not on defining distinct racial (or in this case, cultural) types but, rather, on establishing some basis around which a common or collective identity might be claimed for Lima's urban population. Whereas in the section on race, this common ground was indicated by Fuentes's emphasis on the dilution of pure racial types and their presumed merger into some more pleasingly hybrid type, here a shared identity is provided by the modern culture of Lima's creole elites. The "national dress," for example, is represented by the gowns of Lima's upper-class women, the dress clothes (*fracs*) of its ministers and president, and the habits that distinguish the religious orders. "Artisans, workers, and so on," Fuentes goes on to explain, "do not use any special dress."[39] He does not even mention the distinctive dress of Peru's indigenous peoples.

Religion constitutes another site where Fuentes imagines that the differences between once pure races might be tamed through an advantageous mixture with a national Catholic religion. Thus, Fuentes explains, whereas Lima's "blacks" do retain nominal affiliations with African "tribes" or "castes," today these "tribes" form the *cofradías* (religious brotherhoods) who advance a collective, or national, devotion to Our Lady of the Rosary and Corpus Christi.[40] Whereas European authors had tended to look to the Andes for Peru's pagan past, Fuentes focuses on the blacks or Africans, who outnumber Indians in urban Lima.

As a Limeño, Fuentes also sees African customs as symbolic of all that must be civilized if Peru is to attain the status of a modern nation state. The Africans' savagery is marked, for Fuentes, by their volatility, poor etiquette, and lack of discretion. What is most striking, Fuentes notes, "is the rapidity with which the blacks go from one extreme to the other, from a serious state to screams, from disorder to extravagance."[41] Heading his list of African barbarisms is their "supremely disagreeable" music and dance. "In music, dance, and other things that demand talent and taste," he notes, "the blacks are even more backward, in comparison with the Indians, than the Indians were relative to the Spanish."[42] For his Peruvian readers, Fuentes cautions that "our children must see to the reform of these abuses and others of its kind." For the Europeans, he makes it clear that progress is being made on this front. "Already," he writes, "our authorities have forbidden the blacks from carrying firearms and from shooting during the procession, as they used to do before."[43]

It is in their treatment of women, however, that the blacks reveal their most barbarous side. The blacks, Fuentes claim, believe "it is stupid to mourn the death of a wife since, for each one lost, a hundred can be found. . . . If there is anything that proves the barbarism of this unhappy African, it is the adoption of such an iniquitous maxim. Just and sensible men," Fuentes concludes, "think nothing of the sort."[44] As we will see, women occupy a privileged place in Fuentes's image of the nation. By defining "Africans" as a race that abuses its women, Fuentes makes it clear that this people could never form the basis of a viable national community.

To drive his point home, Fuentes next describes the "civilized" customs that stand as both symbolic opposites and evolutionary improvements over those of the "Africans." Included here are short descriptions of Lima's secular holidays, its professions (medicine, law, journalism), public events, "religious devotions" and typical customs, including visits, condolences, hand-kissing, wakes, burials, memorials, vespers, and cockfights. National foods, beverages, and dances are also described, as are the large public celebrations of Carnival and Corpus Christi, and the upper-class beach resort of Chorrillos.

Fuentes closes the book with a humorous sketch of Limeño customs entitled, in the Spanish edition, "Barbarisms of Word and Deed."[45] The most notorious of these "barbarisms" are committed by the city's unruly lower classes, who block the sidewalks with their packages, burros, and goods. He also singles out Lima's waiters who, he claims, are well known for keeping their customers waiting hours for their lunch. Throughout this section, Fuentes maintains an ironic distance from the practices and customs he describes. Dialogue is used extensively to capture the flavor of life and language in Lima. Much like the costumbrista skits and stories upon which this section is modeled, Fuentes's satire is affectionately, rather than critically, displayed. As an insider to Lima's culture, Fuentes's critique signals the author's familiarity and closeness to the practices he describes. It is a proprietary satire that functions to mark the boundary separating those who belong to Lima's "national" culture from those who do not. Although difference remains as a necessary—because undeniable—element of Lima's public life, diversity is to be tamed by honing its "gross" and "slovenly" extremes.

## THE VISUAL POLITICS OF *LIMA*

The visual politics of Fuentes's *Lima* operates on two related levels. The first takes advantage of the necessarily serial or linear presentation of images in a book to suggest a progression through time from less to more civilized. This level provides a subtle, unspoken narrative coherency to a written text composed of otherwise disconnected vignettes and sketches. The second level grounds Fuentes's statistical and descriptive evidence of racial and civilizational progress in the more elusive domain of visuality and aesthetics. Here gender and race are summoned not as rational ideologies of exclusion, but as part of the aesthetic subconscious of Fuentes's European and Peruvian publics.

On both levels, the basic framework for the book's visual politics is provided by Fuentes's juxtaposition of two distinctive representational technologies: wood engravings and lithographs. The technologies are distinguished by their capacity to convey the tonal gradation and detail that connote "realism." In Fuentes's book they are also distinguished by their relative size and unequal presentation. The lithographs bear the names of both the lithographer (A. Charpentier) and the Parisian printer (Lemercier & Cie). They are also printed on a heavier, gilt-edged paper. Each is cushioned and isolated from the facing text with a semi-transparent sheet of tissue. As a result, a slow, deliberate gesture of unveiling is needed before they can be contemplated and enjoyed. The small woodcuts, by comparison, are printed between the snippets of stories and fragments of sentences through which Fuentes describes his city. They have no border or frame. Most, but not all, bear descriptive captions. Their visual effect is to punctuate the flow of words with glimpses of Lima's picturesque "types"—as opposed to the more contemplative gaze demanded by the lithographs of buildings and portraits. The lithographs evoke art, yet are grounded in the realist necromancy of the camera. As such, they seduce the reader with the competing appeals of aesthetics and science. The drawings' appeal, in contrast, is to neither the pictorialist aesthetics of the lithograph nor the realist magic of photography but, rather, to the more immediate or "gut" aesthetics of physiognomy, race, and type.

On reading through Fuentes's book, one is immediately struck by the rhythm that is created between the full-page lithographs and the small, dark woodcuts of "personalities" and "types." This rhythm—and the emotions it rallies—becomes even more apparent in the sixth and longest section of Fuentes's book. The section opens with a small wood engraving—presumably made from a photograph—of an "Indio por conquistar."[46] Dressed in a feather cape, beads, and headband, the Indian presents his viewer with a three-quarters profile suggesting reluctance. His hesitant stance is reinforced by the partially obscured eyes. His savagery is evoked by the bow and arrow he clutches and the three long spears propped up behind him. Flipping the page, the reader is then confronted with an "Indio conquistado." The more fine grained etching of his engraving reveals a weathered and dark face, rumbled hair, and drooping shoulders. This conquered Indian has no weapons. He instead holds a crumbled hat in his right hand. With his left, he pulls back his shirt to reveal his white and hairless chest.[47]

The photoengravings of an "Indian Muledriver" and "Highland Indian Woman" follow (see Figure 6.6). As we have seen, these plates serve to locate the Indian as an external or transient element in Lima's urban demography. They are followed by small woodcuts of a *china chola* (half Indian, half black) who, in the iconographic tradition of the mulata, has one breast exposed. Next comes a *negro de raza pura* ("a pure black"), who—perhaps in order to emphasize the declining fortunes of his once pure race—leans against a crumbling wall. The two large lithographs of the mulata and samba (Figure 6.4) follow. The next page brings a small wood engraving of a black woman waving a pistol and cane. She intervenes abruptly in a paragraph describing Lima's African "tribes" and their devotion to Corpus Christi. She is followed by a lithograph of a white Limeña, whose folded hands, rosary, and carefully draped dress provide a clear contrast to the dark beauty of the samba and mulata as well as to the questionable intentions of their gun-waving sister.

This graceful señora—who is identified in the list of plates, though not in a caption, as Elisa Mendes de Castro—forms part of a series of thirty-one such portraits of distinguished "Lima beauties." Although the lithographs are not captioned, each woman is identified in the list of plates provided at the end of the book. Of the thirty-one women, three are inserted— along with six similar lithographs of military officers and priests—in the book's early statistical sections. The remaining twenty-eight march in relentless symmetry through the final section, where they provide a marked contrast to the satirical "sketches" and anonymous wood engravings of workers, Indians, and "personalidades" (Figure 6.7). Indeed, the comforting sameness of the Limeñas' poses, gestures, expressions, dress, and coiffures provides a visual coherency to the disparate "sketches" that make up this part of Fuentes's book.

As the most prominent visual element in Fuentes's book, the feminine portraits fulfill several roles.[48] First, and perhaps most obviously, their very whiteness provides a constant visual contrast with the swarthy faces and dark-skinned bodies that people the less orderly sequence of tiny wood engravings. Lest this point be lost on his readers, Fuentes himself points to the women's whiteness in his text: "In Lima," Fuentes writes, "even those men who are immediately descended from the European race have a light brown (*trigueño*) color which is pale and yellowed, although that of the women is much whiter."[49]

Second, the women's faces are offered by Fuentes as examples of perfect physiognomy. "As for [the Limeña's] physical qualities," Fuentes writes,

> the reader can judge by the lithographs that accompany these notes on customs. They are exact reproductions taken from photographs and done by the best artists in Paris. In them, art has done nothing else but to reproduce faithfully nature's work. If physiognomy suffices to judge up to a certain point the good and bad qualities for which it is a mirror, what is lacking in the high and elevated forehead, in the beautiful and wakeful eye, and in the whole ensemble of the face's regular features which are at once fine and expressive?[50]

The rules of physiognomic interpretation would have been well known to Fuentes's readers on both sides of the Atlantic. As we have seen, the prestige

Figure 6.7. "Negress who sells herbal teas" and "Negress who sells *chicha* (corn beer)"

that physiognomy attained as a popular form of knowledge peaked during the decades immediately preceding the publication of Fuentes's book. A large part of this popularity was due to the ways in which the claims of physiognomy dovetailed with the new bourgeois cult of individuality. Here was a formula for deciphering exactly who a person was. By learning the rules of physiognomic method it was possible, the physiognomists claimed, to know not only a person's social background but also the intimate moral and spiritual qualities that constituted that individual's character or personality. Though formulated as a guide to individual character, the rules of physiognomic method were, of course, both aesthetically and racially coded. Features that conformed to classic European canons of beauty were thought to reveal "upright" character and intelligence. Long, narrow noses, for example, signaled a strong character; broader or flatter noses were thought to reveal deceitfulness and moral weakness. Intelligence was marked by a high and preferably receding (as in the balding white European male) forehead. Through such rules, physiognomy effectively transferred the grammar of racial marking from the esoteric domain of biology and ethnology into the bourgeois drawing room. As such, physiognomy offered one of the most important channels through which racial discourse took hold of the European social and aesthetic imagination.

Fuentes's project was peculiarly suited to the discourse of physiognomy. To defend his national project, Fuentes needed to maintain the fiction—so central to the European concept of nation—that Lima (that is, "Peru") was a community made up of individuals or citizens. Though physically different one from the other, these "individuals" formed a pleasingly varied "field of flowers" in which the eye could behold the shared or communal boundary of the field, but not the sharp boundaries separating the flowers' distinctive colors. To defend his particular class and regional project for the nation, however, Fuentes relied on the discourse of racial distinction through which Lima's creole elite had traditionally distinguished itself from both the "barbarian" provinces and the black and Indian plebe. By stressing the women's physiognomy (rather than their whiteness), Fuentes is able to present them as individuals who represent the Peruvian national type, while simultaneously guaranteeing that their beauty would be read as part of the discourse of racial and class distinction that sustained Lima's claims to power.

Leaving nothing to chance, however, Fuentes ensures a particular reading of the women's portraits by subtly changing the physiognomies of the blacks and Indians portrayed in the engravings. Although—as Fuentes himself emphasizes in a note that accompanies the "Conquered Indian"— the wood engravings were based on photographs, a comparison with the original cartes de visites reveals that, in several instances, the subjects' features have been altered to exaggerate particular facial features. Not surprisingly, this alteration conforms to the rules of physiognomy and is, in each case, meant to emphasize the weak character or dishonesty of the figures portrayed. For example, one engraving—signed by the French artist Huyot—is based on a Courret carte de visite in which two policemen stage the arrest of a criminal.[51] In the wood engraving that Fuentes reproduces in *Lima*, the criminal's face has been subtly altered to suggest what a physiognomist would describe as "criminal" features. Other examples include the (unsigned) engravings of a "black melon vendor," "black candle vendor," and "black herbal tea vendor" (*tisanera*; Figure 6.7) whose eyes are drawn with irises that do not reach the bottom eyelids. According to Lavater's physiognomic manual, irises such as these signaled weak character and, in women, prostitution. The particular shape of the melon vendor's eyes—curved at the top, yet with a straight bottom line or lid—provided further evidence of a poor or weak character. The effect is reinforced by the fact that, in the Spanish edition, the melon vendor is printed on a page directly

Figure 6.8. Limeña

facing a portrait lithograph of an upper-class tapada. The tapada's eyes—
which are the only facial feature that can be discerned—have the classic almond shape considered indicative of good character and morals.[52]

Even without alteration, the visual culture of the cartes de visite ensured
that the blacks and Indians portrayed in the wood engravings would be read
as anonymous racial types. By a similar logic, the visual culture of European
portraiture guaranteed that the lithographs, with their tissue overlays and
gilt edges, would be viewed as portraits of individuals, rather than as examples of type. The format of the lithographs also marked the women's features
with the "truth," "naturalness," and modernity associated with photographic
technology.

> The Limeñas' slender bodies, their small and well made feet, the elegance and the
> lightness [désinvolture] of their step, have always been recognized and the object
> of a chorus of praises. That they are beautiful, that they have nothing to envy in

the women of other countries, the portraits which one sees in this book, can say much better than any description. These are not the imaginative reproductions of art, but photographs taken from nature [*prises sur nature*].[53]

As "natural beauties," the women were themselves a sign of the visual regime of transparency through which Fuentes's book purported to translate the physical (that is, visible) surface of Lima into a sign of its true inner character as a modern and civilized nation (Figure 6.8).

## RACIAL AESTHETICS

In the decades leading up to the publication of Fuentes's book, Europeans had witnessed two concurrent—and not always complementary—developments in the arts of social and physical description. On the one hand, Cuvier's once radical notion of the fixed morphological type had achieved an unquestioned hold on popular understandings of race and racial types.[54] This typologizing impulse culminated in the decades prior to Fuentes's work with the publication in 1854 of Gobineau's widely read work on national racial types, the growing popular demand for physiognomy and phrenology handbooks, and the fashionable bourgeois boom market for Disdéri's cartes de visite (see Chapter Five). In Fuentes's own profession of statistics, Fréderic Le Play had also introduced a theory of statistical description based on the notion of ideal or representative types.[55]

On the other hand, the same period that produced Gobineau, Disdéri, and Le Play also brought with it an increasing philosophical and perceptual scrutiny of the individual.[56] In the theory of vision, eighteenth-century concerns with geometric optics were displaced by a new science of physiological optics that located vision in the (mobile and subjective) body of the individual observer.[57] In the arts, realism became the preeminent style of both literary and visual representation.[58] By positing the idea of the artist-observer as an objective or neutral conduit for the perception of immediate physical reality, realism placed apparent limits on the speculative and generalizing acts through which diverse fields such as statistics, medicine, physiognomy, and biology constructed their notions of original or ideal type. Realists emphasized instead the specificity and uniqueness of discrete phenomena and the fleeting and momentary nature of empirical perception. They posited that one could describe only what existed before one's own eyes at a given moment in time. As such, realism challenged the speculative and idealizing enterprise underlying contemporary notions of race and type.

Though in some ways poised at an opposite extreme of the debate surrounding how—or if—individuals could be classified into essential groupings or "types," realism coincided with theories of race and physiognomy in one important domain: both privileged an exclusively physical, or visual, language of social description. Physiognomists and phrenologists studied the visible exterior features of an individual as clues to the interior, or invisible, essence of that person. Racial science came up with a similar solution to the problem of physiological type. As we have seen in the works of Buffon and in the Inca Operatic, Renaissance and Enlightenment societies understood "race" to be an essentially invisible historical lineage that could be traced through genealogies and "blood relations." Nineteenth-century racial theorists, by comparison, literally saw (or read) a person's "racial" identity (and hence history) from a set of visible signs inscribed on the body's surface. Realists made a similar break with eighteenth-century history painting by insisting that only physically tangible (and hence contemporary) subjects could be represented in art. As what Courbet himself defined as "a completely physical language," realism—like both physiognomy and racial theory—saw each object's immediate physical appearance as a sign of its hidden essence or identity.[59] Indeed, many realists—including Courbet and Flaubert—drew on the language of physiognomic type in their descriptions of the "individuals" who were the hallmark of realist method.[60]

By framing his book as an attack on the European travelers, Fuentes seems to point toward a realist strain of critique. "Types," Fuentes seems to argue in his introduction, are too easy. As facile generalities, they reduce—and thus distort—the complex social reality and physical diversity of Peruvian society. To counter this distorted image produced by Europeans, Fuentes claimed to offer a more realistic or "true" portrait of his country—an insider's as opposed to an outsider's view.

Our reading of Fuentes's book, however, reveals his project to be a much more complex one. To correct the Europeans' myopia, Fuentes makes use of a variety of descriptive techniques. Some of these techniques correspond to what we might think of as a realist emphasis on historical specificity and the individual. Others, however, invoke the same classificatory emphasis on "type" to which he seems to object so strongly in his introduction. Indeed, Fuentes's wood engravings make use of the same physiognomic codes by which "appearance" is rendered as "character" in the European accounts.

By situating Fuentes's text in the historical, political, and discursive contexts of mid-nineteenth-century Lima, I have tried to show some of the ways in which Fuentes's apparently "contradictory" position on the issue of realist versus typologizing forms of knowledge was shaped by his political project. Fuentes's outrage in the face of Saint-Cricq's illustrations bears witness to the fact that Peruvians themselves were aware of the dangers inherent in such caricatures and misrepresentations. After all, through their illustrations and texts travelers such as Saint-Cricq were not only commenting on the abstract physical—and physiognomic—character of Peru. More important, they were also pronouncing judgment on the country's prospects as a site for future European investment, immigration, and colonization. That Fuentes was not alone in objecting to European representations is evidenced in an episode that occurred in Paris in 1877, some ten years after the publication of Fuentes's book. In that year, the Peruvian colony in Paris organized to protest the decision to place statues of two Inca warriors on either side of the door to the Peruvian exhibit at the Universal Exposition of 1878. A contemporary French observer noted, "The Peruvians complained before their consulate, insisting on the fact that France, and possibly all of Europe, would certainly mistake these two Indians for modern Peruvian types." In place of the Inca warriors, the Peruvians suggested flanking the door with two mannequins: one of an upper-class criolla in a shawl and the other of a Limeña tapada.[61]

Fuentes's work speaks eloquently for the peculiar position from which such Peruvian elites responded to the growing body of European travel literature on the Andes. As a prominent member of Peru's intellectual elite, Fuentes was in no position to reject the Europeans wholesale. The society in which he lived was one in which British commerce and Paris fashion ruled. The Limeñas, as Fuentes himself proudly proclaims, were known for their devotion to the latest Paris designs. Of the artists and intellectuals with whom Fuentes himself associated, the majority had been educated in Europe and all stayed abreast of the latest developments in European philosophy and science. For these Peruvians, the problem with the Europeans' portrayals of "type" was not that they distorted "reality." Rather the Peruvians objected to the ways in which a European obsession with national types had eclipsed the important racial, cultural, and class divisions that separated upper-class "white" Limeños from the backward social practices—and physiognomies—of their fellow Peruvians.

The almost surreal transparency of Fuentes's statistical and visual account of Lima provides the consummate weapon for constructing such a critique of the European travelers. Caught up in their own egos and blinded by their myths about the "fairyland of Peru," the Europeans, Fuentes seems to say, have been unable to bring their own technologies to bear in describing his and other foreign countries. As a Peruvian, he will use European descriptive techniques to accomplish what the Europeans themselves have been unable to do: compose an accurate, objective, and unmediated description of Peru and its capital city of Lima. Through the modern technologies of statistics, photography, lithography, and photoengraving he will prove his country's parity with other modern nation states by reinserting it into the historical narrative of progress and modernity from which European writers—and illustrators—had effectively divorced it. Bolstered by the implied authority of his status as an "insider" or native, Fuentes recoils completely from the almost obsessive concern with voice and placement through which European authors placed themselves at a scene. Instead, following the brief introduction in which the author situates himself (as native) with respect to—or above—the European travelers, Fuentes virtually disappears from the text. By holding up his objective statistical and visual portrait of Lima, Fuentes, the native, is able to pull back and say "Look, here is the real Lima. *This* is my reality."

Because the book was both addressed to Europeans and made skillful use of the same descriptive technologies that had become associated with European nation building (statistics, physiognomy, realism), it formed a subtle yet skillfully constructed intervention on behalf of a particular conservative project for Peru. Because Fuentes grounded his inherently political argument regarding the Peruvian nation in a modern visual regime that was itself presented as evidence of Lima's "modernity" and "civilization," the book was received within Peru, as well, as part of a statistical—rather than overtly political—project for defining a Peruvian nation.

It is my contention that Fuentes deliberately chose to ground his argument for a national project in this visual, sensuous domain of images, for it was through images—and not words—that Fuentes could rally his readers' inarticulable sensuous and aesthetic responses—their "gut reactions"—to the racial "facts" of Peru. As a statistician, Fuentes's study of Lima focused both on locating and describing the mean or average citizen and on defining the range of variation or deviation by which this "normal" or average type could be discerned. Like Le Play and other contemporary sociologists, Fuentes sought to understand Peruvian society through a portrait of what he took to be its most "representative" individuals: the criollo elite of modern, civilized Lima. To bolster his representation of this class as the representative national citizens of Peru, however, Fuentes had recourse to statistics. By focusing on Lima, he could convincingly erase the indigenous demographic majority. By denying the survival of "pure" blacks in the nation's capital, he could then construct a standard deviation in which "normalcy" would be defined by the relatively small criollo elite of Lima.

For Fuentes, however, race was not a quantitative discourse of heredity and blood but, rather, a qualitative calculus of taste and distinction. By mapping Peru's races onto the statistician's bell curve, Fuentes drew on contemporary aesthetic discourse in which "beauty" was defined as a state of harmony or balance—a middle range of values, tones, and angles in which extremes did not exist. By examining the logic behind these images, we can see the powerful role played by race and gender not as incidental elements of national projects, but as the essential aesthetic and sensuous components explaining how nationalist discourses "took hold"—how, in other words, the abstract notion of "nation" embedded itself in the most intimate realms of sentiment, emotion, passion, and will.

In the literature on vision and visuality, images are often assumed to convey their "messages" through processes that appear strikingly discursive. Yet, as our journey through Fuentes's book suggests, images also operate at a much less articulate or discursive level; and they do so precisely because of the aesthetic discourses to which they make appeal. In the following chapter, we explore the role assigned to visual images, photographic technologies, and aesthetic ideologies in another, substantively different national project of certain early twentieth-century Peruvian *indigenistas*.

## CHAPTER SEVEN

# The New Indians

Four hundred years of European science have compressed the expansion of the original spirit of our people. For this reason, the new ideas which are circulating in contemporary thinking must serve us only as
short term loans or reference points for the
affirmation of our own values.
(*José Uriel García, 1926*)

SOMETIME in the early 1900s, the Peruvian artist Juan Manuel Figueroa Aznar arranged his easel, paints, stool, palette, two open photo-magazines, and two portrait canvases in front of a studio backdrop. On the backdrop, which he also used for occasional work as a commercial photographer, he had painted an arched colonial column and half of a traditional Andean religious altar. Having arranged his utensils and easel in front of this scene, Figueroa then set up his camera, prepared the plate, composed the image, and arranged for another person to release the shutter. He straightened his suit, adjusted the flower on his lapel, and posed, cigarette in hand and one leg crossed casually over the other, to contemplate his work of art (Figure 7.1).

But where, exactly, do we situate the object of this carefully framed and contemplative gaze? Is it the not yet finished painting? The thematic space uniting artist, easel, and paints? Or the still broader frame of an anticipated image that has just been composed on a chemically coated and industrially produced plate of glass? How, in short, are we to understand the relationship of this turn-of-the-century Peruvian dandy, photographer, and painter to the representational technologies he so skillfully wields?

A glance at the embedded pictorial frames of this particular self-portrait suggests that Figueroa was pointing toward questions about the relationship of photography, painting, and art. The stretched and painted canvas is framed by an easel. The easel is in turn framed by a stretched and painted backdrop. This entire scene is then framed by the awkwardly visible and slightly rumpled upper edge of the canvas backdrop. This interior frame—which could easily have been edited from the plate—dismantles the illusion a backdrop is in-tended to convey. Juxtaposed next to the even sharper line left by the negative edge itself, the void left visible by this painted backdrop's edge reveals the photographer's awareness of the technological and artistic artifices enabling

Figure 7.1. Self-portrait (Figueroa Aznar, Cusco)

his own romanticized and introspective gaze into the world of easel, palette, and disguise.

In this chapter, I propose that Figueroa indeed had a very particular interest in understanding and, to a certain extent, dismantling the artifices of both photography and art. Like the dandified self-image he assumed, his approaches to these problems borrowed heavily from the literature and art of European romanticism. Yet contrary to the concept of an amusing colonial mimicry that our own first viewing of this provincial Peruvian dandy might suggest, his reappropriations and reworkings of these borrowed European elements were neither innocent nor misconstrued. Rather, Figueroa created an approach to both photography and modernity that intentionally departed from the dominant mold of European modernism. In discussing his life, I will be particularly interested in the ways in which this tangentially modernist style was shaped by Peruvian understandings of photography and art and by the intellectual and aesthetic project of Cusco's "New Indian" movement.

## PHOTOGRAPHY AND ART IN PERU

Juan Manuel Figueroa Aznar was born in 1878 in the small town of Carás in the Andean highlands of the Peruvian department of Ancash. His father, Juan Manuel Figueroa y Pozo, was from the coastal Peruvian city of Lambayeque and his mother, María Presentación Aznar de Usua, was from Zaragoza, Spain. Although his father continued working in mining ventures in the central highlands until his death in 1910, soon after Juan Manuel's birth the family set up residence in Lima. Juan Manuel spent his youth in the war-torn Lima of the 1880s.[1] Following his studies at a fine arts institution in Lima, Figueroa worked his way through Ecuador, Colombia, and Panama as a portrait painter. While in Colombia, Figueroa may well have learned of newer developments in art photography. Academicism and naturalism, for example, were practiced quite early in Colombia by Antioqueño photographers such as Melitón Rodríguez.[2]

The Peru to which Juan Manuel returned in 1899 or 1900, however, was strikingly different from both Colombia and the western European countries where art photographies first emerged. The vast majority of the country's population consisted of Quechua- and Aymara-speaking peasants employed in small-scale community agriculture or as peons on semi-feudal agrarian estates. The small elite of rural landlords who owned these estates lived in provincial cities that, with few exceptions, were isolated from the modernizing currents of industrial capitalist development.

Lima, the capital of this predominantly rural country, was home to a small but prosperous oligarchy whose wealth was derived from sugar and cotton plantations built from the accumulated profits of the prewar *guano* (bird ma-

nure) and nitrate trade. Production in both the guano fields and the plantations they engendered was based on indentured contract labor from China
and sharecropping by coastal and highland peasantries. Little or none of the
income from these properties was invested in industrial development.[3] Consequently, Lima lacked the bourgeois and emerging middle classes who served
as both the European and the Colombian audiences for pictorialist and
amateur photographies.[4] In these different social and class settings, "art photography" had emerged to fulfill a historically specific set of representational
tasks. These tasks were related to the split between an aesthetic discourse
based on notions of artistic creativity, manual production, and the author, and
the forms of scientific epistemology, mechanized technology, and commodity
production informing bourgeois industrial society.[5] Pictorialist photographies
resolved this problem by transforming the scientific (or industrial) qualities of
photography into "art" through the photographer-artist's personal (or manual)
intervention into the mechanical technology of focus, tone, framing, angle,
and texture. The photographic print was in this respect no longer a reproducible commodity, but a unique "work of art."

In early twentieth-century Lima, by comparison, the ruling class had not
yet been confronted by the challenge of either industrial forms of commodity
production or mass-marketed art (kitsch). In this society of patronage and
family, success as an artist depended on access to both family resources and
the prestigious allure that artistic training in Europe, particularly Paris, gave to
those artists with the means.[6] More specifically, with respect to Figueroa's
personal situation, success as a visual artist meant success as a painter, and
Peruvian painters had not yet been forced to confront the artistic marketplace.
Its traumas had paved the way for both pictorial modernism and art photography in Europe.

The failure of aestheticized and pictorialist photographies to take hold in
Lima must, then, be understood with respect to the specific class and social
structures that defined contemporary Peruvian reality. This fact has two important consequences for reading Figueroa's photographs. First, it suggests
that Figueroa's photographic work was never considered, or perhaps intended, to be "art." Second, it suggests that Figueroa's early decision to turn to
photography was not so much an artistic choice as a practical solution to the
dilemma created by his relatively marginal social position in the closed and
highly stratified society of oligarchic Lima: for an artist with neither upper-
class family ties nor European training, apprenticeship in a successful photography studio was one of the few available routes through which to pursue a
viable career in portraiture, the genre of artistic representation in which
Figueroa had so far specialized.

By 1900 the business of photographic portraiture was a thriving industry in
Lima, with little room for either artistic experimentation or the bohemian
aesthetic that Figueroa had cultivated in his travels abroad. Some forty to fifty

studios competed to serve a market made up of the relatively stable population of Lima's oligarchy and merchant class.[7] These fashionable studios were ranked in accordance with the prestige and class position of their respective clienteles. Together they defined a dominant portrait style based on the rigid poses and stylized theatricality of the ubiquitous carte de visite.

Given the formulaic nature of their composition and content, such photographs' "artistic" qualities were ascribed to the varying qualities of their surface effects. In the early years of Peruvian photography, when the prestigious French studios of Courret, Garreaud, and Manoury dominated Lima's portrait trade, this aesthetic quality was explained in terms of the technical and lighting effects produced within the print itself by the (European-trained) photographer.[8] As photography became more widespread and national, however, the Peruvian photographers—who often could not count on European pedigrees to authorize an artistic status for their machine-made images—began to look toward other means of differentiating the aesthetic value of their commercial products. The favored solution was to transform the machine-produced image into a hand-produced "work of art." This was accomplished through retouching techniques, by which faces and figures were altered in the negative and color added to the final print.

Of these retouching techniques, the most radical was the *fotografía iluminada* ("illuminated photography"), or *foto-óleo* ("oil-photo"). In foto-óleo, oil-based paint was used to idealize the subject's features, add color, and even create backdrops and special effects not present in the original negative. Because of its painterly qualities, the foto-óleo provided both the aura of an original work of art and the allure of modernity ascribed to photography as an industrial and, above all, imported technology. More important, from the point of view of the upper and merchant classes, who at first monopolized the market for foto-óleos, it retained this allure while denying the democratic nature of photography as a mechanically reproducible portrait technology accessible to the working classes. Precisely because of its contradictory combination of exclusivity and availability, foto-óleo rapidly became one of the most popular art forms in Lima. During the first decades of the twentieth century, well-attended exhibitions of fotografía iluminada were regularly held in the major photography studios and reviewed in the national press.

The popularity of the foto-óleo speaks for the extent to which Lima's photographic culture differed from the contemporary Colombian and European art photographies with which Figueroa may also have been familiar. Whereas the pictorialists sought to render photography an art by intervening as artists in the chemical and mechanical process of photographic production, the Peruvians sought to separate completely the photographer's labor from that of the artist. Even this conservative compromise was resisted by Lima's foremost critic, Teofilo Castillo, who as late as 1919 attacked foto-óleos for their "immoral" effects on Lima's popular classes. Castillo claimed that insofar as foto-óleos displayed "a value more industrial than artistic," the public should be protected from their "unculturedness and tackiness."[9] Castillo's virulent defense of traditional aesthetic values in the name of the public good, echoed Baudelaire's 1859 charge in Paris that photography would spread "the dislike of history and painting amongst the masses."[10] The seeming anachronism of the Peruvian critic's attacks on photography sixty years later—when photography was already an accepted artistic form in Europe and North America—reflects not the late arrival of photographic technology and ideas to Lima but, rather, the ways in which analogous class structures informed the two critics' perceptions of photography.[11] For Baudelaire, writing in 1850s France, photography was a threat to painting precisely because it confused the functions of bourgeois industry and the elite art salon. For Castillo, the foto-óleo as "industrial" or bourgeois kitsch had similar resonances for the cultural values of an oligarchical society faced with the prospects of President Augusto Leguía's modernizing state.[12]

Yet neither the technology of photographic portraiture nor the technique of foto-óleo could be forever defended from the demands of Lima's lower classes. As increasing numbers of studios began to offer a commercial version of the prestigious foto-óleo, other critics intervened to ensure that the "artistic" foto-óleo remained a perquisite of the few fashionable studios who used photographers either trained in, or visiting from, Paris, London, and Rome. These in turn depended on the artistic aura assigned to their work to retain both a monopoly on prestige and a loyal, wealthy clientele. The photographs and foto-óleos produced by nationally trained photographers or by the more poorly equipped photograph studios that serviced Lima's working-class and merchant sectors were reciprocally relegated by the critics to a status of technology or "craft."

Although it is not known in which studio Figueroa worked, in 1901 he exhibited two foto-óleos—one of a woman playing the piano, the other of "a young woman half covered with vaporous tulles"—in a department store on Mercaderes Street, where Lima's most fashionable photography studios were located. A review of the exhibit notes that Figueroa's work "reveals the effort to go beyond the routine," but adds that his figures were rigid and lacked the polish of Lima's more accomplished and European-trained studio portraitists.[13] Entry into Lima's exclusive social and artistic circles would clearly not be easy for a newcomer who lacked the sine qua non of a European education.


## A BOHEMIAN AESTHETIC

In 1902 Juan Manuel Figueroa moved to Arequipa, the urban and commercial center of southern Peru's booming wool export trade. At the time of Figueroa's arrival, a small but prosperous oligarchy dominated Arequipeña society. Its members' wealth was based on the commercial export trade. Unlike the Lima oligarchy, they depended very little on the guano trade (and therefore lost little in the war with Chile). And unlike other provincial elites in Peru, they had relatively reduced agrarian holdings; they bought their wool instead from the large haciendas of Puno and Cusco. The city was also home to a relatively large number of foreigners, in particular British agents of the wool export houses and a small Spanish and Arab merchant class.[14] As a result, Arequipa's photographic and artistic establishment, though smaller, was more cosmopolitan and more receptive to new talent than that of Lima.

In this setting Figueroa found work in the new, yet already nationally recognized photographic studio of Maximiliano T. Vargas. In Vargas's studio Figueroa painted backdrops, posters, and foto-óleos for what was to be Arequipa's most luxurious photographic studio. Figueroa learned many of his techniques of studio lighting from Vargas, who was also the instructor for Martín Chambi, another photographer whom Figueroa would meet in Cusco. Vargas's influence on both Figueroa and Chambi can be traced to his skills in photographic portraiture and, perhaps more important, to his early interest in taking studio portraits of Indian subjects.

Although these influences are clear in Figueroa's later work, his early work did not immediately develop Vargas's insights into either the Indian or photographic composition. Instead, during these years Figueroa remained immersed within the world of the foto-óleo and therefore within the all-encompassing dichotomy of photography versus art. In 1903, an exhibit of Figueroa's foto-óleos and landscape and portrait canvases was mounted at the Vargas studio and at a nearby jewelry store. However, it was the "fotografías iluminadas" that the critic for Arequipa's La Bolsa newspaper singled out as most expressive of Figueroa's artistic potential. The young artist, he wrote, "distinguishes himself above all for his good taste in the selection of details which give life to his portraits." Figueroa's "iluminaciones" could compare favorably, he continues, with the paintings of Carlos Baca Flor, Daniel Hernández, and Alberto Lynch—three Paris-based Peruvian artists—were it not for the "small defects [that] originate . . . in large part from his lack of schooling."[15] Other reviews of his Arequipa work focus on the foto-óleos as a means through which the undesirable realism of photography might be sentimentalized and improved. For his growing Arequipeño public, Figueroa was an artist "of the modern school [who] loved reality, albeit embellished and envigorated by art and sentiment."[16]

In 1904 Figueroa moved to Cusco, a smaller city located 11,000 feet above and several weeks' traveling distance from Lima. The Cusco of Figueroa's time was home to about 19,000 Quechua-speaking Indians, a scattering of mestizo and Arab traders, an even smaller group of white landowners, and a half dozen or so Italian and Spanish families engaged in the wool and alcohol trade as well as in a nascent textile industry.[17] The contrast between the luxuriant lifestyles of these landowning and emergent bourgeois sectors and the impoverished Indian peasants upon whose labor and wool the regional economy depended was structured in ways similar to the class and cultural oppositions found in other contemporary Latin American cities.

Figueroa's early work in Cusco seems to suggest that, at least initially, his sympathies sided with the more prosperous pole of Cusco's cultural life. Indeed, the warm reception that Cusco provided the aspiring young photographer and artist must have been a welcome contrast to Lima and Arequipa, where Figueroa had been refused full recognition as an artist. His first Cusco exhibit in October 1905 was of fotografía iluminada, the ambivalent form of art/photography with which he had hoped to appease the taste of Lima's demanding ruling elite. The work was exhibited in the studio of Vidal González, a Cusqueño studio photographer with whom Figueroa had worked since his arrival in Cusco.[18] In his review of the exhibit, the anonymous art critic for Cusco's La Union newspaper predicted Figueroa's future as one in which the artist would have to overturn all of his metropolitan ambitions: although Figueroa's work reflected, he said, a "nobility of the soul," it was restricted in both scope and spirit by the "powerful influence of Lima."[19]

During the next several years, Figueroa established himself as a prominent figure in Cusco's small but vital intellectual circles.[20] His success reflected his ability to resolve the distance between his earlier, more metropolitan notions of art and the locally grounded identity called for by his first Cusqueño critic. An article by José Angel Escalante, a leading Cusco intellectual, describes a visit in August 1907 to Figueroa's atelier on the hacienda Marabamba outside of Cusco.[21]

As a leading local intellectual, José Angel Escalante's comments on Figueroa and the 1907 group exhibit in Cusco in which Figueroa participated, are particularly interesting for what they tell us about Cusqueño attitudes toward photography and art. For Escalante, Figueroa's return to painting while at Marabamba signaled an advance in his artistic formation toward "works of greater scope." This was especially true because while in Cusco "he only occupied himself—it is true that the public so obliged him—in illuminating photographs." Only by visiting him in the fullness of nature at Marabamba, claimed Escalante, was it possible to understand the extent to which this bearded artista with his "Moorish aspect . . . , impressionist tendencies, and fiery and frisky [retozona] blood" excelled in his true vocation as a painter and "quintessential colorist."[22] For this writer, as for many of his contemporaries in Cusco, Figueroa's painting, unlike either his photography or his foto-óleo, was an art because of its intimate and direct relation to the three elements that together were seen to constitute "art": color, nature, and the human spirit.

Similar associations equating the realm of art with that of color, painting with its source in nature, and creative sensibility with individual idiosyncrasy ("frisky blood" and "Moorish aspect") surface again and again in the Cusco reviews of Figueroa's work. They speak of a concept of art and the artist drawn from the discourse of European Romanticism, yet tailored in ways specific to Cusco.

The resultant notion of art was to influence Figueroa's career in two crucial ways. First, the association between color and art placed critical limits on the public acceptability of his photographic work. That Figueroa was accepted and even acclaimed as a photographer at all was due to his skills as a *cromatista*, or colorist. In the days prior to color film, such praise referred, of course, to his manual skill as an oil and pastel painter. As a result, much of Figueroa's best black-and-white photographic work was developed in a strictly private genre: ingenious and experimental self-portraits, sentimentalized family portraits, and academic studies in both lighting and "type" form the core of his photographic opus. This work was done for personal use and limited commercial sales. It was never intended for public exhibition as "art."

Second, the Cusco intellectuals' rejection of Lima's highly academist artistic establishment was formulated as a doctrine of spontaneous artistic creativity. Figueroa, who was criticized in Lima for his lack of European training, was lauded in Cusco precisely because his "pictorial mode . . . follows none of the channeled currents of any school of art."[23] Another critic reflected on the spontaneity and individuality of Figueroa's painting in more philosophical terms, reminiscent of the European Romantics' ideas of art as a cultivated organic growth: "Art consists . . . in making tangible the impressions of the artist, quality, effervescence, as they are felt . . . in translating to the canvas the conceptions of his fantasy, just as they sprout . . . before they are frozen by the coldness of calculation."[24]

In Cusco, then, it was the individual per se, and not his or her social and academic formation (or "calculation"), that was idealized as the source of artistic and general intellectual ability. Sentiment was valued over skill, passion over science, color over form, and instinct over tradition. In later indigenista philosophy, the source of this natural talent would be defined as the Andean landscape itself. In this early period, however, it was expressed primarily through certain consciously contrived bohemian identities associated with the artistic personality. On this front as well, Figueroa's natural status as an outsider to Cusco placed him in a position of artistic advantage. For Cusqueños, Figueroa—four years after moving to Cusco—was still "our guest, the well-known Limeño painter . . . through whose veins runs Andalusian blood and in whose spirit Moorish atavisms endure."[25] This outsider status, an impediment to his artistic acceptance in Lima, buttressed a studied bohemian identity that was to be Figueroa's trademark in Cusco society. "Like all born artists," wrote his fellow indigenista Julio Gutierrez, "Juan Manuel Figueroa led an elegant and refined bohemian life."[26]

The bohemian identity attributed to Figueroa in Cusco of the 1900s borrowed its terms of reference from the earlier nineteenth-century tradition of bohemianism that had originated in the rapidly expanding metropolitan settings of Paris and other European cities. In these cities, and under the pressures of marketplace competition and the mass production of both culture and art, young intellectuals and artists made a conscious endeavor to renounce the materialist values of bourgeois industrial society. Modeling themselves upon such modes of otherness as Gypsies, the bohemians of Paris set the precedent for an emerging modernism based on the cult of individuality, fashion, and "art for art's sake."[27]

The first and in many ways most striking difference between this classic European bohemian setting and rural, seigneurial Cusco is the nearly total absence of the defining structural feature of European Romanticism—the literary and artistic marketplace.[28] Unlike his nineteenth-century European counterpart, the early twentieth-century Cusco artist was not confronted by the challenge of a large new middle-class reading and art-consuming public.[29] Although there was a limited local market for journalism, prior to the university reform of 1909 there was very little public at all for literary journalism and even less for the visual arts. In fact, the first public purchase of works exhibited in the annual show of Cusco's Centro Nacional de Arte e Historia was not until 1922.[30] As a result, the image of marginalized artistic genius used to describe Figueroa and other Cusco artists was inspired not, as in Europe, by an aversion to bourgeois art consumers, but rather by the Cusqueños' rejection of the cultural dominance of Lima. Figueroa was seen by his Cusco contemporaries as a "bohemian" because he was not from Cusco. He was seen as a bohemian "genius" because of the natural affinity for nature and beauty that had drawn him to the Cusco landscape, and because of his personal and aesthetic rejection of Lima society and urban life. In this way, an identity and discourse that, in Europe, had been structured by urban artists' emerging aesthetic and social enmity toward the bourgeois consuming classes was instead tailored in Cusco to fit the quite different needs of a provincial discourse of regionalist demands. The artist as spokesperson for Cusco's own cultural project stood opposed to a place (Lima) and not, as in Europe, to a class (the bourgeoisie).

This slight twist in the Cusco bohemian tradition meant in turn that it would be nature, in the guise of geography or place, that the first Cusco bohemians would privilege in their definition of the sentiment or emotion that inspires artistic genius, and not the Gypsies or other social outsiders upon which the European bohemian ideal was molded. In Cusco, these ideas about nature, individualism, and the bohemian rebel were perhaps best articulated in the popular ideal of the *walaychu*. In Quechua, *walaychu* refers to a man who replaces social or family ties with a restless, wandering existence, yet who, unlike the European bohemian, is neither entirely carefree nor uprooted. Rather, the walaychu replaces his family and community tradition with a deeply sentimental attachment to the land. This emotional attachment to a

Figure 7.2. Bohemians (Figueroa Aznar, Cusco)

province, region, or landscape is then credited as the source of the walaychu's heightened artistic and musical sensibilities. Early twentieth-century Cusco intellectuals saw themselves as building upon this spatially grounded concept of aesthetic sensibility to form a community based on shared artistic sentiment (Figure 7.2). Because of its Andean roots, this community was seen to exclude both Lima and the forms of European mimicry that the Cusqueños believed had undermined Lima's spirit and authenticity.

Figueroa cultivated this bohemian identity in a short but locally remarkable theatrical career in which he chose romantic roles, such as that of Luciano in Joaquín Dicenta's play "Luciano o El Amor de un artista."[31] Offstage, as well, he supplemented his artistic persona with a carefully cultivated image as a "restless spirit, wanderer and adventurer" who continued—despite his upper-class in-laws—to work in the mining ventures that had also been his father's trade.[32] In shaping this public persona of "artist and man of action," Figueroa fused the more down-to-earth profession of miner with the lofty vocation of portrait painter to create a public persona based on the ideal of the artist existing on the fringe of society.[33]

## INDIGENISTA VANGUARD

The end of Figueroa's bohemian career came with his marriage in July 1908 to Ubaldina Yabar Almanza. The Yabars were one of Cusco's most distinguished families. Ubaldina's uncle, for example, was bishop of Cusco and the Yabar family owned several large haciendas in the province of Paucartambo. The bulk of Figueroa's surviving photographic plates are portraits of the Yabar family, taken in the intimate space of their Cusco home or at one of the Pau-cartambo haciendas (see Figure 8.3). Figueroa's favorite space for creating these family portraits was the formal salon where Bishop Yabar received his guests (Figure 7.3). Known as the "Blue Salon" for its richly colored carpet, the remarkable layered imagery of its walls testify to the monumental centrality of visual imagery in the social and religious life of Cusco. Although the extent to which such traditional use of images affected Figueroa's photographic work is unknown, several surviving plates show evidence that Figueroa did experi-ment with re-creating the iconographic space of Cusco school colonial reli-gious paintings (Figure 7.4).

Other family portraits from this same period reveal the uncomfortable con-tradictions of an affluent artistic life in racially divided Cusco. In one photo-graph, for example, we confront a branch of the Yabar family outside its shel-tered hacienda home in Paucartambo (Figure 7.5). Nestled in luxuriant grasses, this family displays all the finery of a Cusco Sunday outing. Emerging from the darkness of the eucalyptus grove behind them, a peasant who is barely perceptible—and certainly far from the consciousness of the group who poses for the camera—peers curiously at the photographer and his subjects. Was he a houseboy, a servant, or simply a peasant who happened by? Did he come with the family from Cusco; and in what capacity did Figueroa know him? Did the photographer place him in the background? Or, more likely, was he excluded from the photograph only to reappear insistently within the frame, as occurs in so many other Cusco photographs from these times?

At first an anecdotal, almost accidental, presence in his photographic work, the shadowy presence of the Indian occupies an increasingly central place in Figueroa's identity, sentiment, and art. His experiences at the Yabar family's Paucartambo haciendas gave him an opportunity to observe the Indians upon whom Cusco's economy depended. It was the intellectual and political dis-course of indigenismo, however, that would determine the ways in which Figueroa would paint and photograph the Indian.

Figure 7.3. Salon Azul of Monseñor Yabar (Figueroa Aznar, Cusco)

Figure 7.4. Altar (Figueroa Aznar, Cusco)

Figure 7.5. Yabar family (Figueroa Aznar, Paucartambo,
c. 1915)

Indigenismo was a pan–Latin American intellectual movement whose stated goals were to defend the Indian masses and to construct regionalist and nationalist political cultures on the basis of what mestizo, and largely urban, intellectuals understood to be autochthonous or indigenous cultural forms. Within this broader vanguard movement, Cusco indigenismo occupied a privileged position because of Cusco's history as capital of the Inca Empire. This history made Cusco a particularly contested site in the battle to wrest a Peruvian national history away from the endless scrutiny and historicizing gaze of the European and North American scientists, archaeologists, and historians whose expeditionary itineraries and reports consistently mapped Peruvian history onto that of a fallen Inca Empire. In reclaiming Inca history and geography as their own, the Cusqueño indigenistas introduced the previously forbidden figure of the contemporary Andean Indian into the Peruvian literary and artistic imagination as well as into Peruvian nationalist discourse, jurisprudence, and domestic policy.[34]

Although the roots of Cusco's indigenista movement can be traced to colonial and nineteenth-century literature about Indians and the Incas, what has been called the "Golden Age" of Cusco indigenismo is more usefully situated in the period from 1910 to 1930.[35] During these years, indigenista writing about the Andean countryside, the Inca past, and Indian culture coalesced with, and responded to, political demands for greater regional autonomy and decentralization. These demands in turn responded to the economic modernization projects and shifting class alliances of President Augusto Leguía's "Patria Nueva." Within this context, the most important factor motivating the Cusqueño intellectuals' interest in the Indian was a series of violent peasant uprisings in the mid-1920s. These revolts in Cusco's high pastoral provinces, together with the processes of economic modernization occurring in the department's agrarian valley provinces, threatened the cultural and social hegemony of Cusco's agrarian-based seigneurial class. In this context, intellectuals from Cusco's upper and middle classes began their campaign to validate an authentic Indian identity for *all* Cusqueños.

Two major works produced during this period were to determine the future course of Cusqueño thinking about the "Indian problem." These were Luís Valcárcel's *Tempestad en los Andes*, published in 1927, and José Uriel García's *El Nuevo Indio*, published in 1930 as a rebuttal to Valcárcel's nationally acclaimed *Tempestad*. Whereas Valcárcel saw postconquest colonial history as a process of racial and cultural degeneration and advocated a return to the values and purity of preconquest Inca society, García saw colonial history as a process of cultural and racial improvement. The true Indian, he argued, was not pure (or "Incaic"), but rather the mixed, or *mestizo*, product of Cusco's colonial past. In conformance with this historical vision, García's indigenista mission was to create a "new Indian." He rejected Valcárcel's vision of Andean culture as a received tradition that could be resurrected according to the historical or archaeological methodologies of empirical description and scientific induction. Instead, García's emergent Andean culture was to be a product of directed *mestizaje* (cultural and racial mixture). The "New Indian" intellectuals who would guide this mission were to be forged by melding the telluric (or spiritual) power of the Andean landscape with the intellectual prowess of a mestizo avant-garde.

The New Indians' notions of telluric power derived from García's theory that Andean culture was a product of the tremendous geologic and organic forces Nature had invested in the Andean landscape. These Cusqueño theories drew, in turn, upon ideas of the geographic or environmental determination of artistic production and cultural spirit, particularly those of Hippolyte-Adolphe Taine. Taine's method, from which both Valcárcel and García borrowed heavily, explained artistic forms as the scientifically determined effects of environment and race.[36] Similar constructs were borrowed from Oswald Spengler, who saw cultural and racial spirit as rigidly bounded by its environment, and Henri Bergson, whose concept of intuition was employed by the indigenistas to explain the causal relation between telluric forces and the Indian art forms that such forces spontaneously induced.[37] For Valcárcel's followers, such theories provided the motivation for their empirical studies of the historical and scientific roots of Andean culture in Inca civilization and the environment.

Two of Taine's propositions were of specific interest to the Cusqueños. The first was his portrayal of the artist as society's most representative figure; the second, his notion that artistic style spoke for society's collective—and hence undifferentiated—spirit. By combining these points from Taine with their particular brand of environmental determinism, the indigenistas were able to posit a uniform and empirically verifiable spiritual connection uniting individuals of all ethnicities and social classes with the "telluric" sources of Andean culture.

These appropriations of nineteenth-century European aesthetic philosophy by Cusqueño intellectuals in the 1920s provided the basis for García's program of directed cultural production. The uniqueness of this program derives from the ways in which the indigenistas combined their philosophical pastiche with a contemporary international discourse of the modernist avant-garde. Between roughly 1910 and 1930, modernist literary journals such as *Prisma*, *Claridad*, and *Proa* entered Cusco from Buenos Aires.[38] The most important of these was *Martín Fierro*, a futurist and *ultraísta*-influenced journal, which first appeared in 1924. The Argentine intellectuals affiliated with *Martín Fierro* advocated the existence of a "natural" disposition for art and culture on the basis of the apparently contradictory ideas of *criollismo* and linguistic purity.[39] This conservative philosophy of national identity provided a model for those Cusco indigenistas who, like García, were grappling with the problem of how to differentiate their Andean nationalism from the national projects of Limeños such as Manuel Atanasio Fuentes (see Chapter Six). By looking to Argentina rather than to Lima for their ideas, the Cusqueños hoped to arm a cultural movement that might successfully oppose the national cultural dominance of metropolitan Lima.

The New Indians' appropriation of modernist discourse was not, however, uncritical. In accordance with their regionalist political agenda and philosophical allegiance to the ideal of an autochthonous Andean culture, they selected only those components of European (and Argentine) modernism that could further their proposition that cultural sentiment and aesthetic creativity emanated from the soil. Thus they eagerly embraced the Europeans' vision of a progressive, constantly changing culture, their questioning of institutional and aesthetic authority, their insistence on the internationalization of culture, and their campaign against both scientific induction and naturalized concepts of tradition and community.[40] Above all they embraced the idea of a cultural avant-garde that defined itself as a transient formation existing outside or beyond both history and tradition. In the visions of Valcárcel and García, the historical roots of Andean culture had been forged by the Indians. Justification of a mestizo avant-garde that might speak for all members of Andean society, including the oppressed and largely voiceless Indian masses, required therefore just this elevation above history and tradition that the modernist conception of an avant-garde offered. In García's vision of indigenismo, the separation of the historical roles of Indian and indigenista followed the well-worn modernist dichotomies of traditionalism versus cultural innovation, popular cultures versus high culture, historicism versus spirituality, and passive community versus a dynamic and forward-looking avant-garde:

> There are, then, in America two Indianities: the Primitive, that which fled, destroyed by the Inca Empire, to the millenarian caverns, and there crouches down; this is the Indianity which sustains the popular spirit of our countryside. . . . The other Indianity is that which is encarnated in the great men representative of the American spirit—thinkers, artists, heroes—all those who with their genius have made of our Continent the possibility of a high [*elevado*] culture. These men who have made or are making the history of America are the legitimate Indians before whom all ideas of an "Inkario" are mere traditionalism.[41]

Some years later, García's colleague Atilio Sivirichi would further harden the vanguardist doctrine of the New Indianism. "Literature, poetry, art in all its manifestations will be converted into spiritual arms for domination," Sivirichi declared. "Poets, intellectuals, artists, men of science form the great indigenista vanguard. . . . The retroguard is formed of the millions of Indians who live along the Andean ranges, working their fields and making the valleys fertile."[42]

In adopting the language of vanguardismo, however, the New Indians were caught at a delicate impasse. From the point of view of the peasant popular cultures that Valcárcel celebrated as a romantic continuation of the Inca past, García's neo-Indianists were forced to define themselves as a modernist avant-garde existing above and beyond the confines of what they saw as the traditionalist cul de sac of Inca history. From the point of view of Lima and its dominant criollo culture, however, their legitimacy as spokesmen for New Indian culture rested precisely on their necessarily historical and geographic ties to the "telluric" forces of the Andes in which they lived. It is this contradiction that both limits the development of "modernist" discourse in Cusco and defines the peculiar emergent qualities of Cusco's indigenismo. Far from being a carbon copy (or much less, an imperialist imposition) of European modernism, indigenismo was a deliberately iconoclastic pastiche of philosophical, aesthetic, and discursive borrowings. The result is a "modernism" that mimics the European only partially and thus appears, from the point of view of European modernism, to have contradictory structures and purposes.

The most visible contradiction that emerges from this process is that which exists between the Cusqueños' enthusiastic subscription to the ideal of an avant-garde and their simultaneous rejection of the formalist and internationalist languages of abstraction and modernity through which the modernist avant-garde constituted itself in European literature, painting, photography, and music. For García's "New Indians," modernity, and in particular the rhythm or velocity of modern life, was perceived as a threat to the very landscape from which Andean peoples drew their spiritual and emotional strength. For them, "indigenism [was] a return to the land . . . an instinctive battle against the new concepts of the twentieth century."[43] Similarly, for New Indianist artists such as Figueroa, abstraction, formalism, and modernity remained taboo.[44] As a result, in the eyes of a European, North American, or Limeño observer, most of the Cusqueño indigenista paintings appear to be strikingly naive, overly stylized, romantic compositions; they appear, in short, to be "bad art."

The Cusqueños' rejection of modernist pictorial idioms, however, cannot be quite so easily dismissed. The artists were exposed to and knowledgeable of modernist pictorial styles. Many, including Figueroa, were trained in European art. Cubist and other abstract formalist styles of painting were exhibited in Cusco and summarily attacked by the Cusco critics.[45] But the Cusqueños' collective decision not to imitate this style was consciously made according to two political criteria. On the one hand, it was precisely the formalism and academicism of European painting that had become most closely identified with the hegemonic culture of Lima. On the other hand, the political and social legitimacy of New Indianist discourse remained necessarily situated in a local history and environment. This political and historical grounding in regionalist, anticoastal politics made the Cusqueños justifiably wary of the European formalist aesthetics that celebrated a disconnectedness from such historical constants as representation and tradition.

This discrepancy in the sites from which European and Cusqueño "modernisms" developed was to determine, as well, the Cusqueños' differently articulated relationship to the other element central to modernist philosophy and Romantic aesthetics: the primitive or peasant icon. European Romanticism developed, in part, through the glorification or aestheticization of the peasant and "the land" at a time when industrial culture threatened both traditional agrarian economies and the nature of artistic production.[46] European modernism made similar uses of a preindustrial other through the appropriation of the art of peoples who had been colonized by Europe. The European modernists' ability to isolate or abstract elements from African and Oceanic art depended on this colonial relation for both the visibility of its iconographic references (the colonial and antiquarian marketplace) and the particular site of power from which it was possible to stand above the primitive and dehistoricize it as a formalist aesthetic.[47]

For the Cusqueño artists, however, the question of cultural difference was conditioned by the artist's spatial as well as social proximity to the Indian. Many of the indigenista intellectuals were themselves hacendados who controlled, and at times lived with, Indian peones on primitive rural estates. Many of them were lawyers or provincial politicians who represented "their" Indians to the state. All of them had paternalistic relationships with Indian servants whom they had known since childhood. Many had had indigenous wet nurses and nannies. All of them lived in the complex urban-rural environment of the city of Cusco, and all were aware of the multitude of ethnic gradations existing between the ideal states of pure mestizo and pure Indian. This lived familiarity with the complexity of cultural and ethnic identity in a modernizing Andean society mediated the ways in which Cusco intellectuals formulated their understandings of cultural difference. These understandings differed from those of the Limeño or European modernist in their refusal to acknowledge the coevality of a primitive Indian "other." In Valcárcel's formulations, for example, absolute cultural difference could be located only in the Inca past and in what was seen as the residual surviving culture of a few existing Indians. Valcárcel believed that this past or residual cultural difference, once isolated through empirical study, could then be consciously resurrected as an archaic revival in the emergent cultural language of neo-Inca indigenismo.

Similarly, for García, an absolute cultural difference between Indian and Spaniard had not existed since before the conquest. Andean culture was a four-century product of colonialism and racial mestizaje, and there were, as a result, no cultural "others" to be found in present-day Cusco. If, therefore, a future Andean Culture was to be constructed, it could be done only by building a united highland identity that would encompass peasant and intellectual alike. For García and his followers, this collective culture of the "New Indians" was to be built around the political realities of an already existing national context: Cusco's collective other could be found, in other words, on the coast and in Lima, and not in the residual survivals of an Inca tradition that Valcárcel sought to revive.[48]

It was this conscious geopolitical mapping of cultural difference onto Peruvian political geography that led Cusco's New Indianist artists to privilege the environment or landscape—rather than the idea of an "authentic" cultural or racial other—as the source of their spiritual and aesthetic intuition. This construction of the telluric Andean landscape was both predated and informed by a local bohemian aesthetic that, as we have seen, defined individual rebelliousness and creativity through reference to the artist's privileged emotional ties to nature. Although this provincial discourse of bohemianism drew on a European Romantic tradition, it differed dramatically from the European bohemian tradition that made explicit iconographic use of Gypsies, *saltimbanques*, primitives, and other "social outcasts" to construct its idioms of both authenticity and individual creativity. In Cusco, by comparison, neither the 1900s bohemians nor the 1920s neo-Indianists sought to link their notions of the artistic individual to the Indian per se. Rather, the Indian, as part of nature, was invoked as evidence of the generalized and environmentally circumscribed cultural intuition that separated all highland peoples from their coastal compatriots.

This homogenizing—and leveling—function of the landscape with respect to cultural, racial, and class differences was best expressed in García's notion of "syncretic tellurism" (*telurismo sincretizante*). This concept was used by García and other neo-Indianists to describe the historical process through which all inhabitants of the Andes—intellectual and Indian alike—would eventually acquire a homogeneous identity centered on the specific form of "emotion" that emanated from the Andean landscape. To escape the dangers of *pasadismo*, or traditionalism, however, Andean emotivity and intuition would require an enlightened and visionary leadership. It is this contradiction that provided an entry point for modernist concepts of the avant-garde élite.

## PHOTOGRAPHY AND THE NEW INDIAN AGENDA

Figueroa's approach to painting and photography was molded both by his personal experiences in Cusco and Paucartambo and by the ways in which the indigenista discourses of Valcárcel and García shaped an understanding of art, ethnicity, and the intellectual avant-garde that was in many ways specific to Cusco. The two decades of indigenista ferment in Cusco (1910–1930) correspond to the period when Figueroa was most active in photography and, although Figueroa left no written records, indigenista concerns clearly informed his studio photos of idealized Indian types, stylized theatrical groups, and bohemian self-portraits (Figures 7.6, 7.7, and 7.8). In carefully composed scenes, Figueroa uses photography to document a precisely constructed

Figure 7.6. Indigenous "type" (Figueroa Aznar, Cusco)

Figure 7.7. Theater group (Figueroa Aznar, Cusco)

Figure 7.8. Self-portrait (Figueroa Aznar, Cusco)

artifice of identity. Each photograph is meticulously composed with backdrops painted by Figueroa for his theatrical and/or portrait work. In front of these backdrops, an "Indian" model is made to recline or the artist himself poses as stalking hunter, Gypsy minstrel, meditative monk, or pensive artist. In another experiment, Figueroa skillfully manipulates and composes his negative so as to render the narrative flow of a sentiment gained and lost (Figure 7.9).

This photographic fascination with the malleability and staging of social identities reflects a broadening of Figueroa's bohemian or walaychu aesthetic to encompass the New Indianists' philosophy of constructed cultural identities. Like the various bohemian selves that Figueroa constructs in his photos, the ethnic and cultural identities celebrated by the New Indians were not natural or historical essences waiting to be empirically discovered and described, as in Valcárcel's indigenismo. On the contrary, the New Indians believed identity should be constructed according to the consciously elaborated criteria of a political and artistic avant-garde.

Photography fit into this philosophy of identity or self as a means to imagine new identities, though not as a medium to represent or to express them.

Figure 7.9. Self-portrait (Figueroa Aznar, Cusco)

Figueroa, for example, often made studio photographs of subjects to be used in future paintings, yet he never exhibited any photographs "as art." As a result, despite the polish and technical sophistication of his work, Figueroa never developed what we might call a "photographic vision" capable of transforming the reality of what the camera recorded into the artifice of illusion achieved by such devices as framing, angle, focus, tone, and composition. Identity and artifice are instead constructed in Figueroa's photographs through theatrical devices and costume. This interest in manipulating the subject rather than the medium of photography is perhaps one reason why "real" Indian or peasant subjects never appear in Figueroa's photographs. For the New Indians, "race" (and hence, the Indian) was not so much a material fact which could be documented and photographed—as it was for both Valcárcel's neo-Inca intellectuals and the European photographers whose work we have discussed in previous chapters. Instead race was transformed in the New Indians' discourse and art into a constantly shifting and historical current of identity. It was an attitude and a pose, rather than an ineluctable or inherited fact of nature.

   This understanding of race helps to explain the differences between Figueroa and his contemporary, Martín Chambi, the only Cusqueño photographer to achieve recognition from European and U.S. photographic historians.[49] The differences between the work of Figueroa and Chambi reveal how photography was appropriated by the two divergent strands of Cusco indigenismo. A first point of comparison involves the effects of class on the uses of photography in Cusco. Chambi was the son of a rural peasant family in Puno, and his position in Cusco society depended very much on his continuing immersion in the work of photography. As an in-law of the landed class, Figueroa had the comparative leisure to abandon the income provided by commercial photography. The effect of these dissimilar class identities on the photographic and artistic philosophies of the two men, however, was articulated primarily in terms of their intellectual allegiances to the two quite different paths taken by Cusco indigenismo. The first of these paths led to Valcárcel's empirical sociology and archaeology for the Andes; the other to García's questioning of scientific authority and the concomitant development of a cultural, aesthetic avant-garde.

Martín Chambi closely followed the first of these two options. He conceived photography as a medium through which to record the existence of what he saw to be a rapidly disappearing historical or "authentic" Andean Indian. His conscious effort to compile a photographic inventory of "ethnic types" resonated with Valcárcel's positivist promotion of scientific and ethnological study of the Inca past. As in other parts of the world, it was the camera that was to provide the most appropriate technology for this scientific quest to inventory, classify, and survey the native world. That Chambi's photography of Indians and Indian fiestas was motivated by such a mission is suggested by his own labeling of the photographs as a "collection" of ethnic "types," as well as by the fact that many of his photographs of Indians approximate the anthropometric poses developed by French anthropology and taught at the University of Cusco by early indigenistas such as Manuel Bueno and José Coello. These photographs were marketed to European and North American tourists.

Indigenismo thus made competing claims on the work of Figueroa and Chambi. Although Chambi sought to give life to an idealized and racially pure Indian type through the pictorial realism of his documentary work, Figueroa eschewed realism and stressed instead the fluid and constructed nature of social identity. In analyzing these differences, I have stressed the affinity of each photographer's work with the distinctive philosophies of Valcárcel and García, respectively. It would be a mistake, however, to pigeonhole them into opposing intellectual camps. Indeed, Figueroa's penchant for theatricality made him a natural ally for Valcárcel's Misión Peruana de Arte Incaica (Peruvian Mission of Incaic Art), a traveling theater group mounted in 1923 to take examples of "neo-Inca" art to Bolivia and Argentina.[50] Figueroa did the sketches for the Mission's stage production of the colonial Quechua drama "Ollantay." He also photographed the rehearsals, costumes, and settings (Figures 7.10 and 7.11). The highly stylized poses used in these mission photographs are reminiscent of those used in his self-portraits, as well as in his photographs of costumed Indian types—many of which used the same model (see Figure 7.6).[51]

Figure 7.10. Study for
Ollantay Theater
Group (Figueroa
Aznar, Cusco)

Throughout his life Figueroa reserved specific media for different representational tasks: photography for self-portraits, theatrical studies, and the costumed Indian types that could be sold to tourists; painting for landscapes and the "art" he would exhibit to Cusco society.[52] In the Cusqueños' romantic conception of art, painters were a conduit through which the emotion or beauty inherent to nature could be transferred to the canvas. Paintings were, therefore, expected to reveal the "truth" of nature. As a modern, mechanically based process, photography interfered with the artist's relation to nature. The fact that photography was not recognized as "art," however, did not mean it could not be used to imagine new and consciously constructed forms of identity (Figure 7.11). This interest in identity was more akin to contemporary forms of European modernist bohemianism than to the nineteenth-century romantic notions of sentiment, nature, and art with which the Cusqueños had circumscribed the artist's relation to paint.

The Cusqueños' doctrinal understandings of the telluric origins of Andean identity placed further limits on Figueroa's ability to imagine his bohemian photographic "studies" as "art." Uriel García, along with the other Cusqueño critics, attributed both the sentiment and the aesthetic success of Figueroa's

Lo que sueña el viajero en el palacio del Almirante

Figure 7.11. "What the
Traveler Dreamed"
(Figueroa Aznar, Cusco)

paintings to his immersion in the rural Andean landscape of Paucartambo.[53] They argued that Figueroa's special bohemian sensibilities made him a fertile medium for translating onto canvas the spontaneous organic powers that Nature had invested in the Paucartambo landscape and that constituted the essence of Andean cultural identity. This aestheticizing or sensitizing effect of the Andean landscape was restricted, however, to the medium of painting and could not pass through the modernizing mechanical medium of the camera. As a result, landscape photography—the first pictorialist form of photography to emerge in Europe and the United States—was never seriously developed in Cusco. Although Cusqueño photographers such as Martín Chambi, Alberto Ochoa, and Pablo Verdamendi made numerous photographs of archaeological sites, these photographs were meant to document the Inca historical past celebrated by indigenista writers such as Valcárcel.[54] The task of expressing the telluric essence of the landscape itself was reserved for the vanguard of indigenista artists who could translate this sentiment into the painterly art of color, emotion, and personal—as opposed to mechanical—sensibility.

Other Cusco artists followed Figueroa's example to the extent that they experimented in both photography and painting. With the exception of Martín Chambi, however, the indigenista photographers of Figueroa's generation always turned back to painting as the preferred medium for expressing what they called "el sentimiento andino." Because, for the indigenistas, beauty was not inherent to the Indian or to the landscape per se, it could not be captured by what Europeans considered to be the "magic" of photographic technology. The reality of the Andean world had to be transformed and reworked, carefully framed and skillfully tinted, before it could serve as an instrument of indigenista philosophy and aesthetics. As one indigenista critic expressed it, "The [indigenista] painters interpret the Indian landscape and carry pure Indianity to the objectivity of plastic arts."[55] Figueroa's importance in framing this aesthetic for both photography and painting is captured in the words of the indigenista writer José Gabriel Cosio, whose elogy for Figueroa lauded him as "among the first to employ the indigenista thematic in a purely aesthetic sense with neither ethnological nor social preoccupations."[56]

## SENTIMENT AND SCIENCE

It is useful to return briefly to my original questions about the universality of the socially constructed divide between photography and art and about Figueroa's specific, culturally and socially situated understanding of his artistic modernity. As the origins of the New Indian movement in which he participated make clear, intellectuals on the "periphery" consciously borrowed and made use of the philosophical and aesthetic philosophies through which, as they were aware, Europe had constructed its hegemonic discourse of art and the artist. They did not naively learn the "neutral" technology of photography and then use it to record subjects appropriate to their own "indigenous" agenda. Even in far off "preindustrial" Cusco, the media of photography and painting were not neutral or transparent technologies acting simply to reflect social ideas and personal inspirations. Rather, as social and aesthetic technologies of representation, painting and photography in early twentieth-century Cusco formed part of the complex discursive strategies of Western art. As the Cusco indigenistas themselves knew, painting and photographs were representational technologies posited on post-Enlightenment forms of Western cultural production in which the aesthetic representation, classification, and idealization (categorization) of social types, natural landscapes, and human forms had come to form an integral part of the humanistic philosophies and scientific knowledge through which the distribution of power in society is regulated and controlled.

Because of photography's close association with colonial expansion and the globalization of bourgeois culture in the late nineteenth and early twentieth centuries, it is a particularly fascinating medium through which to study how intellectuals on the periphery contested this "controlling gaze." Photography was introduced to Cusco through the work of expeditionary scientists and travelers, all of whom represented governmental or private business interests. One of the earliest and most extensive uses of photography in southern Peru, for example, was by a British expedition sent to map the boundary between Peru and Bolivia. Other early uses included those by the archaeological surveys conducted by French, German, Swiss, and U.S. scholars and by the cartes de visite of "Indian types" marketed by French photographers such as Courret and Manoury in the fashionable circles of Paris. These cartes de visite and survey photographs contributed to a scientifically grounded popular image of Peru as an empty land, a Fallen Empire, a country of backward and impoverished Indians whose future progress would depend on both foreign capital and Western progress. What is of most interest about this process, however, is the fact that, without exception, the Peruvian photographers learned their art from these same scientific and studio photographers from Europe. The first photography studio in Cusco—the one in which Figueroa worked upon first arriving in Cusco in 1904—was set up by an English missionary society. The missionaries took photographs of ragged Indians that, in the form of captioned cartes de visite, were used to collect monies in England. Other studios introduced a form of bourgeois studio portraiture whose formal poses and elaborate studio settings contributed to the formation of a certain notion of the bourgeois individual in nineteenth-century Europe.[57]

These uses of photography and their ideological content were neither a secret from the Cusqueños nor uncritically admired by them as emblems of modernity, science, and progress. As we have seen, Cusco New Indians sought to counter this controlling gaze and positivist inventory of their history and

Figure 7.12. Self-portrait with painting "Azares y celos andinos" (Figueroa Aznar, Cusco)

geography by constructing an "imagined community" based on the philosophical and aesthetic values of intuition and sentiment informing their notion of *la emoción andina* (Andean emotion). Integral to this endeavor was the elaboration of a local tradition of the walaychu, or Andean bohemian, as a person who replaces the bonds of social tradition and scientific history (or *pasadismo*) with an aggressive philosophy and aesthetic of nostalgia, sentiment, and music grounded in his close ties to the land. From this tradition came a certain repertoire of ideas regarding both bohemianism and painting as forms of spontaneous sentimental expression enabled by the "telluric" forces of Cusco's mountainous landscape (Figure 7.12).

At the same time, however, the emergence of a pictorial and literary imagery specific to the Cusco indigenistas was only enabled by other contemporary developments in European art and the Latin American vanguardist movement. In Europe, first Romanticism, with its peasants and bohemians, and then modernism, with its "colonial others," emerged as part of a broader discursive structure concerned with the elaboration and reproduction of social and racial difference as "a conscious strategy of exclusion."[58] This "strategy of exclusion" made it possible for European artists and writers to engage both industrial culture and the colonial "other" by transforming the encounter into an aesthetic act of bourgeois cultural production. For the indigenistas of Cusco, it was the exclusionary discourse surrounding both the bohemian aesthetic and its successor, vanguard modernism—and not the modernists' pictorial or representational ideologies—that enabled the Indian to surface as the subject of cultural discourse. This discursive explosion through which "the Indian" entered Peruvians' artistic—and somewhat later, political—imagination was related to debates concerning the desirability of modernizing the traditional (low technology, unsalaried) forms and relations of production, and to the increasingly visible political organization and violence of the Indians themselves. This economic and social backdrop of rapid social change initiated from below provided the institutional incitement for Peruvian intellectuals to speak, finally, about the previously forbidden subject of the Indian.

This discursive shift, however, was also to have specific implications for the development of photography and the modern visual economy in Cusco. Once the hegemonic conceptual divide between photography (technology) and art had been surmounted and the foto-óleo gone out of style, the directions in which Figueroa and other Cusco artists would take photography were determined by a new, regionally focused discourse on art. While President Leguía's "Patria Nueva" (1919–1930) was championing modernization and North American capital, Cusco politicians and philosophers were elaborating an oppositional, regionalist doctrine of sentiment and antimodernity. In accordance with these new doctrines, indigenista critics celebrated the individual creativity and "sentimental realism" of painting for its ties to nature. They focused on both nature and the Indian as subjects whose essence or "sentiment" could not be captured by the technological realism (or "transparency") of photographic representation. What was needed for the indigenistas' cultural agenda was a directed rechanneling of sentiment and spirit to form the newly imagined community of "Cusqueñismo," and not the unmediated realism of either photography or the impoverished Indian that photography revealed. Photographic technology and photographic realism were therefore restricted to the private domain of photographic "studies" for both theater and painting and, in the case of Figueroa, for a remarkable series of self-portraits documenting the indigenistas' concern with constructing the vanguard or bohemian identities that would someday shape the New Indian culture of Cusco.

## CHAPTER EIGHT

# Negotiating Modernity

CONSIDER this photograph of a family in Cusco (Figure 8.1). I don't know their names. I'm not sure when the photograph was taken—probably in the early 1940s. In fact, I'm not even sure who took it. The Cabrera family can't seem to agree which brother was the "real" photographer, Filiberto or Crisanto.[1]

I found the photograph in 1987 among some old dusty boxes of glass-plate negatives that once belonged to the Cabrera family in Cusco, but that had recently been purchased by a research institute there. My friend Fran made a contact print from the plate. She printed it in our Cusco darkroom on nice paper. Portriga, I think. Everyone liked it at the time. I think they were struck by how "modern" the print looked. "Kind of reminds you of Diane Arbus," someone said. "It's the wide-angle lens. The distorted faces." "It's also the stiff poses," I remember thinking in response. "They make people look unnatural." But these stiff poses also reminded me of my own fieldwork portraits from Paruro.

The original negative for this print now belongs to the Fototeca Andina, an archive of historical photographs in Cusco where historians, anthropologists, curators, and politicians can cull images for their books, research, and exhibits. I keep my copy of the print in an old Agfa box—the kind you're not supposed to use to store photographs. Fran probably keeps another one in her house. Maybe stored more securely. Maybe less remembered. Because, for me, somehow, this portrait always sticks in my mind. Among the hundreds of family portraits that Fran and I resurrected from the archives of Cusco and Lima, this one, for some reason, stood out from the rest. So I'll use it, I thought, to introduce this chapter and, in the process, to gain some closure. Having begun the book with my own experience with portraiture and my own initial attempts to understand its meaning, I now consider how my understanding of portraits such as this one has changed after years spent studying other types of Andean images—how it has changed as a result of thinking about it as part of a broader Andean "image world" and an even broader "visual economy of modernity."

But how are we to read this anonymous photograph from Cusco back onto the intentionally dispersed topoi of our excursion into an Andean image world that has so far been configured around such illustrious, upper-class, and above all, named men as Humboldt, Disdéri, d'Orbigny, or Fuentes? To this difficult question I can make several replies. One is that the photograph

Figure 8.1. Family portrait
(Cusco, c. 1935)

evokes quite clearly the fascination we feel as we gaze upon images of people who are both like, and not like, ourselves. This is a fascination that I have tried to understand as I attempted to make sense of Humboldt's, Thibon's, Fuentes's, and Figueroa's very different approaches to looking at "the other." Somewhat more concretely, the photograph also evokes questions about technique, format, pose, and meaning that I have tried to ask of each of the images we have seen. Now, however, after journeying into the world of these other images, it may be easier both to ask and to answer some of the questions. Let's begin with the plaid tablecloths. For me these serve as something like the "punctum" for Roland Barthes—the focal point or object in a given photograph that draws us to the photo, that holds our eye and our heart, and that is seldom the same for any two persons.[2]

Barthes's notion of the punctum, however, only allows me to make emotional sense of the tablecloths and my attraction to them. To make intellectual sense of my interest, I think of the cartes de visite. Indeed, these tablecloths (or are they blankets?) that hang behind the family as an improvised backdrop invite me to "read" this photograph as part of a history in which Disdéri's mass-produced portrait cards introduced the ritual setting of the bourgeois portrait studio into places such as Cusco. When read against this history and social convention, even the photographer's choice of a wide-angle lens takes on additional significance. By simultaneously flattening the space and exaggerating the angle from the image's front plane to its improvised backdrop, this lens has helped the photographer to carve a closed, cubic, and studiolike space from the open—and rather déclassé—space of the outdoor patio in which the picture was taken.

Equally as important as these formal conventions is that once we think at all about the world of images, we begin to realize how familiar we are with this way of reading photographs as part of an archive (or image world) made up of essentially "equivalent" and interchangeable images. We begin to understand the claims that Disdéri's cartes de visite have made on our own photographic culture, and the subtle ways in which this culture intersects with and differs from this family's understanding of photography and portraiture in Cusco half a century ago. We may also, whether we like it or not, have to admit that this format invites us to read it as part of that other shadow archive of racial photography. We look at the photograph and think either to ourselves or out loud, "Well, the woman in the back, the one dressed in black, she looks more Indian than the others." From there we start to scrutinize the other figures. "The man in the middle is taller and has different features. He's probably not in the family." Then, if we're anthropologists, we might conclude, "He's the *padrino* [godfather] of the boy in front." And Cusqueño padrinos, as every anthropologist knows, are usually chosen from a higher class—and if possible, ethnic—group. They are, in short, richer and whiter. Continuing with our calculus of kinship and racial genealogy, we might then decide that the woman with the "most Indian features" is probably the grandmother. The photograph forces us to face the profound inroads that a visual economy based on the logic of equivalency and the language of racial type has made in our own "critical" relationship to this silent image.

Finally, we might want to venture even further into the depths of our critical subconscious and confess the ways in which aesthetic values creep into our reactions to such photographs. The comparison to Diane Arbus is not irrelevant here: Arbus is, of course, known for her photographs of people who are somehow marginal to the standards of what "Western" cultures consider both "normal" and "beautiful." In this photograph from Cusco, the wide-angle lens has foreshortened the bodies and, in the case of the men on each side, distorted their faces. As intellectuals and photographers, we can understand that this is caused by the lens. Nevertheless, the immediate effect of the distortion is strong indeed. As our reading of Fuentes's work suggested, aesthetics, after all, work at the level of the gut and only residually at that of the intellect.

One thing a journey into the history of a visual economy can do, then, is help us to understand the sources of these powerful claims that equivalency, race, and aesthetics exert on both our critical theories and our visual imaginations.

I would not want to close, however, with the idea that either photography or the visual economy with its principles of serialization, equivalency, and type have somehow irremediably colonized either our own or this Cusco family's imaginations. Both modernity and photography are negotiated affairs. Photography, no matter what its claims, cannot "shape" anyone's identity. Nor does "modernity" work in either even or irresistible ways on every individual and culture. These people in Cusco in 1940, for example, have undoubtedly negotiated their own peculiar understanding of the new demands placed on them by Peru's modernizing state. They may also have negotiated their poses, backdrop, and photographic selves with the photographer who was paid to take their picture.

I want to look more closely at these complex negotiations of modernity, race, aesthetics, and gender in a set of photographic portraits taken by Cusco photographers in the early decades of the twentieth century. Like Figueroa— whose work was our concern in the preceding chapter—these photographers learned their craft in the fashionable portrait studios of Lima and Arequipa. Their work also shares with that of Figueroa a concern with portraying, idealizing, and manipulating the fluid racial, cultural, and ethnic boundaries through which identity was constituted in turn-of-the-century Cusco. Although some of the photographers were conversant with the indigenista intellectual debates that fueled Figueroa's work, others worked on the margins of Cusco's literate society. For this latter group of *retratistas* (portraitist), the abstract debates and polemics surrounding contemporary intellectual discussions of Andean culture and the Andean Indian were displaced by the commercial pressures and demands of their working-class and peasant subjects. For these paying clients of the Cusco photography studios, the labels "Indian" and "Andean" resonated less with the redemptive message of the indigenistas' modernist project than with the discriminatory politics of Cusco's ethnic and class-divided society.

## FAMILY PORTRAITS

Families in early twentieth-century Cusco chose their photographer, much as we do today, on the basis of his style, prices, and reputation. This reputation, in turn, was a product of his clientele. One elderly photographer commented in an interview in 1986: "It is useless to exhibit a stupendous, marvelous photograph, even a work of art, of an unknown person. That is for sure. The photographs I use for advertising must always be of individuals who are well known in town."[3] The choice of photographer was thus a conscious decision to affiliate oneself with the "class" of people who also went to that studio. In the small close-knit society of Cusco, this choice was, moreover, a relatively public affair. In such a society it was difficult for family members to have their portrait taken without someone noticing where they went and how much they paid.

In addition to its eventual use as an icon of remembrance (the role we most often associate with family photography), the family photograph in early twentieth-century Cusco was first and foremost a symbolically charged exchange of prestige, as well as cash, between the photographer and the family whose photo he took. It was, in other words, through the family's public act of being photographed, rather than through the relatively private viewings of its members' collective photographic image, that the family made a statement about its identity and status in an ethnically mixed and rapidly changing highland society.

Since its invention in the early nineteenth century, photographic portraiture, as we saw in Chapter Five, has fulfilled the role of a global currency, the circulation of which served to disseminate and cement the representational standards of bourgeois identity as a cultural, pictorial type. One crucial commodity that the most prestigious Cusco studio had for sale was access to these European representational conventions. However, while the Lima-trained studio photographer in Cusco might suggest formats, arrangements, and settings that he felt best conformed to the latest fashions in studio portraiture, the family had, if not an equal, at least an acknowledged voice in the choice of style, setting, pose, and group positioning. Family members' contractual relationship with the photographer gave them a voice in the creation of their photographic selves that the tapadas, mulatas, and Indian "types" seldom, if ever, enjoyed.

As a genre of photographs, the family portraits in this chapter thus differ from the majority of images analyzed in the preceding chapters for two very important reasons. First, the photographs were taken with the collaboration of their subjects. Second, the images were intended to be viewed by the people we see in them, rather than by an unknown and often foreign observer. It is this latter characteristic that lent the studio portrait its privileged status as a medium through which the racial discourses, visual constructs, and cultural nationalisms discussed earlier became incorporated into the self-images and, eventually, the identities of Andean people of widely varying social classes. No longer a passive representation, the portrait photograph was an expression of its subject's conscious will to be seen, reconstituted, and remembered as such by present and future generations.

To an even greater extent than the individual portrait, the family photograph provides an exceptionally provocative arena in which to explore this projection of identities and ideals. As the primary social institution of Cusqueño society, the family provided the necessary backdrop against which an individual's personal aspirations could be both silhouetted and disclosed. This casually revealing intimacy of the family portrait is complemented by the collective social identity formed by those intersecting selves that made up the family group. In an individual portrait, the standardized poses and formulaic props of the sharply compartmentalized bourgeois self often render the specificity of class a successfully disguised component of personal identity. In the family portrait, however, social status and relative class aspirations are divulged through the conflicting or competing claims to identity and photographic presence put forth by individual family members. Personal claims and status aspirations were also expressed in the shifting terrain of racial identity. The construction of race in Andean family portraiture was a product of posture, position, and proportion. These formal conventions formed the limited margins within which individuals could manipulate the racialized ascriptions of ethnicity placed on them by a society in which each social relationship was necessarily framed by the labels mestizo, white, Indian, and cholo.

I begin with portraits of two of Cusco's leading upper-class families. From there we will work our way "down" the social ladder, to consider the rather different ways in which the photographic languages of class, race, and gender were negotiated by members of Cusco's "popular" classes.

Upper-class portraits from Cusco, like upper-class portraits from almost anywhere in the world, reveal a familiarity and ease with the portrait format itself. For these subjects, the formal studio context was a highly malleable and familiar experience. For their family portrait, the Romainville family, for example, chose a format that could speak for their social standing (Figure 8.2). The mother (María de Romainville) and eldest son form the base of a pyramid of children. Her posture and direct gaze serve to differentiate her person and relative power from that of her eldest son, who gazes off somewhere to the left

Figure 8.2. Romainville family (Cusco)

and behind the photographer. The mother meanwhile adopts a distinctively assertive, even domineering, presence. As producer of the photo's other subjects, contractor of the photographer, and owner of the family's lands and factories, María de Romainville constructs a self-contained and self-sufficient image of herself as head of a bourgeois nuclear family. She was, after all, a member of one of the wealthiest landholding and commercial families in Cusco.

The Yabar family was, in comparison, a relatively less moneyed and less imposing family (Figure 8.3). This was, as we will recall, the family into which the photographer Figueroa Aznar had married. Unlike the Romainvilles, whose interests included both manufacturing and capital-intensive agriculture, the Yabars based their claims to class and status upon their traditional agrarian estates in Paucartambo. The extended family grouping shown in Figueroa's photograph of the Yabar family reflects this traditional hacendado culture, with its colonial heritage and oligarchical roots. Particularly striking here is the centrality of the grandmother—who is also the photographer's wife's paternal grandmother. Her status is clearly marked as that of senior generatrix. Through her, the Yabar family, surrounded by their children and centered on their eldest female member, becomes in this photo a self-contained unit for the production of future generations, of time, of longevity, and of remembrance. The expandable circle replaces the self-contained pyra-

Figure 8.3. Yabar family (Figueroa Aznar, Cusco)

mid of the Romainvilles's bourgeois nuclear family, while the open patio and receding space of the arched doorway accentuate the illusion of space and expansivity inherent to the skillfully arranged group portrait.

Upper-class ideals of family and gender were mimicked, transformed, and progressively reinterpreted as one slid down the scale of social class. In Figure 8.4, for example, the mother assumes, like María de Romainville, the posture and position of a founding matriarch at the base of a pyramid made up of her children. Yet unlike María de Romainville, the woman's aspirations to ascending social status are problematically revealed on several fronts. Her traditional Spanish dress and almost comically settled pose contrast with the wealthier woman's assertive engagement with both photographer and self. Unlike the dynamically modern Señora de Romainville, this woman's role as matriarch tends instead toward the lithic or unmoving. Her solidifying attitude toward the family unit she holds together is reinforced by those pictorial elements that signal the members' collectively rising status. These composite signs of status include the cleric son, the suited grandson, the formal painted studio backdrop, and a crumpled rug.[4] In contrast to the plain floorboards and empty back space of the Romainvilles's self-confident family grouping, this family's identity requires that it flaunt these external signs of social status. Similarly, whereas the Romainville children appear as obedient, voluntary,

Figure 8.4. Family portrait (Cusco)

*[handwritten margin note: all three focus on the female head of the household (and thus do not have a father — any meaning?)]*

and docile family participants, defined and united by their mother's passive yet confident presence, here the youngest family member is quite literally held in place by her mother's strong arm.

Portraits of still rising or emergent middle classes reveal these centrifugal forces within the extended family through a somewhat different repertoire of signs. Some appear as purely individual creations of mimicked class pretensions, others as unintentional syntactic errors in the appropriation of European photographic culture. In Figure 8.5, the family group is again that of mother and children.[5] Their class standing is signaled loudly by the conversion of patio into studio, a gesture frequently adopted by families who could not afford the higher-priced photographers. As in European bourgeois studios, the props are of the classic mold. They mimic the columns so prevalent in all nineteenth-century studio portraiture. In addition, the family members display a newspaper, gloves, a watch, a toy rifle, or an attitude compressed into the fashionable newness of their suit, sunglasses, or dress. These personal possessions mark each individual's claim to modernity with respect to the family they collectively compose. The rising station of this family is further

*What is with the pose on the far left (back)*

Figure 8.5. Family portrait (Cusco)

bracketed on one extreme by the apparently professional identities — perhaps as doctor, lawyer, or intellectual — projected by the four standing sons, and, on the other, by the mother's traditional peasant-style dress. The two daughters have whitened their faces for the photograph in a gesture meant, like their poses and attire, to distance themselves from the already nearly invisible mother in their midst.

Facial whitening was a commonly used tool in Andean studio photography. In another example, the two women's faces appear oddly distorted (Figure 8.6). Rather than whitening their faces with cosmetics or even flour, the photographer instead chose to "improve their race" by tampering with the emulsion. This attempt at racial "improvement" is rendered even more awkward by the photographer's misappropriations of European photographic syntax. The son adopts a stylized casual pose reminiscent—and no doubt imitative, perhaps on the part of the photographer—of the ones used in portraits of families such as the Romainvilles. This provincial family's lack of fluency in the photographic idiom of class, however, is emphatically marked by the inclusion of the servant or *muchacha* ("housegirl"). Housegirls were seldom included in contemporary portraiture of upper-class and bourgeois families. The muchacha, who is not herself allotted a position within the space of the backdrop, awkwardly holds the baby out toward the family. She wears neither shoes nor face whitening. In contemporary upper-class family photography,

Figure 8.6. Family portrait (Cusco)

babies were nearly always placed at the center of the photograph. Instead of highlighting the class status for which her presence was meant to speak, the maid's clumsy position draws attention to the adobe walls behind her. For viewers more accustomed than we are to the formulaic modes of studio photography, these walls would, in turn, have drawn attention to the absence of curtains, columns, and props against which more "elegant" studios constructed the moral rectitude and "character" of their posing subjects.

In the provincial, and still quite traditional, society of highland cities such as Cusco, the family was constituted according to its position in both the material realities of Cusco's class hierarchy and the imaginary aesthetic of distinction and color that constituted "race" in the cosmology of urban Cusco. In the family photographs considered so far, this racial component enters most obviously in the photographers' clumsy attempts to whiten women's faces. By creating a permanent record on film of the family as "white"—or, in the language of Cusco, *mejorada* ("improved")—the photograph transforms the imaginary world of racial distinction into a concrete, material fact: the racial identity—mejorada or not—of the family is recorded for posterity, displayed on the mantel, and ritually invoked as irrefutable proof of not only the family's pristine racial status but of the *fact* of race itself.

The question of race, however, extends well beyond the cosmetic tricks of whitening. Indeed, in these portraits race speaks most loudly through a language of negation, for each family has composed its corporate self-image through a studied exclusion of the highland, peasant, and Indian world beyond its frame. Although the manner of exclusion varies in both degree and kind with the class aspirations of its proponents, the effect is largely the same. Both emergent middle-class and bourgeois family portraits are visually and socially constituted as a palisade intended to fend off or deny each family's actual complicity in the rural, provincial, and decidedly nonbourgeois setting in which they lived. By translating this aspiration into an enduring material and visual artifact, the photographic portrait played a pivotal role in sedimenting the ideological construction of race—as a supposedly biological and physiological boundary that separates and thus constitutes distinct populations. This fetishistic role of the photographic portrait would have been especially marked in a city such as Cusco, where the actual, lived distinctions between ethnic or cultural groups were much messier than such portraits (and many anthropologists) would lead us to believe.[6]

But how did this bounding or framing mechanism work for working-class or peasant subjects? Several Cusco photographers catered exclusively to the peasant and working-class trade. Their photographs, like those of the more well-to-do families of Cusco, represented a compromise between the acquired standards of trained studio photographers and the needs and identities of the posing subjects. The women portrayed in these photographs, for example, exert a calm, demanding presence. Their attitude toward the camera is at once less formal, and more contained, than that of the upper-class women. For them the photograph was a luxury, and an event; yet—and it is here that their difference from the upper- and middle-class family women appears—it was not in itself an act of self-definition.

In Figure 8.7, for example, we see a peasant or, perhaps, working-class woman and her children. The relation between the two older women—who may be sisters or mother and daughter—is uncertain. Similarly, other relationships among the sitters are not formally marked in the composition of the photograph. The children are no longer the well-dressed ornaments or testimonials of family life that they were in, say, the Romainville portrait. Instead they are persons whose social and photographic presence speaks in and of its own right. The boys appear in the caps that mark them as urban children who perhaps work, or soon will, in the textile factories of Cusco. The older girls project a personality and presence that neither depends on nor rejects the equally self-confident person(s) of their mother(s).

A majority of the portraits of Cusco's lower classes, however, are about events—confirmations, marriages, deaths, first communions (Figures 8.8). Unlike the carefully arranged portraits of upper-class families, it is difficult to discern hierarchies and relationships in these photos. The sitters obviously belong to some extended family, yet their precise composition is not calculated to form an image that could serve as a photograph of the family per se. In other images, the meticulously preserved separation of family and frame characterizing the bourgeois family portrait as genre is missing (Figure 8.9).

Figure 8.7. Family portrait (Cusco)

Figure 8.8. Family portrait (Cusco)

Figure 8.9. Family portrait (Cusco)

The photographs are not about framing, but about events where groups have no fixed or rigid boundaries. As if forecasting modern-day peasant attitudes toward photography, all those who can possibly manage to do so have squeezed themselves into the picture's frame.

This differing relation to the frame is, more than any other factor, what divides photos of peasant and working-class families from those of their upper-class compatriots. On the one hand, this discrepancy speaks for very real differences in family structure. The Andean peasant family included as an intimate part of its social identity the various networks of ritual kin through which family members established alliances with other social classes and ethnic groups. Similarly, owing in part to the requirements of agrarian labor, relations of reciprocity and cooperation between collaterals and affines were at once more intimate and more extended than in the ideally self-sufficient bourgeois family. In short, the nuclear family, though important as the household with whom one lived, was not the enclosing, self-constituting fortress of identity that it was for the members of Cusco's rising and upper classes.

The Cusco middle-class family, by comparison, identified itself both socially and photographically as different from—and better than—the Indian masses that surrounded it. As a result, the very act of being photographed became a means of consolidating, or even inventing, the racial difference that could ensure this separation. In this respect, it was at least partially through the highly naturalistic and status-heavy "art" of photography that middle-class Cusqueños came to assume cultural difference as more than just a conscious gesture of repeated self-assertion, something learned and carefully cultivated so as to set oneself and one's family apart from the rest. Both "culture" and its constant companion, race, through their formalization as part of the photographic representation of self and family, acquired the aura of real, concrete, observable, and scientifically quantifiable things. The Andean peasant family, in contrast, had no particular investment in proving either its cultural or its racial identity. Neither its photographic nor social self was conceived of as an act of exclusion or opposition. For these families, neither "culture" nor "race" had yet been naturalized as a fetishized marker of difference.

## VISION, RACE, AND MODERNITY

This brief glance at the rich archive of Andean family portraits speaks for the crucial role that the visual economy in general and photography more specifically have played in the formation of modern racial subjects. "Race" in and of itself has always been and remains a contested and, above all, slippery concept. Even in the nineteenth century, when "biological racism" supposedly reigned supreme, no two theorists agreed on the content or even the definition of race. An even more contradictory field of meanings was at play in popular understandings of race. There, ideas about visual appearance, skin color, physiognomy, and heritage intersected with the subterranean ebbs and flows of historically motivated prejudices, emotions, sentiments, and beliefs. Foucault has pointed out that race is a "discourse of vacillations."[7] With no clear-cut basis in either biology or physical appearance, "race" (like sexuality for Foucault) must be constantly reinvented, reinvoked, and resurrected by being incessantly spoken of, referred to, defined, and denied. Nowhere was this dynamic clearer than in early twentieth-century Cusco, where devastating declines in the regional wool market and a series of violent peasant uprisings in the 1920s were followed locally by indigenista projects calling for a re-invented cultural identity and nationally by the incursions of Peru's first modern, normalizing state. In such a context, it is no exaggeration to say that race was on everybody's mind as all struggled to make sense of the shifting politics of culture and class.

Family portraiture from Cusco suggests that photography helped to transform this vacillating discourse of "race" into the concrete, observable, and scientifically quantifiable characteristics or traits that the popular imagination desired in order to make sense out of the concept. Photography accomplished this by formalizing and codifying the language of pose and gesture through which Andean individuals and families represented and saw themselves.

The photographs also, however, suggest that there are two ways to think about the intersection between subject formation and the racially informed languages of photographic portraiture. The first, animated by the writings of Foucault, sees the process of racial sedimentation in photographic portraiture as a disciplining of vision, as a technology that molds subjectivities in accordance with a vision of modernity that has been, for the most part, scripted and centered in Europe. This reading informs my understanding of how (and why) the upper and "middle" classes in Cusco appropriated European photographic conventions and their language of distinction. My second reading follows a somewhat more utopian strand in modernity to look for what Paul Gilroy has called the "cultural mutation and restless (dis)continuity that exceed racial discourse and avoid capture by its agents."[8] This reading follows from my understanding of the way that portraits of the popular classes seem to dismantle and subvert the framing devices inherent in studio photography. It suggests that, in these portraits of working-class and peasant subjects, the embodying and enframing technologies of race, type, and photography itself have been rerouted and resisted.[9]

As an anthropologist, I am skeptical about my ability to answer these questions concerning Cusqueños' modernities, selves, resistances, and identities simply by looking at pictures. Even after my excursion into the historical archive, I retain a residual unease about speaking for these mute Andean subjects. What I do hope to convey by looking at these peoples' images is an idea of the power that both visual ideologies and visual technologies have to sediment and materialize the abstract and frequently contradictory discourses of racial, ethnic, and class identity that crisscross our own lives as they do those of the photographs' Andean subjects. In the field of ambiguity and fluidity that is "race," photography and the visual technologies of "type" that preceded it played a crucial role in producing the truth of "race." They did so by producing the material evidence that "race" and its enabling logic of comparability, interchangeability, equivalence, and exchange existed not only out there in the world but, more immediately, here in the bodies of ourselves and those around us. Equally important, photography provided, as we have seen in the otherwise very different cases of the Cusco indigenistas and the Cusco studio photographers, a format through which each individual could change his or her racial identity by recording it in the concrete, realistic, technologically based, and hence scientific medium of the photographic print.

As I have argued, this technology and the racial ideology it helped to realize and concretize formed part of a visual economy in which two principles reigned supreme. The first concerns the disciplining of vision as a spatializing technology. This disciplinary impulse ensured that our "views" of the world, like those of Humboldt, would include a framing device by which images could be spatialized, segregated, fetishized, and eventually dislodged from the world they "represent." This particular aspect of the visual economy of modernity has been theorized elsewhere as a product of changes internal to European modernity. I have posited that it is not possible to understand the economic logic of equivalence and exchange animating both modern visual regimes and modern languages of "difference" without taking into consideration European experience with the "non-European" world.

The second principle of the visual economy concerns the flow or circulation of images. This circulation, in turn, demanded an uprooting of images from their material referents such that images could be compared with other images and, through this logic of equivalency, come to constitute a "reality" of their own. This logic is perhaps clearest in the period of Disdéri's cartes de visite. The cartes and their circulation, however, were enabled by the earlier visual philosophies of type articulated by men like Humboldt, d'Orbigny, Rugendas, and Angrand well before the invention of photography. For our purposes, what is most interesting in this history is the fact that these regimes for disciplining vision and articulating "types" were not always clearly affiliated with racial projects or even, in the case of Humboldt, with any particular interest in race. Rather, following Foucault, we must think about the intersections of visual and racial discourse as features of an epistemic formation in which vision and race were organized through the same principles of equivalence and exchange without being necessarily causally or historically linked.

The Andean or South American case is a fascinating one for thinking about the ways in which racial and visual discourses converged in the nineteenth century. D'Orbigny's *L'Homme américaine* was published in Paris in the same year in which Dominique François Arago made his famous announcement of Daguerre's invention of photography. Although this timing was purely coincidental, it had important implications for how race would be simultaneously theorized and visualized in South America. For anthropologists and critical theorists interested in the history of vision and/or race, South America becomes an especially interesting—though not necessarily unique—site for interrogating the place of visual technologies and regimes in modern racial thought.

As Raymond Williams has eloquently pointed out in his study of images of the city and the country, the origin of any particular image or idea forms a constantly receding horizon.[10] In my attempt to come to terms with the meaning of both vision and race in the Andean context, I have located a tenuous point of origin in France's Enlightenment romance with the Incas. During this period when operas, novels, and natural histories explored the meaning of Inca history and the sensuous possibilities of the European-Andean encounter, a diffuse yet discernible set of images emerges of the Andes as a space of unrealized utopian possibilities.

By beginning my journey in the Inca Operatic, I have also made a statement about where I think we should place the "origins" of both modern racial thought and the visual economy of modernity. Much ink has been spilt trying to decide whether the idea of "race" is old or new; where it was "born"; how continuous it has been in the history of European societies. Of course "racism"—which I would define as the mobilization of (unequal) power according to principles of prejudice that may or may not have anything to do with what a person looks like—is certainly not new. What I have argued in this book, however, is that a certain understanding of race emerged in Europe over a period stretching from the late eighteenth to the early nineteenth centuries. This period coincides with the epistemic break that Foucault has mapped between classical and modern regimes of knowledge. It also coincides with the periodization of his history of modern (European) sexuality. In placing the origins of modern racial thought at this same conjuncture, I do not want to say that everything about the modern idea of race was "new." Ann Stoler and Foucault have both argued that racial discourse is powerful precisely because of the ways in which it continually rephrases and mobilizes older understandings of difference, appearance, physiognomy, and morality.[11] To argue for the "newness" of modern racial regimes, therefore, I have chosen to look not only at transformations in the meanings assigned to "race" itself but also at the parallel transformations that occurred in visual discourses and spatializing technologies such as type or view. Thus, in looking at Buffon's understanding of race, I focused on his concept of species. For Humboldt, I looked at his ideas of "view" and "physiognomic space." Finally, to understand how the Peruvians Fuentes and Figueroa mobilized racial discourse, I looked at their ideas of nation, beauty, landscape, and art. In each case, changes in the idea of "race" could be read as part of a parallel and enabling history of visual and spatial technologies.

In the end, I suggest that the mysterious, even subterranean ways in which racial discourse moves through history are more difficult—if not impossible—to grasp if we focus only on "race." The very slipperiness of "race" is the strongest indication of its power, its hold on our own social and political imaginations, and its presence in the shaping of modernity. It is also an indication that "race" may never be understood in its own terms. By charting race's tortured course through a history of vision, this book argues not so much for a tight fit between the histories of race and visuality. Much less does it argue for any simple causal relation between the two. But by situating race firmly within the visual economy of modernity, we may rethink the ways in which we study and theorize race—and the ways in which we think of it as a necessary, even enabling, component of European modernity.

# Notes

## Chapter One

1. Salgado 1986.

2. Pollock 1994, 14.

3. Williams 1983, 1985, and 1977, 11–20. For critical genealogies of the culture concept in American anthropology see, among others, Roseberry 1989, and Stocking 1992, esp. 114–177.

4. On the society of the spectacle, see Debord 1977. Debord (1988) dates the emergence of the society of the spectacle in the late 1920s, a date which, as Crary (1989) points out, corresponds to both the invention of television and the rise of the European fascist regimes.

5. I focus in this book on French thinking about the Andes. While recognizing the necessarily porous nature of the national boundaries we place around cultural and (especially) intellectual traditions, a focus on France is justified in the Andean case by several historical considerations, including the central role played by French intellectuals in the production of a certain utopian image of the New World in the eighteenth century; the predominance of French photographers and travelers in nineteenth-century South America; the wealth of Andean images held in French archives; and, finally, the importance of French cultural influence on nineteenth-century Andean elites. Throughout I approach French images, texts, and intellectuals as in some respects representative of "European" ideas about vision, race, and the Andes. Whenever possible, however, I have tried to respect the specificity of French intellectual, scientific, aesthetic, and cultural traditions.

6. Among the nineteenth- and twentieth-century artists and travelers whom I have reluctantly excluded from this book's discussion of the Andean image world are Ephraim George Squier, Frederic Edwin Church, Paul Marcoy, Pancho Fierro, Agustín Guerrero, Francisco Laso, Adolphe Bandelier, Hiram Bingham, and Martín Chambi. The extent of this list expresses the difficulties of presenting any selection of images as representative of the diverse world of materials that have circulated through our scientific and popular imaginations as constitutive of "the Andes." On Squier, Church, and Bingham, see Poole 1995.

7. For histories of photography in the Andean countries, see Antmann 1983; Benavente 1995; Chiriboga and Caparrini 1994; McElroy 1985; and Serrano 1983.

8. When assessed as part of this value system, historical shifts in technique, genre, and format appear in retrospect to have been the inevitable outcome of an impulse—originating in Renaissance perspectivalism and Cartesian rationalism—toward greater realism or "truth" in the domain of visual representation. For critical discussions of realist discourse in art and photographic history, see, among others, Bryson 1983; Crary 1990; Krauss 1989; Mitchell 1986; Sekula 1984; and Tagg 1988.

9. My concept of exchange value is indebted to recent work on the commodity character of photographs. For different approaches to this problem, see Bourdieu 1965; Krauss 1989; Metz 1985; Rouillé 1982; Sekula 1983, 1984; Tagg 1988; and Taussig

1993. Benjamin's (1969, 1980) essays on photography and mechanical reproduction have been key to recent rethinking of the photograph as commodity form.

10. Compared with the virtual revolution in literary and cultural studies that followed the publication of Edward Said's *Orientalism*, surprisingly little serious attention has been paid to exploring the specific role of visual imagery in European colonialism and U.S. imperialism. Important exceptions include Alloula 1986; Edwards 1992; Graham-Brown 1988; Lutz and Collins 1993; Maurel 1980; Monti 1987; Pinney 1992a; Prochaska 1990; and Solomon-Godeau 1981.

11. On the postcard, see especially Alloula 1986 and Schor 1992. On ethnographic survey photography, see especially Pinney 1992b.

12. Some of the most important work on the photographic archive as a technology of imperial power has focused on U.S. western land survey photography; see, for example, Krauss 1989 and Trachtenberg 1989, 119–163. On the photographic archive as theoretical and discursive concept, see Sekula 1989. I discuss the elision of colonial photography from Sekula's history of the European archive in Chapter Five.

13. Following what has become accepted usage among postcolonial critics, the term "colonial" is used here and elsewhere in this book as a gloss for "non-European." The advantages of such usage is that it points toward the hierarchical relations and histories that connect Europe with "non-Europe." As the Andean and Latin American case makes clear, the disadvantage is that it obscures the important chronological discrepancies that shaped "colonial" histories and cultures in different areas of the world.

14. Benjamin 1969, 1980.

15. Crary 1990, 11.

16. Foucault 1980a, 142–144. On biopower, see also Foucault 1991.

17. Stoler 1995. On race and colonialism, see also Alatas 1977; Breman 1990; Hobsbawm 1987, 252–254; Kiernan 1969; McClintock 1995; and Pieterse 1992.

18. Foucault 1980a, 127. See also Pollock 1992.

19. Foucault 1991, 1992. Stoler (1995, 55–94) provides a summary of Foucault's unpublished lectures on race. It is difficult to reconstruct Foucault's understanding of the history of racial thought in large part because the very nature of his project effectively dismisses the possibility of defining absolute chronologies or origins. Instead Foucault presents what Stoler (1995, 61) characterizes a "discursive bricolage" in which "an older discourse of race is recovered, modified, encased, and encrusted in new forms."

20. Taussig 1993, 188.

21. See, for example, Bryson 1983; Crary 1990; Fabian 1983; Foucault 1973b, 1979, 1980b; Keller and Grontkowski 1983; Rorty 1979; and Tagg 1988. In extending this critique to the study of vision and visual technologies in the colonial or non-European world, Foucault's work on surveillance and disciplinary power has been especially important. See, for example, Chow 1995; Mitchell 1988, esp. pp. 1–62; and Shohat 1991.

22. Barthes 1977.

23. Jay 1988, 115.

24. Jay 1988, 123.

25. Barthes 1981.

26. On Benjamin's visual theory, see Buck-Morss 1989.

27. See, for example, Rose 1986; Keller and Grontkowski 1983.

28. Attempts to do this are rarer than one might expect, although for two very different exceptions to this rule, see Chow 1995 and Gutman 1982. This is perhaps because, in embracing postcolonial theory, visual anthropology has also tended to focus on European visual forms (see, for example, Lutz and Collins 1993; Taylor 1994).

29. Said 1993.

30. I am grateful to Gary Urton for pointing out the perils of *assuming* a "silent" indigenous subject in even the most "repressive" sorts of nineteenth-century photography. Recent anthropological studies of photography have tried to work their way around this impasse by stressing a relational notion of vision. Lutz and Collins (1993), for example, speak of the multiple intersecting gazes at work in photographs of non-Europeans. In his otherwise very different analysis of colonial photography Taussig (1993, 186) also emphasizes the "impulses radiating from each side of the colonial divide."

31. Pollock 1994, 4.

32. For histories of the period, see, among others, Burga and Flores-Galindo 1987; Flores-Galindo 1977; Gootenberg 1989; Larson 1988; Mallon 1983; and Walker 1992.

33. See, for example, Adorno 1986, 1991; Cummins 1988; MacCormack 1991; Stern 1982; and Urton 1990.

34. On the colonial origins of Andean racial ideologies, see, among others, Manrique 1993; Rivera Cusicanqui 1993; and Stern 1982. On the nineteenth-century roots of Andean racial discourse, see Callirgos 1993; Platt 1984; and Poole 1990, 1994.

35. See, for example, Banton 1987.

36. See Cohen 1980 for a detailed history of the racial, aesthetic, and visual languages through which Africans have seemingly always been viewed in French political and cultural discourse.

37. These racial theorists are discussed in Chapter Three.

## Chapter Two

1. Epigraph source: *Lettre sur Alzire*, May 1736; cited in Braun 1989, 12.

2. La Condamine 1745.

3. La Condamine 1778. At the time of La Condamine's visit, Cuenca—which is today located in the country of Ecuador—belonged to the Viceroyalty of Peru.

4. Rudwick 1976.

5. According to La Condamine, the dispute began when Seniergues went to the woman's home to care for her epileptic father. The mayor's son then accused him of having seduced his fiancée (the epileptic man's daughter).

6. Owing to the expense, it was rare for books published at this time to include more than one illustration, inserted near the front of the book. This limitation lent an extraordinary significance to the illustration as a "visual summary of the book" (Rudwick 1976, 154).

7. Juan and Ulloa 1748.

8. La Condamine 1751, vii.

9. He also published a longer official account of the expedition, intended for a more restricted public (La Condamine 1751).

10. On the impact of the La Condamine mission in France, see Broc 1969, 174–177; Broc 1974, 38–41; Conlon 1967; Duviols 1978, 20–21, 150–156; Macera 1976, 51–

57; and Mercier 1969. Throughout this book, I use the term "bourgeois" to refer to the cultural formation that emerged along with the French bourgeoisie, but that, as a discourse of distinction, was not confined to that class. For more on the nineteenth-century bourgeoisie as an international class and culture, see Chapter Five. On the problematic class definition of the pre-Revolutionary bourgeoisie and its cultural affiliations with the aristocracy, see Hobsbawm 1990a, 7–8, and Tocqueville 1967, 153–158.

11. La Condamine 1778, i-ii.

12. La Condamine 1778, 257.

13. Hobsbawm (1990b) places the origins of modern nationalist sentiment in the period immediately following the French Revolution. Anderson (1991) explores more fully the non-European origins of nationalist discourse. On nineteenth-century French nationalism, see Girardet 1972; Noiriel 1988, 1992; Tocqueville 1967; and Todorov 1994.

14. Foucault 1980a, 124. See also Noiriel 1992, 8.

15. Hobsbawm 1990b, 14–17. On nation as community, see Anderson 1991 and Chatterjee 1993.

16. Figlio 1975. On related eighteenth-century theories of perception, see Crary 1990, 25–66.

17. Figlio 1975, 181.

18. Cuvier, cited in Figlio 1975, 184. On Cuvier, see Chapter Three.

19. For critical discussions of eighteenth-century Orientalist fictions, see Kiernan 1969; Mannsaker 1990; Martino 1906; Netton 1990; and Pucci 1990. On Orientalism as a discursive and political formation, see Said 1979.

20. Rousseau in turn relied on the sixteenth-century accounts of the Tupinambá by de Léry ([1578] 1990) and Montaigne ([1580] 1892).

21. While various European countries vied for access to Spain's carefully guarded colonial markets, the French proved particularly tenacious as smugglers. "The quantity of French ships that trade in these seas is extraordinary," the Royal Audience of Lima complained in 1708. "They intimidate with threats those who would prevent the unloading of their goods; they land their cargo with force of arms, and they forge by force or violence a freedom for their commrce." Archive Nationale de la Marine: B. 7 251; cited in Dahlgren 1909, 496–497.

22. Feuillée 1714; cited in Duviols 1978, 149.

23. Frezier 1982, 226–235.

24. Bachelier (Durret) 1720.

25. Bachelier (Durret) 1720, I:168.

26. Bachelier (Durret) 1720, I:166.

27. Las Casas's most widely read work outside of Spain was the *Brevisima relación de la destrucción de las Indias* (1552). On French uses of Las Casas, see Hanke 1952, 59–64.

28. Although the theory has roots in much older sources, Montesquieu's *L'Esprit des lois* (1748) was probably the most influential eighteenth-century popularizer of climatic determination. For discussion of theories of climatic determination in South America, see Chapter Three.

29. Garcilaso's work was first published in Spanish in 1609. A French translation appeared in 1632 and was followed by new editions in 1633, 1672, 1704, 1737, and 1744 (Atkinson 1972, 124). On Garcilaso's influence on seventeenth-century French

images of Peru, see Atkinson 1972, 100, 123–126. On Peruvian intellectuals' uses of Garcilaso during roughly the same period, see Flores-Galindo 1987, 50–53, and Rowe 1976.

30. See, for example, Voltaire 1769, III:23–30. On Enlightenment anthropology, see, among others, Duchet 1971; Malefijt 1974, 73–93; and Todorov 1994.

31. In this respect, the European encounter with the New World was markedly different from that with Africa, where racial and aesthetic stereotypes about Africans predated extensive colonial contact. For the French case, see Cohen 1980.

32. Voltaire 1769, I:25. The two "races" he suggests were the Eskimo (who had facial hair) and all other Americans.

33. *Les Indes galantes* remained in the Academy's repertoire and was performed regularly up through the end of the eighteenth century (Chinard 1913, 233–237). For contemporary reviews, see Masson 1972, 68.

34. Masson 1972, 124.

35. Masson 1972, 124–125.

36. On opera and colonialism, see Said 1993, 111–132.

37. Gay 1966. On seventeenth-century French deism and paganism and their roots in travel literature, see Atkinson 1972, 110–162.

38. The chorus of sun virgins laments: "Sun, your superb sanctuaries have been destroyed. There remains for you no other temple than our hearts. Deign to hear us in these peaceful deserts. Zeal is for the Gods the richest of honors" (Rameau and Fuzelier 1971, 184–185). On Inca virgins of the sun, see note 46.

39. Rameau and Fuzelier 1971, 169.

40. Rameau and Fuzelier 1971, 174–177.

41. Pougin 1971, 7–8.

42. Chinard 1913, 235.

43. Masson 1972, 131. I have been unable to locate descriptions or illustrations of the costumes from *Les Indes galantes*, which were probably designed by the official Opéra designer, Martin et Bouquet.

44. Masson 1972, 128. See also Braun 1989, 57.

45. Mannsaker 1990.

46. In Inca society, the sun virgins or *acllas* were cloistered women who lived in a special palace called the *acllawasi* ("house of the acllas"). In the eighteenth-century literature discussed here, the acllas are conflated (erroneously) with "Inca princesses" and are said to have lived in the Temple of the Sun. *Tapadas* were creole women who covered their heads with dark shawls. They are discussed in detail in Chapter Four. On royal women and acllas in Inca society, see Silverblatt 1987.

47. For detailed histories of the "black legend," see Carbia 1943; Gibson 1971; and Juderías 1954.

48. *Alzire* ran through 238 performances, including two for the Court and remained in the repertory of the Comédie Française until 1830 (Braun 1989, 45–47). *Alzire* also inspired at least three parodies (*Les Sauvages*, *Alzirette*, and *La Fille obéissante*), all of which faulted Voltaire for not making the Incas savage enough. *Alzire* was later adapted by Verdi as the basis for his 1845 Neopolitan opera *Alzira*.

49. Voltaire makes use of nearly identical romantic plots in his earlier works *Adélaïde du Guesclin* (1734) and *Zaïre* (1732). While *Zaïre*—the play with the most striking

similarities in both plot and character to *Alzire*—was set in the then more fashionable Orient, *Alzire* was timed to coincide with the shifting exotic interests of France in the aftermath of La Condamine.

50. Voltaire owned copies of Las Casas and Garcilaso, as well as an eighteenth-century translation of the conquest chronicler Zarate (Perkins 1943). In addition to Garcilaso and Las Casas, Voltaire (1769, III:23–30) also cites the conquest accounts of Herrera and Zarate in his account of the Inca conquest. He would presumably have also been familiar with Frezier's plates and journal. The costumes for *Alzire*, however, showed little concern for historical accuracy. Alzire, for example, wore a feather skirt and cloak more evocative of the generic "America" than of the Inca figures described by Garcilaso, Frezier, and others (Braun 1989, 57). In *Candide* (1759), Voltaire shows a similar disregard for historical detail in his portrayal of a utopian land modeled after Peru.

51. The different humanist values which Europeans assigned to Inca and Aztec religions informed the very different images and representations of the two empires. On Aztec representations in European literature and art, see Chiapelli 1976; Keen 1971; and Honour 1975.

52. Braun 1989, 3. Voltaire's strategy was successful. *Alzire* not only was staged twice for the Court, but was also well received by the same powerful clergy whom Voltaire would continue to offend in his later works.

53. Grafigny's novel appeared in over seventy French, English, and Italian editions between 1747 and 1835 (Nicoletti 1967, 49–67) and was the third most frequently encountered book in a study of eighteenth-century European libraries (Macera 1976, 67).

54. Feminist and literary critics have tended to focus their analyses of the *Lettres d'une péruvienne* on de Grafigny's feminism, her use of the epistolary form, and the charges that she modeled her novel on Montesquieu's *Persian Letters*. See, for example, Hartmann 1989; Nicoletti 1967; Robb 1992; Rustin 1989; and Schneider 1989. As with other works of the Inca Operatic—most notably *Alzire*—the Peruvian setting is given curiously little importance in the critical literature on the *Lettres d'une péruvienne*. For exceptions, see Douthwaite 1991 and especially Altman 1990.

55. Grafigny 1990, 59.

56. Marmontel began writing *The Incas* in 1767, during the height of the scandal over an earlier work, *Le Bélisaire*. Although he completed the novel in 1771, he delayed publishing it until 1777. In *Le Bélisaire*, Marmontel had offended the censors by arguing in favor of a larger tax burden for the aristocracy, by defending a theological argument that God pardons pagans, and by suggesting that the king (like God) should be more tolerant (Renwick 1974). Although *The Incas* was also concerned with tolerance and the salvation of virtuous pagans, it never provoked scandal.

57. Kaplan (1987, 366) suggests Marmontel also drew on Masonic ritual and symbols for the Inca ceremonies in *Les Incas*. Other sources cited by Marmontel (1777, I:183, II:42) include La Condamine and the abbé Prévost's 1750 *Histoire générale des voyages*.

58. In the opening of *Les Incas*, Marmontel laments that the Spaniards opted for violence rather than trade. Through the "new needs and pleasures" brought by trade, he writes, "the Indian would have become more industrious, more active; and gentleness would have obtained from him what violence could not" (Marmontel 1777, I:2). On

trade as a sign of the triumph of reason over passion in eighteenth-century France, see Hirschmann 1977, 70–80.

59. Marmontel 1777, II:17.

60. Marmontel 1777, II:21.

61. The heart was the most frequently targeted organ for the elusive sensorium commune. See Figlio 1975.

62. Marmontel's best known erotic work was *La Neuvaine de Cythère* (1765). See Kaplan 1973.

63. Marmontel 1777, II:29–30.

64. Marmontel 1777, II:30–31.

65. The principal subplot involves a group of exiled Mexican nobles who arrive during the Inca Sun Feast to warn the Incas of their fate.

66. Marmontel 1777 II:356–357.

67. Marmontel 1819, 217–218.

68. La Condamine also builds on contemporary anticlerical sentiments in naming the vicar of Cuenca the "prime mover" (1778, 234) behind Seniergues's murder. He accuses the vicar of refusing last rites to Seniergues, thereby inciting a general revolt against the "heretical" French (1778, 241).

69. Foucault 1980a, 116.

70. Foucault 1980a, 127–128. See also Pollock 1992 and 1994, 25–37.

71. See note 50.

### Chapter Three

1. Epigraph source: D'Orbigny 1854, 311.

2. The essence of Buffon's argument about New World species appears in the essay "Animaux communs aux deux continents," published in 1761 in the *Histoire naturelle*, vol. IX (Buffon 1749–1809). On American exceptionalism, see Gerbi 1982.

3. Buffon 1749–1809, XV:443–444.

4. Buffon, "Animaux comuns," 106.

5. D'Orbigny 1839, 250.

6. Foucault 1973a, 1973b.

7. D'Orbigny 1839, 86–87.

8. My account of Buffon's life draws on the excellent biography by Jacques Roger (1989). On the Jardin du Roi, see Laissus 1964. After the Revolution, the Jardin du Roi was converted into the Muséum d'Histoire Naturelle.

9. The American collections included Andean specimens brought back by Feuillée and the La Condamine mission.

10. The Jardin differed from other institutions of higher education on several counts: lectures were in French, rather than in Latin; classes were open to foreign students; and no academic credentials or prior registration were required (Laissus 1964, 314–417). On French colonial aspirations and eighteenth-century life sciences, see Broc 1974; Moravia 1967, 1980; Mornet 1911; and Roger 1993.

11. The *Histoire naturelle* (hereafter *HN*) is divided into seven series published between 1749 and 1809.

12. On Buffon's theories of human variation, see Roger 1989, 223–247, and Todorov 1994, 96–106. On the American races, see "Variétés," *HN*, III (1749):509–512.

13. Glacken 1967, 681–682. On Latin American responses to Buffon, see Brading 1991, 450–462, and Gerbi 1982.

14. Buffon, cited in Roger 1989, 546.

15. To refer to what we now understand as climate in the sense of atmospheric conditions, Buffon used the term *air*. See Broc 1969, 173.

16. "Le Lion," *HN*, IX (1761):2; cited in Roger 1989, 391.

17. The notion of the "country of origin" is developed in the *Époques de la nature* (Epochs of Nature), published in 1787 as volume V of the seven-volume *Supplément* to the *Histoire naturelle*. See also Roger 1989, 544–555.

18. On the interior mold, see *HN*, IV (1753). On Buffon's general theory of generation, see Bowler 1973 and Roger 1993, 542–558.

19. Bowler 1973, 275–276; Glacken 1967, 518–519; and Roger 1989, 378–389.

20. "Premier discours," *HN*, I (1749):13.

21. Roger 1989, 242.

22. "Premier discours," *HN*, I (1749):13. On the Buffon-Linnaeus debate, see Sloan 1976. Foucault (1973b, 135) dismisses the debate and emphasizes the two men's shared discourse of classification. Their very dissimilar understandings of type and species, however, speak to the unevenness of the epistemological break that Foucault posits between eighteenth-century natural history and modern biology.

23. "De l'asne," *HN*, IV (1753); cited in Sloan 1976, 370–371.

24. Roger 1989, 240.

25. See Sloan 1976 and Stafleu 1971, 267–336.

26. "De la description," *HN*, IV (1749); cited in Reynaud 1990, 364.

27. Sloan 1994, 475.

28. "Histoire générale des animaux," *HN*, II (1749); cited in Sloan 1976, 368, emphasis mine.

29. "Des sens en général"; cited in Roger 1989, 214. On the importance of touch for Buffon, see also Roger 1989, 561. On the prevalence of touch in eighteenth-century perceptual regimes, see Crary 1990, 59–64.

30. "Premiers discours," *HN*, I (1749); cited in Sloan 1976, 360.

31. Reynaud 1990, 365; Roger 1993, 528–542.

32. Cited in Reynaud 1990, 366.

33. Reynaud 1990, 365.

34. On Humboldt's life and education, see Botting 1973; Bruhns 1873; and Minguet 1969.

35. On La Condamine's influence on Humboldt, see Minguet 1991.

36. See especially Letter to Don Ignacio Checa, 1803; in Humboldt 1980. Lima was also one of the few places in Spanish America where Buffon's theories of American inferiority found active supporters (Brading 1991, 449). On Lima creole identification with Europe, see Chapter Six.

37. Humboldt 1814–1825; English translation, Humboldt 1852.

38. On Humboldt's influence in Latin America, see Brading 1991, 514–534, and Pratt 1992, 111–143; Pratt also discusses his aesthetic and narrative style. On Humboldt and modern plant geography, see Cannon 1978 and Nicolson 1987.

39. Humboldt 1850, 234.

40. Humboldt 1850, 234.

41. Humboldt 1852, I:x.

42. Humboldt 1850, 236.

43. On Humboldt's theories of plant geography, see Cannon 1978, 73–110; Glacken 1967, 543–548; and Nicolson 1987.

44. Humboldt 1850, 236–7; emphasis mine.

45. Humboldt 1850, 1.

46. *Views* was Humboldt's only work that featured graphic images as its principal mode of describing the New World. The plates were engraved in Paris and Stuttgart by artists who worked from Humboldt's sketches. Roughly two-thirds illustrate archaeological materials. The second-largest group consists of landscapes, waterfalls, and volcanoes in the Ecuadorian and Colombian Andes. Finally, a handful of plates depicts urban scenes or curiosities, such as the swimming mail couriers of northern Peru. Following the plates, Humboldt provides commentaries explaining the circumstances, events, artifacts, and places depicted in the engravings.

47. Buffon's *Epochs of Nature* (see note 17) contained what was considered to be the most complete inventory of mountains in the world. In that work he described the mountains of the New World as a continuous single chain, with the highest point located on the equator. See Broc 1969, 49–53.

48. Humboldt 1850, 3.

49. Humboldt 1810, 3; see also Humboldt 1850, 144.

50. The influence of the German Romantics on Humboldt's work has been noted by Nicolson 1987, 176–179, and criticized by Pratt (1992, 137–138).

51. Humboldt 1810, plate 25. At the time Humboldt traveled to South America, Chimborazo was believed to be the highest mountain in the world (Broc 1974, 117).

52. Humboldt 1810, 200.

53. For his ideas regarding the effects of altitude on vision and light, Humboldt was indebted to Henri Saussure, whose four-volume *Voyage dans les Alpes* (1780–1796) he "reread, word by word" before leaving for South America, marking "all those experiences that [Saussure] would wish one to have" (Humboldt, cited in Broc 1969, 262).

54. Humboldt 1810, 41.

55. On the notion of singularity in eighteenth-century landscape theory, see Stafford 1984.

56. Humboldt 1980, 111.

57. Bruhns 1873, I:78.

58. Blumenbach 1795, esp. 227–234.

59. Humboldt 1850, 432.

60. Humboldt 1850, 431.

61. Humboldt 1852, I:304. Humboldt is describing the Chaymas Indians in a Venezuelan mission.

62. The question of how, or if, savages registered expression was widely debated in late eighteenth- and early nineteenth-century Europe. See Courtine and Haroche 1989.

63. Humboldt 1852, I:305.

64. On nineteenth-century travel to Peru and the Andes, see Macera 1976; Nuñez 1989; and Duviols 1978.

65. D'Orbigny 1839, ix.

66. D'Orbigny 1839, 2; see also Blumenbach 1795, 271–273.

67. Blumenbach 1795, 160–161, 271.

68. D'Orbigny 1839, xxii.

69. D'Orbigny 1839, xxiv.

70. D'Orbigny 1839, 10.

71. D'Orbigny 1839, 75.

72. D'Orbigny 1839, 74, 264.

73. D'Orbigny 1839, 83–84.

74. D'Orbigny 1839, 271.

75. Crary 1990, 26–66.

76. Crary 1990, 55; Foucault 1973b; see also Rorty 1979, 131–164.

77. Foucault 1980b, 149.

78. D'Orbigny (1839, v) dedicates *L'Homme américain* to Humboldt, "whom Europe has proclaimed the example and model of the philosopher-traveler."

79. Foucault 1973b, 264.

80. Cuvier 1828; cited in Coleman 1964, 102.

81. Humboldt's and Cuvier's visual and spatial methodologies also converged in the fields of geology and cartography, where Cuvier developed new mapping conventions for illustrating invisible or subterranean structures. See Rudwick 1976, 161–162, 169–170.

82. Cuvier 1836, I:98.

83. Cuvier 1836, I:103.

84. Cuvier 1836, II, plates 1–16.

85. Cuvier, in Hervé 1910, 305. Cuvier also instructed travelers to collect as many anatomical pieces as possible, first taking care "to boil the bones in a solution of soda or caustic potash" before storing them in linen bags (ibid., 306).

86. Foucault 1980b, 146.

## Chapter Four

1. Epigraph source: Anonymous 1748, 49.

2. Tapadas were also common in Santiago de Chile and Buenos Aires. For general histories of the Limeña tapada, see Bromley 1944, 17–25, and Martin 1983, 299–306.

3. Published catalogues and compilations of Rugendas's work include Rugendas 1968, 1966, 1975; Lago 1960; and Richert 1959.

4. The original watercolors and sketches form part of the Collection Angrand at the Bibliothèque Nationale in Paris.

5. In colonial Peru, *mulato* referred to a person of African and indigenous ancestry. For most of the European travelers discussed in this chapter, however, "mulata" referred to any of a number of racial mixtures, including what Peruvians would have distinguished as the *samba* (African, European, and indigenous ancestry) and the *negra* ("black" or African). For these Europeans, it was the mulata's appearance rather than ancestry (or *casta*) that determined her "race."

6. *Criollo*, or creole, referred to persons of Spanish descent who had been born in the Americas. Because criollos were either of a relatively light skin color or, more important, thought of themselves as such, criollo can be glossed as "white" in the racial ideology of Lima. Most European travelers, however, did not perceive creoles as "white."

7. Because the imported textiles used at home were easily recognized, women usually chose old shawls and ragged skirts (*sayas picadas*) when dressing as tapadas. The old clothes allowed them to "to disguise themselves as poor" (Flores Araoz 1975, 56) and to move anonymously in public spaces.

8. Bromley 1944, 19–23; Martin 1983, 301–305; and d'Orbigny and Eyriés 1842, II:11–12. The Spanish Crown had similar difficulties controlling its women at home. Despite repeated attempts to outlaw its use, Spanish women in those areas of southern Spain with heavy Moorish influence adopted the veil for the greater freedom it allowed them in public streets and outside the home.

9. Radiquet 1874, 87; and Baxley 1865, 111.

10. See also Angrand 1972, plates 11 (pp. 45–46), 23 (p. 54), 112 (p. 133), and 110 (p. 132).

11. See Gilman 1986. Much of the speculation regarding African female physiology was based on Cuvier's 1812 dissection of the "Hottentot Venus."

12. Earlier travelers to Lima described the tapadas's freedom of movement as a source of general corruption and decay. See, for example, Frezier 1982 (1716), 220–221.

13. Radiquet 1874, 84.

14. Angrand 1972, 172.

15. Angrand 1972, 172; Radiquet 1874, xii. See also Bresson 1886, 99.

16. D'Orbigny and Eyriés 1842, II:11.

17. For depictions of tapadas and prayer rugs, see Rugendas 1975, plates 90 (p. 172), 55 (p. 135), 62 (pp. 139–40), 65 (pp. 141–142), 67 (p. 154), and 74 (p. 164).

18. See Angrand 1972, plates 16 (p. 50), 17 (p. 51), 56 (p. 83), and 36 (pp. 65–66); and Rugendas 1975, plates 17 (p. 103) and 99 (p. 179).

19. See Angrand 1972, plates 107 (p. 130) and 110 (p. 132).

20. Radiquet 1874, 158.

21. Radiquet 1874, 157.

22. Rugendas 1975, plate 50 (p. 132).

23. Radiquet 1874, xiii.

24. Bresson 1886, 100. See also Radiquet 1874, xiii.

25. Baxley 1865, 110.

26. Radiquet 1874, 84; Flores Araoz 1975, 22.

27. Radiquet 1874, 103–106.

28. Radiquet 1874, 108.

29. Gootenberg 1991, 111. See also Flores-Galindo 1977.

30. Baxley 1865, 113.

31. Radiquet 1874, 86.

32. Rugendas 1975, plate 73 (pp. 161–162); see also plates 75 (p. 156), and 168 (p. 190).

33. Angrand 1972, 163–173.

34. For examples of mulatas nursing, see Angrand 1972, plates 114 (p. 135) and 116 (pp. 136–137); and Rugendas 1975, plates 140 (p. 195) and 143 (p. 196). It is probable that the mulata's place as wet nurse for the creole upper classes played an important role in this imagery. See Rugendas's "Ama de leche" (Rugendas 1975, plate 146, p. 197).

35. Baxley 1865, 142–143. In European observations, the mulata's threatening sexuality was consistently associated with her economic trade. Many travelers, for example, comment on barter as the market woman's ruse to force (white) men to engage in conversation with her.

36. Squier 1877, 54–55.

37. Radiquet (1874, 87) considered the tapada's dainty slippers the "touchstone of

elegance, the merciless weapon of seduction" (*l'arme sans merci de la séduction*). Other, earlier observers of Lima social life, however, considered this obsession with small feet to be a fetish peculiar to Spanish (or Peruvian) men. They compared it unfavorably with their own more "natural" interest in women's breasts. See, for example, Frezier 1982 (1716), 223.

38. See Angrand 1972, plates 50 (pp. 77–78) and 51 (pp. 79–80).

39. See Alloula 1986 and Graham-Brown 1988.

40. See also Angrand 1972, plate 169 (p. 55).

41. Rugendas 1975, plate 49 (p. 126); see also plates 55 (p. 135) and 61 (pp. 137–138).

42. Nochlin 1983, 122–123.

43. On Peruvian creole nationalism, see Chapter Six. On the wars between Peru's regional military strongmen, or *caudillos*, see especially Gootenberg 1989 and Walker 1992.

44. Nochlin 1988; Pollock 1988; Pollock and Parker 1981.

## Chapter Five

1. While the standard 18 × 24 cm portraits sold for 100 francs each, the new format allowed Disdéri to sell 25 portraits with two different poses for less than a third the price (Gernsheim 1988, 191). Epigraph source: Daguerre 1980 (1839), 12.

2. Rouillé (1982) analyzes the economic discourse of the carte-de-visite trade.

3. Holmes 1863, 8.

4. Rouillé 1984.

5. Disdéri 1862, 290–291.

6. For histories of physiognomy, see Courtine and Haroche 1989; Cowling 1989; and Wechsler 1982.

7. The reception hall exhibited portraits of Nièpce, Daguerre, Talbot, and della Porta. Gernsheim 1988, 191.

8. See especially Rouillé 1982, 1984; Freund 1980; Sekula 1989; and Trachtenberg 1989.

9. Disdéri; cited in Rouillé 1982, 172.

10. Disdéri; cited in Rouillé 1982, 178.

11. Williams 1977, 132–134.

12. Disdéri 1862.

13. Freund 1980, 57. In 1861 the French state accepted Disdéri's proposal for a military photography department.

14. The European passion for collecting cartes de visite in sets or albums began with the Royal Album sold in London in 1860 (Gernsheim 1988, 193). Shortly after, Disdéri marketed a collection of cartes de visite of celebrities called the "Galerie des contemporains" (Gernsheim 1987, 192).

15. First introduced in 1830—nine years before Daguerre's invention of the photographic process—the stereograph began to grow in popularity following a display of photographic stereographs at the Crystal Palace Exhibition in London in 1851. With the perfection of inexpensive paper printing processes in the mid-1850s, the stereograph market soared.

16. Stereographs sold in Paris in 1857 for 15 francs a dozen (Rouillé 1987, 41).

17. Holmes 1980.

18. Holmes 1980, 77.

19. Holmes 1980, 72.

20. Holmes 1980, 81.

21. See, for example, Holmes 1863, and Poe 1980.

22. In the collections surveyed for this study, it was unusual to find photographs of Andean Indians without hats. The only other cartes of bareheaded Indians occur under the themes of "lice gathering" and "domestic servants." The bareheaded look, however, would become *de rigeur* in the anthropometric photography discussed later in this chapter.

23. See Chapter Six. This was less the case in Bolivia or Ecuador, whose capital cities were located in the highlands and where it was consequently much less easy for painters to ignore the presence of an indigenous Andean culture. See, for example, costumbrista paintings of indigenous types from the 1850s by the Ecuadorian Juan Agustín Guerrero (Guerrero 1981; see also Muratoria 1994). On nineteenth-century Ecuadorian photography, see Chiriboga and Caparrini 1994.

24. "Portraits de personalités de l'Amérique du Sud," album en 8°, s/f (S.XIX), Estampes et photographies, Bibliothèque Nationale (Paris).

25. Although produced (and perhaps sold) in the Lima studio of the French photographer Eugene Courret, this photograph appears to have been taken during the photographer's travels through Polynesia. The caption "Type péruvien" was probably added by the album's owner.

26. See, for example, "Personnages et costumes du Pérou," album en 8°. v. 1870, Collection Sirot, Estampes et photographies, Bibliothèque Nationale (Paris). Photographs labeled "gauchos" and even "Argentine gauchos" were included in nearly every nineteenth-century Peruvian and Bolivian album.

27. "Types Indigènes d'Amérique," album, Collection Sirot, Estampes et photographies, Bibliothèque Nationale (Paris).

28. International Museum of Photography, George Eastman House, Rochester, N.Y. The album's complete title is "Pérou et Bolivie—types et coutûmes indiens du Pérou et de la Bolivie (Quichuas Aymaras). Métis (cholos et cholas). Nègres et métis divers." *Rabonas* were one of the most popular carte-de-visite subjects.

29. Although the album title refers to Peru and Bolivia, the majority of the photographs show subjects in Bolivian indigenous dress. The fact that several of these images match photographs marketed as cartes de visite by the Courret Hermanos in Lima suggests that photography studios sold cartes made from other studios' negatives.

30. The album moves through eleven categories of poses: (1) full-body standing pairs ; (2) full-body pairs of men in which one sits and the other stands; (3) full-body pairs in which both are seated; (4) full-body pairs in which one sits on a box and the other on the floor; (5) full-body groups of more than two; (6) full-body single standing men; (7) full-body single seated men (including squatting and kneeling poses); (8) full-body standing single women; (9) full-body pairs of Indian women; (10) half-body shots of single men (shot from the knees up); (11) half-body seated single men.

31. "92 photographies de Bolivie offertes à la Société de Géographie par M. le Dr. L. C. Thibon, consul de Bolivie à Bruxelles, 27 juin 1885," Bibliothèque Nationale (Paris).

32. Gernsheim 1987, 200.

33. In modern usage, *chola* (or *cholo*, masculine) usually carries a derogatory or insulting connotation.

34. Wiener 1880. Selected chapters of Wiener's book were serialized in the popular travel magazine *Le Tour du Monde.*

35. Today the cartes are filed geographically under "Types and Vêtements" in the photography collection at the Musée de l'Homme. Because the cartes have been mounted on museum board for filing purposes, it is not possible to check provenance (such as photographer's studio) or any additional comments that Wiener himself may have written directly on the back of the cartes. The captions for the different cartes on each sheet are listed on the back of the museum card and presumably follow Wiener's originals. I was unable to ascertain if the cartes were ever exhibited at either the Palais or the museum that took up its collections.

36. As presently archived, the cartes are arranged six to a sheet according to occupational categories. It is unclear whether this was Wiener's organization or a grouping imposed later by the museum following Wiener's original captions.

37. For example, a model posed seated in one carte de visite is labeled "farm hand" (*garçon de ferme*). Another, larger, photograph of the same man standing against the same studio backdrop is labeled "landowning Indian."

38. See Banton 1987, 28–64; and Gould 1981, 73–112. On French racial theory, see especially Cohen 1980, 210–222; Kremer-Marietti 1984; and Todorov 1994.

39. The Agassiz cartes were from the Ricardo Villalba studio in La Paz (Bolivia). His collection is now held at Harvard University's Peabody Museum.

40. The Haddon cartes were from the Castilla studio in Lima. The collection is now held at the Cambridge University Museum of Archeology and Anthropology. I am grateful to Christopher Pinney for providing me with photocopies of Haddon's Andean cartes.

41. Chervin 1908, I:52. Chervin's interest in Bolivia's mixed races was inspired by the work of his teacher and mentor Paul Broca (to whom all of Chervin's published works are dedicated). By questioning Gobineau's 1854 treatise (in which national identity is equated with racial purity), Broca's famous 1856 memoir on racial hybridity placed both the colonial question and the problem of racial mixture at the center of European anthropologists' research agenda (Broca 1864; see also Williams 1985).

42. Chervin 1908, I:vii.

43. Chervin later cautions scientists and travelers against using such "picturesque" photographs, because although they "are very attractive, very interesting from the picturesque, aesthetic or curiosity point of view, they unfortunately have no documentary character, no scientific character since they cannot be compared one with the other" (Bertillon and Chervin 1909, 5).

44. By prescribing the precise focal distance, angle, lighting conditions, and pose to be used in making photographic portraits, Bertillon proposed to elevate photography to an exact, statistical science. His system, which was taught at the Service Anthropométrique de Paris, became the basis of modern criminological identification systems. Bertillon 1885; Phéline 1985.

45. See for example, Bertillon and Chervin 1909, Figures 37–38, pp. 100–101.

46. Chervin 1908, xxviii.

47. Bertillon and Chervin 1909, 112.

48. Bertillon and Chervin 1909, 153.

49. Bertillon and Chervin 1909, 153.

50. Bertillon and Chervin (1909, 112) recommended that all measurements, including skin color—which they recommended be recorded in such quantitative terms as "very small, small, . . . large, very large"—be calculated "on the basis of the average French type." This type was, in turn, defined by Bertillon on the basis of 25,000 measurements recorded by him at the Service Anthropométrique de Paris.

51. Chervin 1908, III, esp. 31–34. Broca (1875) thought that the stereoscope was the only medium capable of providing the geometric perspective he believed to be fundamental for the study of skulls. In response to Broca's objections that two-dimensional images could not adequately address the geometric methods of craniology, Chervin prescribed the use of multiple images taken from six different optical angles. "One must reason as if there were six identical cameras placed around the skull and oriented along the six faces of a hypothetical cube" (1908, III:13).

52. Between 1877 and 1883, the Prefecture accumulated an archive of over 75,000 cartes de visite (Phèline 1985, 34).

53. Bertillon 1882.

54. Sekula 1989, 346.

55. Sekula 1989, 346; emphasis in original.

56. See, for example, Bolton 1989; Rouillé 1982, 1984; Squiers 1990; and Tagg 1988.

57. Baudrillard 1981, 93.

## Chapter Six

1. Epigraph source: Letter to Don Ignacio Checa; in Humboldt 1980, 107.

2. Fuentes 1867b, iii–iv.

3. Fuentes 1867a, vi.

4. Although not identified by Fuentes, the woodcuts come from a widely read account of travel in Peru written by the Viscount Laurent Saint-Cricq, and published in *Le Tour du Monde* under the pseudonym of Paul Marcoy (Saint-Cricq 1862–1866). The illustrations were by "Riou," the artist who illustrated many other articles published in *Le Tour du Monde*.

5. Fuentes 1867a, vi.

6. On the rabona, see Chapter Five, p. 121.

7. Fuentes 1867a, vii.

8. Fuentes 1867a, viii.

9. Fuentes 1867a, b, c. The editions, however, are not identical: the anecdote about the French traveler is tactfully omitted from the French-language edition.

10. Flores-Galindo 1984, 99–108. Gootenberg (1991) discusses the difficulties of estimating "ethnic" demography from Peruvian censuses of the time.

11. On class and racial relations in early republican Lima, see Flores-Galindo 1984.

12. Gootenberg 1989, 80–85. On Lima's colonial aristocracy and opposition to free trade, see also Flores-Galindo 1984.

13. Basadre 1968; Gootenberg 1989; Walker 1992.

14. Anderson 1991, 47–65; Brading 1991.

15. Méndez 1993; Rowe 1976.

16. Melgar 1878, 102–103.

17. Melgar 1878, 102.

18. Herrera; cited in Basadre 1968, II:856. On Herrera, see also Delgado 1980, 66–68.

19. Basadre 1968, II:902; Gootenberg 1989, 65–66. On the economic and intellectual history of Lima during this period, see Basadre 1968; Bonilla 1974; Cornejo Polar 1980; Delgado 1980; Gootenberg 1993; and Quiroz 1987.

20. Anderson (1991) has defined "print capitalism" as a mechanism through which shared territorial identity was created in European nationalism.

21. On Palma and the Lima romanticists, see Cornejo Polar 1980, 43–66; Delgado 1980, 73–77; and Flores-Galindo 1984, 179–184. The Andean Indian did not emerge as a subject of literary or political interest until after the War of the Pacific; see Chapter Seven.

22. Pease 1988, 1

23. Basadre 1968, III:1419. The 180-page biography was published anonymously in Chile in 1856 as *Biografia del Excelentísimo señor Ramón Castilla, Libertador del Perú, escrita por el mas fiel adorador.*

24. In one Fuentes cartoon reproduced in Basadre (1968, V:71), a politician's corruption is shown occurring in three stages. Each is marked by his girth, which grows fatter and fatter, and his nose, which evolves from the "Greek" aquiline nose considered by physiognomists as a sign of intelligence to the bulbous nose of the fool to the protruding nose of the ass.

25. Fuentes 1866.

26. Gootenberg 1993, 71.

27. Information on the book's reception at the time is unavailable. Its luxurious format and multiple language editions would have guaranteed it at least some visibility in Europe. The Parisian *imprimeur* and Fuentes's reputation would have guaranteed its appeal for the Peruvian elite.

28. The sections are titled: 1. Foundation and Description of Lima; 2. Churches; 3. Government, Administration, Public Instruction, Welfare, and Military Establishments and Offices; 4. Other Buildings, Private Enterprises, Productions, Business and Industry; and 5. Buildings for Public Entertainments, Decorative Works (*Obras de Ornato*) and Strolling Places (*Lugares de Paseo*).

29. Fuentes 1867a, 80.

30. Fuentes (1867a, 80–81) defines Peru's three "original races" as "white" (European), "yellow" (Indian), and "black" (African).

31. Fuentes 1867a, 83.

32. Fuentes 1867a, 93.

33. Fuentes 1867a, 102.

34. Fuentes 1867a, 184.

35. Fuentes 1867a, 82. In fact, according to Fuentes's own statistics (Fuentes 1858), in 1857 nearly a fifth (or 10,000) of Lima's total population of 55,000 was classified as "black" (cited in Gootenberg 1993, 67).

36. Although not credited as such by Fuentes, the lithographs of the samba, mulata, and Indian women are based on photographs from the Courret studio in Lima. The popularity of these particular images is suggested by the fact that both the photographs and the lithographs crop up in many other contemporary collections. See for example, "Costumes et Moeurs. Amérique du Sud," Estampes et photographies, OF 4e,

III, Bibliothèque Nationale (Paris). Fuentes (1867a, 81) defines the *samba* (which he spells, following nineteenth-century usage, as *zamba*) as the offspring of one black and one white parent. The *mulata* is, then, the offspring of a samba (or a sambo) with a white.

37. Fuentes 1867a, 97.

38. Fuentes also describes Indian muledrivers as vagrants. Like other statisticians of his time, Fuentes was very interested in and wrote on vagrancy as a statistical and political problem. In his 1858 *Estadística de Lima*, he identifies one-fifth of Lima's adult males as "without employment" or "vagrant" (cited in Gootenberg 1993, 67).

39. Fuentes 1867a, 110.

40. Fuentes 1867a, 83–84.

41. Fuentes 1867a, 88.

42. Fuentes 1867a, 90.

43. Fuentes 1867a, 87.

44. Fuentes 1867a, 92.

45. In the French edition (1867a, 233), the section is titled: "Customs That Reveal the Lack of Civilization."

46. Fuentes 1867a, 79.

47. Europeans were fascinated by the supposed fact that American Indians had no body hair.

48. No other category of public figure or "popular type" is accorded a similar quantity of plates. The next most prominent category is that of bishops and archbishops, of whom Fuentes includes only five, all in the first, statistical, chapters. Fuentes includes only two portraits of political and military men.

49. Fuentes 1867a, 104.

50. Fuentes 1867a, v.

51. Fuentes 1867a, 191. The original Courret photograph is reproduced in McElroy 1985, Fig. 37.

52. Although two other lithographs do show white women with irises that do not reach the bottom lid, their eye shape has in each case been drawn in the more "classic" almond shape.

For the black melon vendor (*melonera*) see Fuentes 1867a, 217; for the candle seller (*velero*), see Fuentes 1867a, 206. Given Fuentes's indignant introduction, perhaps the most striking example of physiognomic alteration is the caricatured faces of two of the four rabonas he portrays (1867a, 185, 187). Their features and overall "character" are remarkably similar to those in the Riou woodcut Fuentes cites as an example of European caricature.

53. Fuentes 1867a, 105.

54. Although the idea of fixed types was, of course, rejected by Darwinian evolutionists, it greatly influenced popular understandings of the constancy and visual predictibility of racial "types."

55. Hacking 1990, 135–141.

56. Foucault 1973a, 1979.

57. Crary 1990.

58. Nochlin 1971.

59. For nineteenth-century realists, all "essence" was necessarily fleeting or transitory. See Nochlin 1971.

60. For example, Balzac in literature and Frith in painting, among others. See Cowling 1989 and Wechsler 1982.

61. Bresson 1886, 589–590. The Peruvian exhibit was mounted by French ethnologists, including Charles Wiener.

## Chapter Seven

1. Peru was at war with Chile from 1879 to 1883.

2. Serrano 1983 and Mejía Arango 1988.

3. See Burga and Flores-Galindo 1987.

4. Regarding the class origins of European pictorialist photography, see Hassner 1987 and Melón 1987. Medellín, where the pictorialist-influenced photographers Melitón Rodríguez and Benjamín de la Calle lived and worked, was also home to a relatively progressive industrial and commercial bourgeoisie who distinguished themselves culturally, socially, and racially from the rest of Colombia.

5. See Benjamin 1969; Sekula 1983, 1984.

6. See Ugarte Eléspuru 1968 and Lauer 1976.

7. See McElroy 1985.

8. F. Castro 1990.

9. "Incultura i cursilería"; Castillo 1919.

10. Baudelaire 1980; see also documents concerning this debate in Rouillé 1989, 92–135. Like Baudelaire as well, Castillo (1919) charged that art was necessarily private, visionary, and manual, and that while "photography can serve as a document to reconstruct a lost semblance . . . in no way can it [serve] to transform the semblance into a basic element of serious composition." Similar debates regarding the foto-óleo took place in Colombia in the 1890s (see Serrano 1983, 213, 218–219).

11. Photography appeared in Lima only a few years after its invention in 1839. See McElroy 1985.

12. Castillo's articles attacking the foto-óleos correspond to a period of dramatic change in Lima. The year 1918 was marked by a series of violent strikes by workers and artisans. The next year brought crisis for the traditional agricultural export economy of Lima's oligarchy. In July of 1919 August O. Leguía took office, promising to build a modern, antioligarchical state to be known as the "Patria Nueva" (Flores-Galindo 1987 and Burga 1987, 125–142).

13. Undated newspaper clipping from El Comercio (Lima), 1901; Luis Figueroa Yabar, personal archive.

14. Flores-Galindo 1977.

15. "Un Artista nacional," La Bolsa (Arequipa), 12.III.1903.

16. "Progresos fotográficos," La Bolsa (Arequipa), 13.I.1904.

17. See Tamayo Herrera 1981, 107–108; Valcárcel 1981.

18. This photography studio was founded in the 1890s by a group of English evangelical missionaries, who left the studio and all its equipment to the González family as payment for back rent. J. G. González retained the name "Fotografía Inglesa" for his business, which was inherited by his sons and grandsons (interview with Washington González, Cusco, July 1986).

19. "Arte Nacional. Plumadas," La Union (Cusco), 10.V.1905.

20. He was, for example, associate director of Cusco's Academia de Arte. He was also

close to the circle of scholars who made up the Centro Científico del Cusco, an organization devoted to promoting progress through the reclamation of Cusco's jungle resources. Figueroa would later serve as subprefect for one of these lowland provinces.

21. Escalante 1908.

22. Escalante, 1908.

23. "Notas de arte," *El Ferrocarril* (Cusco), 30.I.1908.

24. J. Castro 1908.

25. "Notas de arte," *El Ferrocarril* (Cusco), 30.I.1908.

26. Obituary, 1951 (typescript).

27. Graña 1964; Graña and Graña 1990; Brown 1985.

28. See Williams 1983 and Graña 1964.

29. Similar discrepancies emerge between the European Romantic tradition and its contemporary imitators in oligarchic Lima of the 1840s. Whereas European bohemians became associated with a secular public sphere of cultural discussion, Lima artists relied on the personal patronage of wealthy sponsors such as don Miguel del Carpio. One Peruvian critic has described the period: "Peruvian romanticismo germinates . . . not in a *café*, nor on the street corner, but rather in an elegant mansion, perfumed and enriched by an atmosphere of patronage [*mecenazgo*] and protection" (Arriola Grande 1967, 19).

30. "La Exposición de Arte," *El Comercio* (Cusco), 4.X.1922.

31. "Teatro," *La Union* (Cusco), ?.X.1907; theater poster dated Cusco, 30 May 1907, in the collection of Sra. Ubaldina Yabar de Figueroa, Lima. In Dicenta's play, written in 1893, Luciano is an artist "guided by reverie, poetry and the world of the muses" who battles a world of materialism and shallow bourgeois women (Mas Ferrer 1978).

32. Obituary, *La Prensa* (Lima), 20.II.1951.

33. "Ante unos cuadros de J. M. Figueroa Aznar," *El Comercio* (Lima), ?.IV.1951. In a 1937 interview, for example, Figueroa describes himself as an "enemy of publicity" who had just arrived at his Arequipa exhibit from mines in "the furthest corner of the earth . . . removed from all contact with the civilized world" ("Una Exposición de más de 40 cuadros . . .," *Noticias* [Arequipa], 20.I.1937).

34. Prior to the 1920s Indians appear in the work of only one Peruvian painter, Francisco Laso, and even these appearances are not based on authentic models. In 1868 Laso photographed himself dressed in Indian clothes as a model for his paintings. Although the similarities between Laso's and Figueroa's self-portrait work are suggestive, it is doubtful that Figueroa would have known about Laso's photographs, which were never publicly exhibited. Laso's photographs are reproduced in McElroy 1985, plates 41–42. More precedents exist for indigenista literature; see Delgado 1980 and Cornejo Polar 1980.

35. In 1910 the American Alberto Giesecke was appointed rector of the University of Cusco. The new curriculum he imposed emphasized European philosophers such as Spengler, Ortega y Gasset, Froebenius, Taine, and Simmel. See Tamayo 1980, 187; Tamayo 1981, 123–126; and Valcárcel 1981. At the other end of the "Golden Age," 1930 marks the end of President Augusto Leguía's dictatorship.

36. Taine 1875. Similar theories regarding national identity and the telluric landscape were developed by Bolivian indigenistas during roughly the same period; see Queiser Morales 1984.

37. On Bergson, see Sivirichi 1937 and Valcárcel 1981, 217.

38. Tamayo 1981, 102.

39. The Argentines' concern with both linguistic purity and criollismo came out of the context of massive state-supported European immigration to Buenos Aires in the early twentieth century. See Romero 1965 and Sarlo 1983.

40. The Cusco indigenistas insisted that Andean culture transcended national boundaries. This would influence the Aprista doctrine of "Indo-America" (Haya de la Torre 1935).

41. García 1973, 90–91; emphasis in original. Inkario was Valcárcel's term for his vision of a restored Inca culture.

42. Sivirichi 1937, 21.

43. Yepez Miranda 1940, 30.

44. Cusco's neo-Indianist painting is best described as costumbrista in both style and composition (see Chapter Four). Influences came from Spanish localism and the indigenista painting of northern Argentina.

45. In one review, Cubism—which the author describes as the "craziness [chifladura] of a few"—is derided for portraying "what appears rather than what is" (Fernando Mollinedo, "Notas del Día. Palique," El Sol [Cusco], 6.V.1911).

46. Williams 1983.

47. Early twentieth-century coastal Limeño artists were similarly situated with respect to their primitive or peasant "other." Criollo artists such as José Sabogal, Camilo Blas, and Julia Codesido used the Indian to develop a formal pictorial style based on woodcut technology, stylistic borrowings from European expressionist painting, and imitation of popular iconography. These abstract representations of Indians and Andean culture formed part of a leftist political revindication of peasant culture during the 1920s and 1930s. See Mariategui 1987c, d.

48. The clearly defined historical and cultural dichotomy of Inca versus Spaniard in Valcárcel's brand of indigenismo facilitated its acceptance in Lima. Valcárcel's writings influenced the ideas of José Carlos Mariátegui and the Socialist Party he helped to form. Valcárcel himself moved to Lima in 1931, where he served as director of the National Museum and Minister of Education. García meanwhile remained in Cusco as a member of the Communist Party. It is partly because of his allegiance to the local politics and regionalist claims of Cusco that García's "New Indian" movement predominated over Valcárcel's brand of "Incaism" as the philosophy shaping a distinctively Cusqueño discourse of indigenismo during the 1930s and 1940s. In later decades, however, and in part as the (ironic) result of his political influence in Lima, Valcárcel's vision of the Inkario would come to dominate Cusqueño cultural discourse (see Nieto Degregori 1995).

49. Exhibitions of Chambi's photographs have been mounted in the Museum of Modern Art in New York as well as in Europe. For a critical analysis of Chambi's work written from the perspective of European photographic history, see Kozloff 1985, 155–166.

50. Valcárcel 1981, 218–221. In Valcárcel's doctrine of indigenismo, "neo-Inca" art was to be based on the careful scientific study and adoption of authentic Inca styles and motifs.

51. An advertisement for Figueroa's commercial photography studio in the 1921 Guia del Sur del Perú offers photographs of indigenous types and includes reproductions of two such photographs.

52. In the early 1910s, a shift occurs in Figueroa's work from foto-óleos, landscapes, nudes, and copies of religious themes to paintings focused almost exclusively on themes pertaining to Indian and Inca subjects. For examples of the type photographs Figueroa sold to tourists, see Figure 7.6 and the advertisements for his studio in the 1921 edition of the *Guía general del Sur del Perú* (pp. 130, 189, 195). The *Guía* was a guide for businesses, tourists, and travelers.

53. Uriel García, *El Sol* (Cusco), 2.VII.1908. José Gabriel Cosio similarly describes Paucartambo's influence on Figueroa's work as a product of its "reverie and tragedy because it is in the solemnity of its snow-capped mountains and in the plasticity of its forests that the tragedy of emotion resides" (*El Pueblo* [Arequipa], 17.II.1957). Another critic traces Figueroa's fame as a landscape artist to "that exuberant Paucartambo region [which is] near the domain of the jungle, yet also, on the other side, nestled [*encajada*] in the ruggedness of the Andes" (*El Comercio* [Cusco], 4.X.1922).

54. Even in the case of such archaeological landscapes, the New Indianists—for whom the camera was an instrument of modernity and therefore anathema to the telluric sentiments of Cusco—claimed that it was the landscape itself and not the camera that "captured" the scene. Thus, for example, in a recent film about Martín Chambi, Atilio Sivirichi describes a process whereby an (archaeological) landscape "casts a spell" (*hechizo*) upon Chambi's film (Atilio Sivirichi interviewed in the film "Martín Chambi and the Heirs of the Incas," by Andy Harris and Paul Yule, 1986).

55. Sivirichi 1937, 21.

56. José Gabriel Cosio, "Obituario," *El Comercio del Cusco*, 1951; undated clipping, Luis Figueroa Yabar, personal archive.

57. See Chapter Five.

58. Huyssen 1986, vi.

## Chapter Eight

1. Both brothers took photographs, although only Crisanto, who had studied with Martín Chambi, was able to work full time as a photographer (Benavente 1995, 11).

2. Barthes 1981.

3. Interview with David Salas, Cusco 1986.

4. Sending a son into the clergy was one common way for aspiring families in the lower rungs of the landed classes to better their social standing. The larger landholding and incipiently bourgeois families, such as the Romainvilles, by comparison, rarely sent sons into the seminary.

5. On the one hand, the overwhelming majority of the family portraits that we found in the Cusco archives did not include adult males. On the other hand, the archives included an almost equally large number of photographs of public or official events in which women figured hardly at all.

6. My understanding of the photographic frame builds on Christian Metz's concept of the "off-frame effect" through which photographs acquire their fetishlike qualities. Metz argues that the photograph differs from film owing to the nature of its frame and the ways in which the frame "marks the place of an irreversible absence, a place from which the look has been forever averted" (1985, 87).

7. Foucault; paraphrased in Stoler 1995, 72.

8. Gilroy 1993, 2.

9. On the other (more pessimistic) hand, the portraits can just as easily be read as inept appropriations of the languages of style and distinction that shaped a modern European photographic self.

10. Williams 1973.

11. Foucault 1991, 1992; Stoler 1995.

# References

Adorno, Rolena (ed.). 1986. *Guaman Poma: Writing and Resistance in Colonial Peru.* Austin: Univ. of Texas Press.

————. 1991. *Transatlantic Encounters: Europeans and Andeans in the Sixteenth Century.* Berkeley: Univ. of California Press.

Alatas, S. H. 1977. *The Myth of the Lazy Native.* London: F. Cass.

Alloula, Malek. 1986. *The Colonial Harem.* Minneapolis: Univ. of Minnesota Press.

Altman, Janet Gurkin. 1990. "Making Room for Peru: Graffigny's Novel Reconsidered." In C. Lafarge (ed.), *Dilemmas du Roman: Essays in Honor of Georges May*, pp. 33–46. Saratoga, Calif.: Anma Libra.

Anderson, Benedict. 1991. *Imagined Communities.* London: Verso.

Angrand, Leonce. 1972. In C. Milla Batres (ed.), *Imagen del Perú en el siglo XIX*. Lima: Milla Batres.

Anonymous. 1748. *A True and Particular Relation of the Dreadful Earthquake which hapen'd at Lima, the Capital of Peru, and the neighbouring Port of Callao, on the 28th of October, 1746.* London: T. Osborne.

Antmann, Fran. 1983. "Sebastián Rodríguez's View from Within: The Work of an Andean Photographer in the Mining Town of Morococha, Peru, 1928–1968." Doctor of Arts dissertation, New York Univ.

Arriola Grande, Maurilio. 1967 [1948]. *José Arnaldo Marquéz y Martín Fierro.* Junin: Festival del Libro.

Atkinson, G. 1972 [1924]. *Les Relations de Voyage du XVIIᵉ siècle et l'evolution des idées.* Geneva: Slatkine Reprints.

Bachelier, D. (ed. Durret). 1720. *Voyage de Marseilles à Lima.* Paris: Jean Baptiste Coignard.

Banton, Michael. 1987. *Racial Theories.* New York: Cambridge Univ. Press.

Barthes, Roland. 1977. *Image, Music, Text.* New York: Hill & Wang.

————. 1981. *Camera Lucida.* New York: Hill & Wang.

Basadre, Jorge. 1968. *Historia de la República del Perú, 1822–1933.* Lima: Edit. Universitaria.

Baudelaire, Charles. 1980 [1859]. "The Modern Public and Photography." In A. Trachtenberg (ed.), *Classic Essays on Photography*, pp. 83–89. New Haven: Leete's Island Books.

Baudrillard, Jean. 1981. *For a Critique of the Political Economy of the Sign.* St. Louis: Telos Press.

Baxley, H. Willis. 1865. *What I Saw on the West Coast of South and North America and at the Hawaiian Islands.* New York: D. Appleton & Co.

Benavente, Adelma. 1995. "Photography in Southern Peru, 1900–1930." In *Peruvian Photography: Images from the Southern Andes, 1900–1945*, pp. 8–12. Colchester: Univ. of Essex.

Benjamin, Walter. 1969 [1936]. "The Work of Art in the Age of Mechanical Reproduction." In Benjamin, *Illuminations*, pp. 217–251. New York: Schocken.

Benjamin, Walter. 1980 [1931]. "A Short History of Photography." In A. Trachtenberg (ed.), *Classic Essays on Photography*, pp. 199–216. New Haven: Leete's Island Books.

Bertillon, Alphonse. 1882. *Les Races sauvages*. Paris: G. Masson.

———. 1885. *Instructions signalétiques*. Paris: Melun.

Bertillon, Alphonse, and Arthur Chervin. 1909. *Anthropologie métrique: Conseils pratiques aux missionaires scientifiques sur la manière de mesurer, de photographier et de décrire des sujets vivants et des pièces anatomiques*. Paris: Imp. Nationale.

Blumenbach, Johannes Friederich. 1795. "On the Natural Variety of Mankind." In *The Anthropological Treatises of Johann Friedrich Blumenbach*, pp. 65–276. London: Anthropological Society of London.

Bolton, Richard (ed.). 1989. *The Contest of Meaning: Critical Histories of Photography*. Cambridge: MIT Press.

Bonilla, Heraclio. 1974. *Guano y burguesía en el Perú*. Lima: IEP.

Botting, Douglas. 1973. *Humboldt and the Cosmos*. New York: Harper & Row.

Bourdieu, Pierre. 1965. *Un Art moyen*. Paris: Minuit.

Bowler, Peter J. 1973. "Bonnet and Buffon: Theories of Generation and the Problem of Species," *Journal of the History of Biology*, 6 (2):259–281.

Brading, D. A. 1991. *The First America: The Spanish Monarchy, Creole Patriots, and the Liberal State, 1492–1867*. Cambridge and New York: Cambridge Univ. Press.

Braun, T.E.D. 1989. "Introduction." In *The Complete Works of Voltaire*, vol. 14, pp. 1–103. Oxford: Voltaire Foundation.

Breman, J. (ed.). 1990. *Imperial Monkey Business: Racial Supremacy in Social Darwinist Theory and Colonial Practice*. Amsterdam: VU Univ. Press.

Bresson, André. 1886. *Sept années d'explorations, de voyages et de séjours dans l'Amérique Australe*. Paris: Challamel Aîné.

Broc, Numa. 1969. *Les Montagnes vues par les géographes et les naturalistes de langue française au XVIIIᵉ siècle*. Paris: Bibliothèque Nationale.

———. 1974. *La Géographie des philosophes: Géographes et voyageurs français au XVIIIᵉ siècle*. Paris: Edition Ophrys.

Broca, Paul. 1864 [1856]. *On the Phenomena of Hybridity in the Genus Homo*. London: Longman, Green, Longman & Roberts.

———. 1875. "Instructions craniométriques," *Bulletins de la Société d'Anthropologie*, 10:337–367.

Bromley, Juana. 1944. *Virreyes, cabildantes y oidores*. Lima: P. Barrantes.

Brown, Marilyn R. 1985. *Gypsies and Other Bohemians: The Myth of the Artist in Nineteenth-Century France*. Ann Arbor: UMI Research Press.

Bruhns, Karl. 1873. *Life of Alexander von Humboldt*. 2 vols. London: Longmans, Green & Co.

Bryson, Norman. 1983. *Vision and Painting: The Logic of the Gaze*. New Haven: Yale Univ. Press.

Buck-Morss, Susan. 1989. *The Dialectics of Seeing: Walter Benjamin and the Arcades Project*. Cambridge: MIT Press.

Buffon, Georges-Louis Leclerc, Comte de. 1749–1809. *Histoire naturelle, générale et particulière*. Vols. 1–44. Paris.

Burga, Manuel, and Alberto Flores-Galindo. 1987. *Apogeo y crisis de la república aristocrática*. 4th ed. Lima: Ed. Rikchay Perú.

Callirgos, Juan Carlos. 1993. *El Racismo: La Cuestión del otro y de uno*. Lima: Desco.

Cannon, Susan Faye. 1978. *Science in Culture: The Early Victorian Period*. New York: Dawson & Science History Publ.

Carbia, Romulo D. 1943. *Historia de la leyenda negra Hispano-Americana*. Buenos Aires: Ed. Orientación Española.

Carrey, Emile. 1875. *Le Pérou: Tableau descriptif, historique et analytique des êtres et des choses de ce pays*. Paris: Garnier Frères.

Castillo, Teófilo. 1919. "Palos y palmas," *El Comercio* (Lima); reprinted in "Los Triunfos artísticos de Figueroa Aznar en Lima," *El Comercio del Cusco*, May 8, 1919.

Castro, Fernando. 1990. "Photographers of a Young Republic: Being French in Courret's Lima," *Lima Times*, Dec. 14, pp. 6–7.

Castro, Julio. 1908. "Culto por el arte," *El Sol*, Jan. 30.

Chatterjee, Partha. 1993. *The Nation and Its Fragments: Colonial and Postcolonial Histories*. Princeton: Princeton Univ. Press.

Chervin, Arthur. 1908. *Anthropologie bolivienne*. 3 vols. Paris: Imp. Nationale.

Chiapelli, F. (ed.). 1976. *First Images of America*. Berkeley: Univ. of California Press.

Chinard, Gilbert. 1913. *L'Amérique et le rêve exotique dans la littérature française du XVIIᵉ au XVIIIᵉ siècle*. Paris: Lib. Hachette.

Chiriboga, Lucía, and Silvana Caparrini. 1994. *Identidades desnudas: Ecuador, 1860–1920*. Quito: Abya-Yala, Ildis, and Taller Visual.

Chow, Rey. 1995. *Primitive Passions: Visuality, Sexuality, Ethnography, and Contemporary Chinese Cinema*. New York: Columbia Univ. Press.

Cohen, William B. 1980. *The French Encounter with Africans: White Response to Blacks, 1530–1880*. Bloomington: Indiana Univ. Press.

Coleman, William. 1964. *Georges Cuvier, Zoologist*. Cambridge: Harvard Univ. Press.

Conlon, Pierre M. 1967. "La Condamine the Inquisitive," *Studies on Voltaire and the Eighteenth Century*, 55:361–393.

Cornejo Polar, Antonio. 1980. *Literatura y sociedad en el Perú: La Novela indigenista*. Lima: IEP.

Courtine, Jean-Jacques, and Claudine Haroche. 1989. *Histoire du visage, XVIᵉ début XIXᵉ siècle*. Paris: Editions Rivages.

Cowling, Mary. 1989. *The Artist as Anthropologist: The Representation of Type and Character in Victorian Art*. New York: Cambridge Univ. Press.

Crary, Jonathan. 1989. "Spectacle, Attention, Counter-Memory," *October*, 50:97–107.

———. 1990. *Techniques of the Observer: On Vision and Modernity in the Nineteenth Century*. Cambridge: MIT Press.

Cummins, Tom. 1988. "Abstraction to Narration: Kero Imagery of Perú and the Colonial Alteration of Native Identity." Ph.D. dissertation, Univ. of California, Los Angeles.

Cuvier, Georges. 1836–1849. *Le Regne animal*. Paris: Fortin, Masson et Cie.

———. 1828. *Histoire naturelle des poissons*. Paris: Levrault.

Daguerre, Louis Jacques Mandé. 1980 [1839]. "Daguerreotype." In A. Trachtenberg (ed.), *Classic Essays in Photography*, pp. 11–13. New Haven: Leete's Island Books.

Dahlgren, E. W. 1909. *Les Relations commerciales et maritimes entre la France et les côtes de l'Océan Pacifique: Le Commerce de la Mer du Sud*. Paris: Champion.

Debord, Guy. 1977. *Society of the Spectacle*. Detroit: Red and Black.

———. 1988. *Commentaires sur la société du spectacle*. Paris: Gérard Lebovici.

Delgado, Washington. 1980. *Historia de la literatura republicana*. Lima: Ed. Rikchay Perú.

de Lery, Jean. 1990 [1578]. *History of a Voyage to the Land of Brazil*. Berkeley: Univ. of California Press.

Deustua, José, and José Luis Rénique. 1984. *Intelectuales, indigenismo y descentralismo en el Perú, 1897–1931*. Cusco: CERA Bartolomé de Las Casas.

Diderot, Denis. 1966 [1772]. "Supplement to Bougainville's Voyage." In L. G. Crocker (ed.), *Diderot's Selected Writings*. New York: Macmillan.

Disdéri, André Adolphe Eugène. 1862. *L'Art de la Photographie*. Paris: Disdéri.

d'Orbigny, Alcides Dessaignes. 1839. *L'Homme américain (de l'Amérique méridionale) considéré sous ses rapports physiologiques et moraux*. Paris: Pitois-Levrault.

———. 1854. *Voyage dans les deux Amériques*. Paris: n.p.

d'Orbigny, Alcides Dessaignes, and J. B. Eyries. 1842. *Viaje pintoresco a las dos Américas, Asia y África*. Barcelona: Juan Oliveres.

Douthwaite, Julia V. 1991. "Relocating the Exotic Other in Graffigny's *Lettres d'une Péruvienne*," *Romanic Review*, 82 (4):456–474.

Duchet, M. 1971. *Anthropologie et histoire au siècle des Lumières*. Paris: Maspéro.

Duviols, Jean-Paul. 1978. *Voyageurs français en Amérique: Colonies espagnoles et portugaises*. Paris: Bordas.

Edwards, Elizabeth. 1992. *Anthropology and Photography, 1860–1920*. New Haven and London: Yale Univ. Press and the Royal Anthropological Institute.

Escalante, José Angel. 1908. "Impresiones de arte." *El Sol* (Cusco), Jan. 31.

Fabian, Johannes. 1983. *Time and the Other: How Anthropology Makes Its Other*. New York: Columbia Univ. Press.

Feuillée, Louis. 1714. *Journal des observations physiques, mathematiques et botaniques, faites par l'ordre du Roy sur les Côtes Orientales de l'Amérique Meridionale et dans les Indes Occidentales, depuis l'année 1707 jusques en 1712*. 5 vols. Paris.

Figlio, Karl M. 1975. "Theories of Perception and the Physiology of Mind in the Late Eighteenth Century," *History of Science*, 12:177–212.

Flores Araoz, José. 1975. "Presencia de Rugendas en el Perú." In Rugendas 1975, pp. 9–88.

Flores-Galindo, Alberto. 1977. *Arequipa y el Sur Andino*. Lima: Univ. Pacífica.

———. 1984. *Aristocracia y plebe: Lima, 1760–1830*. Lima: Mosca Azul.

———. 1987. *Buscando un Inca: Identidad y utopia en los Andes*. Lima: Instituto de Apoyo Agrario.

Foucault, Michel. 1973a [1963]. *The Birth of the Clinic: An Archaeology of Medical Perception*. New York: Vintage.

———. 1973b [1966]. *The Order of Things: An Archaeology of the Human Sciences*. New York: Vintage.

———. 1979 [1975]. *Discipline and Punish: The Birth of the Prison*. New York: Vintage.

———. 1980a [1976]. *The History of Sexuality*. Vol. 1. New York: Vintage.

———. 1980b [1977]. "The Eye of Power." In Foucault, *Power/Knowledge: Selected Interviews and Other Writings, 1972–1977*, pp. 146–165. New York: Pantheon.

———. 1991. "Faire vivre et laisser mourir: La Naissance du racisme," *Les Temps Modernes*, no. 535:37–61.

———. 1992. *Genealogia del racismo*. Madrid: La Piqueta.

Freund, Gisèle. 1980. *Photography and Society*. Boston: Godine.

Frezier, Amadeus. 1982 [1716]. *Relación del viaje por el Mar del Sur*. Caracas: Biblioteca Ayacucho.

Fuentes, Manuel Atanasio. 1858. *Estadística general de Lima*. Lima: Tip. Nacional.

——. 1866. *Mémoire sur le coca du Pérou*. Paris: Imp. de Ad. Lainé et J. Havard.

——. 1867a. *Lima: Esquisses historiques, statistiques, administratives, commerciales et morales*. Paris: Lib. de Firmin Didot Frères et Fils.

——. 1867b. *Lima: Apuntes históricos. estadísticos, administrativos, comerciales y de costumbres*. Paris: Lib. de Firmin Didot.

——. 1867c. *Sketches of the Capital of Peru: Historical, Statistical, Administrative, Commercial and Moral*. London: Trubner & Co.

García, Uriel. 1973 [1930]. *El Nuevo Indio*. Lima: Colección Autores Peruanos.

Garcilaso de la Vega, El Inca. 1632. *Le Commentaire royal*. Paris: A. Courbé.

Gay, Peter. 1966. *The Enlightenment: An Interpretation*. Vol. 2, *The Rise of Modern Paganism*. New York: Alfred A. Knopf.

Gerbi, Antonello. 1982 [1955]. *La Disputa del nuevo mundo: Historia de una polémica, 1750–1900*. Mexico City: Fondo de Cultura Económica.

Gernsheim, Helmut. 1988. *The Rise of Photography, 1850–1880: The Age of Collodion*. London: Thames & Hudson.

Gibson, Charles (ed.). 1971. *The Black Legend: Anti-Spanish Attitudes in the Old World and New*. New York: Knopf.

Gilman, Sander L. 1986. "Black Bodies, White Bodies: Toward an Iconography of Female Sexuality in Late Nineteenth Century Art, Medicine, and Literature." In H. L. Gates (ed.), *"Race," Writing, and Difference*, pp. 223–261. Chicago: Univ. of Chicago Press.

Gilroy, Paul. 1993. *The Black Atlantic: Modernity and Double Consciousness*. Cambridge: Harvard Univ. Press.

Girardet, Raoul. 1972. *L'Idée coloniale en France, de 1871 à 1962*. Paris: La Table Ronde.

Glacken, Clarence J. 1967. *Traces on the Rhodian Shore: Nature and Culture from Ancient Times to the End of the Eighteenth Century*. Berkeley: Univ. of California Press.

Gobineau, Joseph Arthur de. 1854. *Essai sur l'inégalité des races humaines*. Paris: Firmin Didot.

Gootenberg, Paul. 1989. *Between Silver and Guano: Commercial Policy and the State in Post-Independence Peru*. Princeton: Princeton Univ. Press.

——. 1991. "Population and Ethnicity in Early Republican Peru," *Latin American Research Review*, 26 (3):109–157.

——. 1993. *Imagining Development: Economic Ideas in Peru's Fictitious Prosperity of Guano, 1840–1880*. Berkeley: Univ. of California Press.

Gould, Stephen Jay. 1981. *The Mismeasure of Man*. New York: W. W. Norton.

Grafigny, Françoise de. 1752. *Lettres d'une péruvienne*. Paris: Duchesne Lib.

——. 1990 [1747]. *Lettres d'une péruvienne*. Paris: Côtes-Femmes.

——. N.d. *Letters of a Peruvian Princess with the Sequel*. London: Aspin Printers.

Graham-Brown, Sarah. 1988. *Images of Women: The Portrayal of Women in Photography of the Middle East, 1860–1950*. New York: Columbia Univ. Press.

Graña, Cesar. 1964. *Bohemian versus Bourgeois: French Society and the French Man of Letters in the Nineteenth Century*. New York: Basic Books.

Graña, Cesar, and Marigay Graña. 1990. *On Bohemia: The Codes of the Self-Exiled*. New Brunswick, N.J.: Rutgers Univ. Press.

Guerrero, Juan Agustín. 1981 [1852]. *Imágenes del Ecuador del siglo XIX*. Quito: Fundación Hallo.

Gutman, Judith Mara. 1982. *Through Indian Eyes*. New York: ICP.

Hacking, Ian. 1990. *The Taming of Chance*. Cambridge: Cambridge Univ. Press.

Hanke, Lewis. 1952. *Bartolomé de Las Casas, Bookman, Scholar and Propagandist*. Philadelphia: Univ. of Pennsylvania Press.

Hartmann, Pierre. 1989. "Le Lettres d'une Péruvienne dans l'histoire du roman epistolaire." In *Vierge du Soleil/Fille des Lumières: La Péruvienne de Mme. de Grafigny et ses suites*, pp. 93–111. Strasbourg: Presses Universitaires de Strasbourg.

Hassner, Rune. 1987. "Amateur Photography." In Jean-Claude Lemagny and André Rouillé (eds.), *A History of Photography*, pp. 80–102. Cambridge: Cambridge Univ. Press.

Haya de la Torre, Víctor Raúl. 1935. *A dónde va Indoamérica?* Santiago de Chile: Editorial Ercilla.

Hervé, G. 1910 [1800]. "A la recherche d'un manuscrit: Les Instructions anthropologiques de Georges Cuvier," *Revue de l'Ecole d'Anthropologie de Paris*, 20:289–306.

Hirschman, Albert O. 1977. *The Passions and the Interests: Political Arguments for Capitalism before Its Triumph*. Princeton: Princeton Univ. Press.

Hobsbawm, Eric. 1987. *The Age of Empire, 1875–1914*. New York: Pantheon.

————. 1990a. *Echoes of the Marseillaise*. New Brunswick, N.J.: Rutgers Univ. Press.

————. 1990b. *Nations and Nationalism since 1780*. Cambridge: Cambridge Univ. Press.

Holmes, Oliver Wendell. 1863. "Doings of the Sunbeam." *Atlantic Monthly*, 12 (69), July 1863, pp. 1–15.

————. 1980 [1859]. "The Stereoscope and the Stereograph." In A. Trachtenberg (ed.), *Classic Essays on Photography*, pp. 71–82. New Haven: Leete's Island Books.

Honour, Hugh. 1975. *The New Golden Land: European Images of America from the Discoveries to the Present Time*. New York: Pantheon.

Hulme, Peter. 1986. *Colonial Encounters: Europe and the Native Caribbean, 1492–1797*. New York: Methuen.

Humboldt, Alexander von. 1805. *Essai sur la géographie des plants*. Paris.

————. 1810. *Vues des cordillères et monumens des peuples indigènes de l'Amérique*. Paris: Chez F. Schoell, 1810.

————. 1814–1825. *Relation historique du voyage aux régions équinoxiales du nouveau continent*. 3 vols. Paris: G. Dufour.

————. 1850 [1826]. *Aspects of Nature, in Different Lands and Different Climates with Scientific Elucidations*. Philadelphia: Lea and Blanchard.

————. 1852. *Personal Narrative of Travels to the Equinoctial Regions of America during the Years 1799–1804*. 3 vols. London: Henry G. Bohn.

————. 1978. *Kosmos*. Stuttgart: Brockhaus Komm. Antiquarium Series.

————. 1980 [1803]. "Carta a Don Ignacio Checa." In Charles Minguet (ed.), *Cartas americanas*, pp. 106–107. Caracas: Ayacucho.

Huyssen, Andreas. 1986. *After the Great Divide: Modernism, Mass Culture, Postmodernism*. Bloomington: Univ. of Indiana Press.

Jay, Martin. 1988. "Scopic Regimes of Modernity." In Jay, *Force-Fields: Between Intellectual History and Cultural Critique*, pp. 115–133. New York and London: Routledge.

Juan, Jorge, and Antonio de Ulloa. 1748. *Relación histórica del viaje a la América meridional*. 5 vols. Madrid.

Juderias, Julian. 1954 [1914]. *La Leyenda negra*. Madrid: Editora National.

Kaplan, James M. 1973. *"La Neuvaine De Cythère*: Une Démarmontélisation de Marmontel," *Studies on Voltaire and the Eighteenth Century*, 113.

———. 1987. "The Stockholm Manuscript of Marmontel's *Les Incas*," *Studies on Voltaire and the Eighteenth Century*, 249:359–378. Oxfordshire: Voltaire Foundation.

Keen, Benjamin. 1971. *The Aztec Image in Western Thought*. New Brunswick, N.J.: Rutgers Univ. Press.

Keller, Evelyn Fox, and Christine Grontkowski. 1983. "The Mind's Eye." In S. Harding and M. B. Hintikka (eds.), *Discovering Reality: Feminist Perspectives on Epistemology, Metaphysics, Methodology, and Philosophy of Science*, pp. 207–224. Dordrecht: D. Reidel Publishing.

Kiernan, V. G. 1969. *The Lords of Human Kind: Black Man, Yellow Man, and White Man in an Age of Empire*. New York: Columbia Univ. Press.

Kozloff, Max. 1985. *The Privileged Eye*. Albuquerque: Univ. of New Mexico Press.

Krauss, Rosalind. 1989. "Photography's Discursive Spaces." In R. Bolton (ed.), *The Contest of Meaning: Critical Histories of Photography*, pp. 286–301. Cambridge: MIT Press.

Kremer-Marietti, Angèle. 1984. "L'Anthropologie physique et morale en France et ses implications idéologiques." In B. Rupp-Eisenreich (ed.), *Histoire de l'anthropologie (XVIe-XIXe siècles)*, pp. 319–351. Paris: Klinck-Sieck.

La Condamine, Charles Marie de. 1745. *Relation abrégée d'un voyage fait dans l'intérieur de l'Amérique méridionale*. Paris: Veuve Pissot.

———. 1751. *Journal du voyage vait par ordre du Roi a l'Equateur*. Paris: L'Imprimerie Royale.

———. 1778. *Relation abrégée d'un voyage fait dans l'intérieur de l'Amérique méridionale*. Maastricht: Jean Edma du Four et Phillippe Roux.

Lago, Thomas. 1960. *Rugendas: Pintor romántico de Chile*. Santiago de Chile: Ed. Universidad de Chile.

Laissus, Yves. 1964. "Le Jardin du Roi." In René Taton (ed.), *Enseignement et diffusion des sciences en France au XVIII siècle*, pp. 287–319. Paris: Hermann.

Larson, Brooke. 1988. *Colonialism and Agrarian Transformation in Bolivia. Cochabamba, 1550–1900*. Princeton: Princeton Univ. Press.

Lauer, Mirko. 1976. *Introducción a la pintura peruana del siglo XX*. Lima: Mosca Azul.

Lutz, Catherine, and Jane L. Collins. 1993. *Reading National Geographic*. Chicago: Univ. of Chicago Press.

MacCormack, Sabine. 1991. *Religion in the Andes: Vision and Imagination in Early Colonial Perú*. Princeton: Princeton Univ. Press.

Macera dall'Orso, Pablo. 1976. *La Imágen francesa del Perú (siglos XVI–XIX)*. Lima: Instituto Nacional de Cultura.

Malefijt, Annemarie de Waal. 1974. *Images of Man: A History of Anthropological Thought*. New York: Knopf.

Mallon, Florencia. 1983. *The Defense of Community in Peru's Central Highlands: Peasant Struggle and Capitalist Transition, 1860–1940*. Princeton: Princeton Univ. Press.

Mannsaker, Frances. 1990. "Elegancy and Wildness: Reflections of the East in the Eighteenth-Century Imagination." In G. S. Rousseau and R. Porter (eds.), *Exoticism in the Enlightenment*, pp. 175–195. Manchester: Manchester Univ. Press.

Manrique, Nelson. 1993. *El Universo mental de la conquista de America*. Lima: DESCO.

Mariategui, José Carlos. 1987a [1926]. "Arte, revolución y decadencia." In Mariategui, *El Artista y la época*, pp. 18–22. Lima: Amauta.

———. 1987b [1930]. "El Balance del suprarrealismo." In Mariategui *El Artista y la época*, pp. 45–52. Lima: Amauta.

———. 1987c [1928]. "La obra de José Sabogal." In Mariategui, *El Artista y la época*, pp. 90–93. Lima: Amauta.

———. 1987d [1928]. "Julia Codesido." In Mariategui, *El Artista y la época*, pp. 97–98. Lima: Amauta.

Marmontel, Jean-François. 1777. *Les Incas, ou la destruction de l'Empire du Pérou*. 2 vols. Berne: Société Typographique.

———. 1819. *Les Incas ou La Destruction du Pérou*. 2 vols. Paris: Chez Verdière.

Martin, Luis. 1983. *Daughters of the Conquistadores: Women of the Viceroyalty of Perú*. Albuquerque: Univ. of New Mexico Press.

Martino, Pierre. 1906. *L'Orient dans la littérature française au XVIIᵉ et XVIIIᵉ*. Paris: Hachette.

Mas Ferrer, Jaime. 1978. *Vida, teatro, y mito de Joaquín Dicenta*. Alicante: Instituto de Estudios Alicantinos.

Masson, Paul Marie. 1972 [1930]. *L'Opéra de Rameau*. Reprint. New York: Dacapo.

Maurel, Christian. 1980. *L'Exotisme colonial*. Paris: Laffont.

McClintock, Anne. 1995. *Imperial Leather*. New York: Routledge.

McElroy, Keith. 1985. *Early Peruvian Photography: A Critical Case Study*. Ann Arbor: UMI Research Press.

Mejía Arango, Juan Luis. 1988. "La Fotografía." In Jorge Orlando Melo (ed.), *Historia de Antioquía*, pp. 447–453. Medellín, Colombia: SU.

Melgar, Mariano. 1878. *Poesías*. Nancy: Crépin-Leblond.

Mélon, Marc. 1987. "Beyond Reality: Art Photography." In Jean-Claude Lemagny and André Rouillé (eds.), *A History of Photography*, pp. 80–102. Cambridge: Cambridge Univ. Press.

Méndez, Cecilia. 1993. "Incas Sí, Indios No: Apuntes para el estudio del nacionalismo criollo en el Perú." Lima: Instituto de Estudios Peruanos, Documento de Trabajo no. 56.

Mercier, Roger. 1969. "Les Français en Amérique du Sud au XVIIIᵉ siècle: La Mission de l'Académie des Sciences (1735–1745)," *Revue Française d'Histoire d'Outre-Mer* (1969):327–374.

Metz, Christian. 1985. "Photography and Fetish," *October*, 34:81–90.

Minguet, Charles. 1969. *Alexandre de Humboldt, historien et géographe de l'Amérique espagnol, 1799–1804*. Paris: Maspéro.

———. 1991. "La Condamine en la obra de Alejandro de Humboldt." In R. Thiercelin (ed.), *Cultures et sociétés Andes et Méso-Amérique*, vol. 2, pp. 599–624. Aix-en-Provence: l'Université de Provence.

Mitchell, Timothy. 1988. *Colonising Egypt*. Cambridge and New York: Cambridge Univ. Press.

Mitchell, W.J.T. 1986. *Iconology, Image, Text, Ideology*. Chicago: Univ. of Chicago Press.

Montaigne, Michel de. 1892 [1580]. "Of Cannibals." In C. W. Hazlitt (ed.), *The Essays of Michel de Montaigne*, pp. 214–230. London: George Bell & Sons.

Montesquieu, Charles-Louis de Secondat, Baron de. 1964 [1721]. *The Persian Letters*. New York: Bobbs-Merrill.

Monti, Nicholas. 1987. *Africa Then: Photographs 1840–1918*. New York: Knopf.

Moravia, Sergio. 1967. "Philosophie et géographie à la fin du XVIII^e siècle," *Studies on Voltaire and the Eighteenth Century*, 57:937–1011.

————. 1980. "The Enlightenment and the Sciences of Man," *History of Science*, 18:247–268.

Mornet, D. 1911. *Les Sciences de la nature en France, au XVIII^e siècle*. Paris: Armand Colin.

Muratoria, Blanca. 1994. "Nación, identidad y etnicidad: Imágenes de los Indios ecuatorianos y sus imagineros a fines del siglo XIX." In B. Muratoria (ed.), *Imagenes e imagineros: Representaciones de los indígenas Ecuatorianos, siglos XIX y XX*, pp. 109–196. Quito: FLACSO.

Netton, Ian Richard. 1990. "The Mysteries of Islam." In G. S. Rousseau and R. Porter (eds.), *Exoticism in the Enlightenment*, pp. 23–45. Manchester: Manchester Univ. Press.

Nicoletti, Gianni (ed.). 1967. *Lettres d'une Péruvienne*. Bari: Adriatica Editrice.

Nicolson, Malcolm. 1987. "Alexander von Humboldt, Humboldtian Science, and the Origins of the Study of Vegetation," *History of Science*, 25:167–194.

Nieto Degregori, Luis. 1995. "Tres Momentos en la evolución del Cusqueñismo," *Márgenes*, año 6 (13/14):113–161.

Nochlin, Linda. 1971. *Realism*. London: Penguin Books.

————. 1983. "The Imaginary Orient." *Art in America* (May 1983):119–189.

————. 1988. *Women, Art, and Power*. New York: Harper & Row.

Noiriel, Gérard. 1988. *Le Creuset français: Histoire de l'immigration XIX^e–XX^e siècles*. Paris: Seuil.

————. 1992. *Population, immigration et identité nationale en France, XIX–XX siècle*. Paris: Hachette.

Nuñez, Estuardo. 1989. *Viajes y viajeros extranjeros por el Perú*. Lima: Concytec.

Pauw, Cornelius de. 1771. *Recherches philosophiques sur les Americains*. 3 vols. London.

Pease, Franklin. 1988. "Prólogo." In Manuel A. Fuentes, *Lima: Apuntes históricos, descriptivos, estadísticos y de costumbres* (1867), pp. 1–3. Lima: Banco Industrial del Perú.

Perkins, Merle E. 1943. "The Documentation of Voltaire's *Alzire*." *Modern Language Quarterly*, 4:433–436.

Phèline, Christian. 1985. *L'Image accusatrice*. Paris: Les Cahiers de la Photographie.

Pieterse, Jan Nederveen. 1992. *White on Black: Images of Africa and Blacks in Western Popular Culture*. New Haven: Yale Univ. Press.

Pinney, Christopher. 1992a. "The Parallel Histories of Anthropology and Photography." In E. Edwards (ed.), *Anthropology and Photography, 1860–1920*, pp. 74–95. New Haven and London: Yale Univ. Press and Royal Anthropological Institute.

————. 1992b. "Underneath the Banyan Tree: William Crooke and Photographic Depictions of Caste." In E. Edwards (ed.), *Anthropology and Photography, 1860–1920*, pp. 74–95. New Haven and London: Yale Univ. Press and Royal Anthropological Institute.

Platt, Tristan. 1984. "Liberalism and Ethnocide in the Southern Andes," *History Workshop Journal*, 17:3–18.

Poe, Edgar Allan. 1980 [1840]. "The Daguerreotype." In A. Trachtenberg (ed.), *Classic Essays on Photography*, pp. 37–38. New Haven: Leete's Island Books.

Pollock, Griselda. 1988. *Vision and Difference: Femininity, Feminism, and Histories of Art.* New York: Routledge.

———. 1992. "Painting, Feminism, History." In M. Barrett and A. Phillips (eds.), *Destabilizing Theory: Contemporary Feminist Debates*, pp. 138–176. Stanford: Stanford Univ. Press.

———. 1994. "Feminism/Foucault-Surveillance/Sexuality." In N. Bryson, M. A. Holly, and K. Moxsey (eds.), *Visual Culture: Images and Interpretations*, pp. 1–41. Hanover, N.H.: Wesleyan Univ. Press.

Pollock, Griselda, and L. Parker (eds). 1981. *Old Mistresses: Women, Art, and Ideology.* London: Pandora.

Poole, Deborah. 1990. "Ciencia, peligrosidad y represión en la criminología indigenista peruana." In C. Walker and C. Aguirre (eds.), *Bandolerismo, criminalidad y sociedad en Peru y Bolivia*, pp. 335–367. Lima: Instituto de Apoyo Agrario.

———. 1995. "Landscape and the Imperial Subject: U.S. Images of the Andes, 1859–1930." Paper presented at the conference "Rethinking the Post-Colonial Encounter," Yale University, Oct. 1995.

Poole, Deborah (ed.). 1994. *Unruly Order, Violence, Power, and Cultural Identity in the High Provinces of Southern Perú.* Denver: Westview Press.

Pougin, Arthur. 1971. "Introduction." In J.-P. Rameau and L. Fuzelier, *Les Indes galantes: Ballet héroique*, C. Poisot (ed.), pp. 1–9. Paris: Théodore Michaelis Editeur.

Pratt, Mary Louise. 1992. *Imperial Eyes: Travel Writing and Transculturation.* New York and London: Routledge.

Prochaska, David. 1990. "The Archive of *Algerie Imaginaire*," *History and Anthropology*, 4: 373–420.

Pucci, Suzanne Rodin. 1990. "The Discrete Charms of the Exotic: Fictions of the Harem in Eighteenth-Century France." In G. S. Rousseau and R. Porter (eds.), *Exoticism in the Enlightenment*, pp. 145–174. Manchester: Manchester Univ. Press.

Queiser Morales, Waltraud. 1984. "Philosophers, Ideology, and Social Change in Bolivia," *International Philosophical Quarterly*, 24:21–38.

Quiroz, Alfonso W. 1987. *La Deuda defraudada: Consolidación de 1850 y dominio económico en el Perú.* Lima: Instituto Nacional de Cultura.

Radiquet, Maximilian. 1874. *Souvenirs de l'Amerique espagnole: Chili-Pérou-Bresil.* Paris: Michel Lévy Frères.

Rameau, Jean-Phillipe, and Louis Fuzelier. 1971 [1735]. *Les Indes galantes.* New York: Broude Brothers Ltd.

Raynal, Guillaume-Thomas. 1770, 1774, 1781. *Histoire philosophique et politique, des éstablissmens and du commerce des européans dans les deux Indes.*

Renwick, John. 1974. *Voltaire and the Bélisaire Affair.* Studies on Voltaire and the Eighteenth Century, vol. 121. Oxfordshire: Voltaire Foundation.

Reynaud, Denis. 1990. "Pour une théorie de la description au 18è siècle," *Dix-Huitième Siècle*, 22:347–366.

Richert, Gertrude. 1959. *Johann Moritz Rugendas: Ein Deutscher Maler des XIX.* Berlin: Rembrandt-Verlag.

Rivera Cusicanqui, Silvia. 1993. "Anthropology and Society in the Andes," *Critique of Anthropology*, 13 (1): 77–96.

Robb, Bonnie Arden. 1992. "The Easy Virtue of a Peruvian Princess," *French Studies*, 46 (2):144–59.

Roger, Jacques. 1989. *Buffon: Un Philosophe au Jardin du Roi*. Paris: Fayard.

―――. 1993. *Les Sciences de la vie dans la pensée française du XVIII siècle*. 3rd ed. Paris: Albert Michel.

Romero, José Luis. 1965. *El desarrollo de las ideas en la sociedad argentina del siglo XX*. Mexico and Buenos Aires: Fondo de Cultura Económica.

Rorty, Richard. 1979. *Philosophy and the Mirror of Nature*. Princeton: Princeton Univ. Press.

Rose, Jacqueline. 1986. *Sexuality in the Field of Vision*. London: Verso.

Roseberry, William. 1989. *Anthropologies and Histories*. New Brunswick, N.J.: Rutgers Univ. Press.

Rouillé, André. 1982. *L'Empire de la photographie: Photographie et pouvoir bourgeois, 1839–1870*. Paris: Le Sycomore.

―――. 1984. "Les images photographiques du monde du travail sous le Second Empire," *Actes de la Recherche en Sciences Sociales*, no. 54 (Sept. 1984):31–44.

―――. 1987. "The Rise of Photography." In Jean-Claude Lemagny and André Rouillé (eds.), *A History of Photography*, pp. 29–52. New York: Cambridge Univ. Press.

―――. 1989. *La Photographie en France: Textes et controverses—Une Anthologie, 1816–1871*. Paris: Macula.

Rowe, John H. 1976. "El movimiento nacional inka del siglo XVIII." In A. Flores-Galindo (ed.), *Tupac Amaru II, 1780*, pp. 11–66. Lima: Retablo de Papel.

Rudwick, Martin, S.J. 1976. "The Emergence of a Visual Language for Geology, 1760–1840," *History of Science*, 14:149–195.

Rugendas, Juan Mauricio. 1968. *Rugendas a viagem pitoresca atraves do Brasil*. Rio de Janeiro: Ed. de Ouro.

―――. 1966. *J. M. Rugendas, Exposición de sus obras*. Buenos Aires: Museo Nacional de Bellas Artes.

―――. 1975. *El Perú romantico del siglo XIX*, C. Milla Batres (ed.). Lima: Milla Batres.

Rustin, Jacques. 1989. "Sur les *Suites* françaises des *Lettres d'une Péruvienne*." In *Vierge du Soleil/Fille des Lumières: La Péruvienne de Mme. de Grafigny et ses suites*, pp. 123–146. Strasbourg: Presses Universitaires de Strasbourg.

Said, Edward W. 1979. *Orientalism*. New York: Pantheon.

―――. 1993. *Culture and Imperialism*. New York: Knopf.

Saint-Cricq, Laurent, Viscomte de ("Paul Marcoy"). 1862–1866 [1848–1860]. "Voyage de l'Ocean Atlantique à l'Ocean Pacifique a travers l'Amerique du Sud," *Le Tour du Monde*, 6 (1862):81; 7 (1863):225–304; 8 (1863):97–144; 9 (1864):129–225; 10 (1864):129–193; 11 (1864):161–234; 12 (1865):161–221; 14 (1866):81–152.

Salgado, Sebastiao. 1986. *Other Americas*. New York: Pantheon.

Sarlo, Beatriz. 1983. "Vanguardia y criollismo: La Aventura de *Martín Fierro*." *Revista de Crítica Literaria Latinoamericana* (1983):39–69.

Schneider, Jean-Paul. 1989. "Les *Lettres d'une Péruvienne*: roman ouvert ou roman fermé?" In *Vierge du Soleil/Fille des Lumières: La Péruvienne de Mme. de Grafigny et ses suites*, pp. 7–48. Strasbourg: Presses Universitaires de Strasbourg.

Schor, Naomi. 1992. "Cartes Postales: Representing Paris 1900," *Critical Inquiry*, 18 (Winter 1992):188–244.

Sekula, Alan. 1983. "Photography between Labour and Capital." In B. Buchloh and B. Wilkie (eds.), *Mining Photographs and Other Pictures: A Selection from the Negative*

*Archives of Shedden Studio, Glace Bay, Cape Breton, 1948–1968.* Halifax: Nova Scotia College of Art and Design.

Sekula, Alan. 1984. *Photography against the Grain.* Halifax: Nova Scotia College of Art and Design.

―――. 1989. "The Body and the Archive." In R. Bolton (ed.), *The Contest of Meaning: Critical Histories of Photography*, pp. 343–389. Cambridge: MIT Press.

Serrano, Eduardo. 1983. *Historia de la fotografía en Colombia.* Bogotá: Museo de Arte Moderno.

Shohat, Ella. 1991. "Imaging Terra Incognita: The Disciplinary Gaze of Empire," *Public Culture*, 3 (2):41–70.

Silverblatt, Irene. 1987. *Moon, Sun, and Witches: Gender Ideologies and Class in Inca and Colonial Peru.* Princeton: Princeton Univ. Press.

Sivirichi, Atilio. 1937. "El Contenido espiritual del movimiento indigenista," *Revista Universitaria del Cuzco*, no. 72 (1937):21–22.

Sloan, Phillip R. 1976. "The Buffon-Linnaeus Controversy," *Isis*, 57:356–375.

―――. 1994. "Buffon Studies Today," *History of Science*, 32:469–477.

Solomon-Godeau, Abigail. 1981. "A Photographer in Jerusalem, 1855: Auguste Salzmann and His Times," *October*, 18:91–107.

Squier, Ephraim George. 1877. *Perú: Incidents of Travel and Exploration in the Land of the Incas.* New York: Harper & Brothers.

Squiers, Carol (ed.). 1990. *The Critical Image.* Seattle: Bay Press.

Stafford, Barbara Maria. 1984. *Voyage into Substance: Art, Science, Nature, and the Illustrated Travel Account, 1760–1840.* Cambridge: MIT Press.

Stafleu, Frans A. 1971. *Linnaeus and the Linnaeans: The Spreading of Their Ideas in Systematic Botany, 1735–1789.* Utrecht: Oosthoek.

Stern, Steve. 1982. *Peru's Indian Peoples and the Challenge of Spanish Conquest: Huamanga to 1640.* Madison: Univ. of Wisconsin Press.

Stern, Steve (ed.). 1987. *Resistance, Rebellion, and Consciousness in the Andean Peasant World, 18th to 20th Centuries.* Madison: Univ. of Wisconsin Press.

Stocking, George. 1992. *The Ethnographer's Magic and Other Essays in the History of Anthropology.* Madison: Univ. of Wisconsin Press.

Stoler, Anne Laura. 1995. *Race and the Education of Desire. Foucault's History of Sexuality and the Colonial Order of Things.* Durham: Duke Univ. Press.

Tagg, John. 1988. *The Burden of Representation.* Amherst: Univ. of Massachusetts Press.

Taine, Hippolyte-Adolphe. 1875. *Lectures on Art.* Trans. J. Durand. New York: AMS Press, 1971.

Tamayo Herrera, José. 1980. *Historia del indigenismo cusqueño.* Lima: Instituto Nacional de Cultura.

―――. 1981. *Historia social del Cusco republicano.* Lima: Editorial Universo.

Taussig, Michael. 1993. *Mimesis and Alterity.* New York: Routledge.

Taylor, Lucien (ed.). 1994. *Visualizing Theory.* New York and London: Routledge.

Tocqueville, Alexis de. 1967 [1856]. *L'Ancien Régime et la Revolution.* Paris: Gallimard.

Todorov, Tzvetan. 1994. *On Human Diversity.* Cambridge: Harvard Univ. Press

Trachtenberg, Alan. 1989. *Reading American Photographs: Images as History, Matthew Brady to Walker Evans.* New York: Noonday Press.

Ugarte Eléspuru, Juan M. 1968. "Notas sobre la pintura peruana entre 1890 y 1930."

In J. Basadre, *Historia de la República del Perú*, vol. 16, pp. 149–64. Lima: Edit. Universitaria.

Urton, Gary. 1990. *The History of a Myth: Pacaritambo and the Origin of the Incas*. Austin: Univ. of Texas Press.

Valcárcel, Luís. 1981. *Memorias*. Lima: IEP.

Voltaire (François Marie Arouet). 1989 [1736]. *Alzire*. Critical edition by T.E.D. Braun. In *The Complete Works of Voltaire*, vol. 14, pp. 105–210. Oxford: Voltaire Foundation/Taylor Institution.

———. 1769 [1756]. *Essai sur les moeurs et l'esprit des nations* Geneva.

Walker, Charles F. 1992. "Peasants, Caudillos, and the State in Peru: Cusco in the Transition from Colony to Republic, 1780–1840." Ph.D. dissertation, Univ. of Chicago.

Wechsler, Judith. 1982. *A Human Comedy: Physiognomy and Caricature in Nineteenth-Century Paris*. Chicago: Univ. of Chicago Press.

Wiener, Charles. 1880. *Pérou et Bolivie: Récit du Voyage*. Paris: Lib. Hachette.

Williams, Raymond. 1977. *Marxism and Literature*. New York: Oxford Univ. Press.

———. 1983 [1958]. "The Romantic Artist." In Williams, *Culture and Society, 1780–1950*, pp. 30–48. New York: Columbia Univ. Press.

———. 1985. *Keywords: A Vocabulary of Culture and Society*. New York: Oxford Univ. Press.

Yepez Miranda, Alfredo. 1938. "Indigenismo i [sic] serranismo," *Revista Universitaria del Cuzco*, 74:87–100.

———. 1940. "El Proceso cultural del Perú: La Unidad geográfica y cultural de la costa," *Revista Universitaria del Cuzco*, 78:27–37.

ABOUT THE AUTHOR

Deborah Poole is Associate Professor of Anthropology at the Graduate Faculty of the New School for Social Research in New York. Her previous publications include *Unruly Order: Violence, Power, and Cultural Identity in the High Provinces of Southern Peru* and *Peru: Time of Fear*.

## DATE DUE